PRAISE FOR NEW YORK AUTHOR APHRODITE JONES AND

The Embrace

"Parents of teens may want to read *The Embrace* just to heed the warning signs."
—*Denver Rocky Mountain News*

"Readers . . . will get some sense of the shadowy fantasy lives of 'kids fallen through life's crack.'"
—*Kirkus Reviews*

"Jones reports the story carefully. . . . She has obviously done her research. . . . The writing is smoothly competent. . . . For those who question the true story behind the horrific headlines, Jones provides a clear understanding of what moves a 'strawberry blond, normal-looking kid, to being this dark figure lurking in the night.' Parents would be wise to see *The Embrace* as a cautionary tale: take an active part in raising your child, and know about his or her friends. It may someday save your life."
—*Sun-Sentinel* (Ft. Lauderdale, FL)

"Jones provides a good overview of the facts surrounding voyeuristic intensity."
—*Publishers Weekly*

All She Wanted

"This fragile family background has been compellingly documented by the true-crime writer Aphrodite Jones."
—*The New Yorker*

"The book sizzles. . . . A gripping read."
—*The Herald* (Lake Worth, FL)

By Aphrodite Jones

The Embrace
All She Wanted
Della's Web
Cruel Sacrifice
The FBI Killer

THE
EMBRACE

A True Vampire Story

APHRODITE JONES

POCKET BOOKS

New York   London   Toronto   Sydney   Singapore

POCKET BOOKS, a division of Simon & Schuster Inc.
1230 Avenue of the Americas, New York, NY 10020

ISBN: 0-671-03467-7

First Pocket Books paperback printing June 2000

10 9 8 7 6 5 4 3 2 1

POCKET and colophon are registered trademarks of
Simon & Schuster Inc.

Front cover photos by John Pendygraft/The Advocate/Silver
Image; Index Stock. All interior photographs courtesy of the
author except where otherwise indicated.

Printed in the U.S.A.

For Jared and Joshua

ACKNOWLEDGMENTS

The one constant in my professional life has been my agent, Matt Bialer, who has provided me with balance, courage, and faith, particularly in these past two years, a trying period, during which I composed The Embrace. For this, I thank him.

For her immense confidence, her tireless enthusiasm, and for being a wonderful and caring friend, I also thank my editor, Jane Cavolina of Pocket Books. If it hadn't been for Jane's vision, this book would never have existed.

For other forms of advice, counsel, and blessings, I owe a great debt to several attorneys. In alphabetical order, they are Howard Babb, Thomas Carle, Greg Galloway, Michael Graves, Harry Hackney, David Harrington, Candace Hawthorne, Brad King, David Norris, Jeffery Phister, Mary Ann Plecas, and Lou Tally. Other blessings came from John Parsons, who encouraged me to travel to Murray with an HBO crew, and from David Hered, who made me realize just how important it was to spend time behind bars, talking face-to-face with these teens.

I also wish to thank Debbie Allen of the state attorney's office, who was instrumental in supplying me with essential court documents; Deputy Linda Ward, the evidence supervisor, who offered me access to everything, including Rick's knife, Ruth's pearls, and Heather's teddy bear; and Sheriff Stan Scott, who shared with me various diaries, artworks, and letters, confiscated from the residence of Roderick Ferrell.

Of the countless media sources I used for reference material, I thank the news teams of WESH-TV, WFTV, WKMG, Fox 35, and Court TV, Henry Stephens of the Daily Commercial, Walter Apperson and Jim Mahanes of the Murray Ledger & Times, and Frank Stanfield of the Lake Sentinel. I also thank my hosts at Mission Inn Golf and Tennis Resort and the Lakeside Inn of Mount Dora, two beautiful Lake County lodging establishments, where I was treated with kid gloves.

For their transcriptions, phone calls, extreme efforts, and loyalty, I would like to thank my assistants Cathlyn Baker, Louis Flores, Amy Sims, and Lynn Balthazor. These people became my life's blood during the research-gathering process, but above all, I wish to single out Cathlyn and Louis, whose work involved creative input as well.

For their cooperation, and for having the strength to see the bigger picture and make sense of this tragedy, I thank Heather and Jennifer Wendorf, Paula and Samantha Queen, Charity Kessee, Jeanine LeClaire, and Matt Goodman.

Finally, more than anyone realizes, it has been my close friends who have seen me though this work. Without their love and emotional support, I would never have been able to produce it. I love you, I thank you, and I need you in my life.

No one holds command over me. No man. No God. No Prince. What is a claim of power for ones who defy death? Call your damnable hunt. We shall see whom I drag screaming to hell with me

—VAMPIRE: THE MASQUERADE

My soul vast, filled with the evils of the world.
My eyes cold with pain and suffering.
What is to become of these foolish mortals
who dare to cross my path?

—RODERICK JUSTIN FERRELL

TO THE READER

The characters in this book are real. The story is true, the dialogue comes from recollections of the participants, but it bears mentioning that I have altered certain details. Though this is a work of nonfiction, I have taken certain storytelling liberties in writing the narrative, and, in one case, combined two characters into one. These alterations apply strictly to the innocent and exist primarily to disguise people's identities. In terms of the court and police proceedings, the narrative remains faithful to the events as they really happened. I have drawn upon court records, psychological reports, sworn depositions, and news stories, all of which allowed me to re-create the events and words of the participants.

Though I have utilized proven sources of journalistic research, this book also relies on hundreds of hours of interviews with dozens of people who were kind enough to share their secrets. It is through their remembrances and thoughts that I have been able to imagine Roderick and re-create the essence of his being. I did manage to meet with Rod's mother once. As we spoke, she sat clutching a copy of *Interview with the Vampire*. I also met with Rod face-to-face, at the Lake County Jail. For what it's worth, he still believes he is immortal.

THE
EMBRACE

prologue

It was cold in central Florida the day Rod arrived back in Lake County. He knew the place as well as anyone could; the ridges in the roads, the little bridges crossing over lakes, the Spanish moss dangling above orange groves. The passengers with Rod could feel the old red car go clip-clop, like the wheels of a wagon crossing over a bridge that was carrying them to some prehistoric time.

He had promised them an ancient place. Lake County was foreign to Rod's friends, and the waters of Little Lake Harris made things feel like they were traveling through a gray mist. It almost seemed like they were in a fog, with smoke lifting up from the lakes, large mirrors to the gray sky. It sure wasn't the sunny Florida any of these kids from Kentucky had dreamed about. Even though they were only thirty minutes north of Orlando, the place felt ominous. It wasn't any Disney World . . . not even close.

Charity was disappointed. She'd been hearing about Lake County for nine months now, but it turned out it was just a hick stomping ground, with farms and groves and little church steeples, where the people moved slow and the weeds grew high. She and Rod planned to be married, and she had so hoped Lake County would have more to offer than golfing and tennis and a bunch of fruit stands. When Rod turned off the highway onto Main Street in Tavares, he made a stop at a seedy place called Tom's Grocery.

Charity let Rod know she felt homesick. She and her girlfriend Dana wanted to head back to Kentucky. But Rod didn't seem to hear her. Instead, he motioned to his buddy, Scott, to take the wheel. Rod needed cigarettes, he was edgy. Rod was tired of being nagged. After hours of nonstop driving in a junky Buick, the four of them were getting on each other's nerves.

The girls complained they were hungry, but Rod came out of the grocery empty-handed. He requested that Scott drive a couple more miles down the road to Eustis, where there was a K Mart, so he could pick up razor blades. While Rod was in there, he grabbed a box of Little Debbie cakes and a few Dr Peppers, hoping that would keep Dana and Charity quiet. As he stood at the pay phone in front of K Mart, Rod scrounged for change and fumbled through the white pages. The neon and glare of the business district was a far cry from the creepy setting they had first come upon.

Things seemed dismal, but Charity figured they wouldn't be hanging around Eustis for long. Rod was right, Lake County wasn't what Charity had in mind. She wanted excitement. Already, she'd seen enough of central

Florida, and she suddenly understood why Rod had promised to come get Heather. No wonder Heather wanted out of this place. There was nothing to do—no big malls, no movie complexes, not even an arcade.

As Rod ran his long nails through his thick hair and waited for someone to pick up the phone, he seemed nervous. Rod trusted that his friend Shannon would let them all clean up, but deep down he knew that, if her parents were home, it might be a problem.

As it turned out, Shannon was in the house alone, and she offered to let them drop by. As he spoke on the phone, Rod threw a sarcastic glance over at Scott. Shannon was cute, with a button nose and blond hair, a high-class preppy. She had a large home and was just the type Rod needed so he could show off. He wanted his little Kentucky group to see that people in Lake County lived better. As he spoke into the receiver, Rod had a smirk on his face.

Looking a combination of half-punk, half-Gothic, Scott and the girls hid behind their dark sunglasses. Scott didn't say much, but then, he never felt he had to. He was the quiet one among them. He basically did whatever Rod told him to, copying Rod's style of dress, his mannerisms, everything he could, right down to Rod's Marilyn Manson T-shirts. Scott was Rod's lackey. Having him along was fun, especially when Scott would go off into his dreamworld and act freaky. Scott liked to play fantasy games.

Dana hoped life would be better once they retrieved Heather and began their journey to New Orleans. The only legal adult in the group, nineteen-year-old Dana had most of her stuff packed in the car. She was ready to start a new existence, and she didn't really care what town they all ended up in, just as long as they stuck to their plan to be a "family."

Charity had her own ideas about life with Rod. She saw herself set up in an apartment with him, preferably somewhere on the West Coast, maybe in Oregon, where she could find work in a beauty shop, and Rod could work as an artist. Charity wanted to move far away because she didn't trust Rod. She knew he was sleeping with girls up and down the East Coast. She couldn't wait for Rod to get off the phone so she could find out about this chick, Shannon.

Up until then, Charity only knew about Heather and Jeanine. For almost a year, Rod had told her stories about these girls being his "children." Rod said Jeanine had a son with him, but had given the baby up for adoption. Charity was under the impression that these girls had a weird bond with Rod. She disliked the idea of having to accommodate Heather and dreaded the possibility that Jeanine might wind up tagging along with them too.

As for Scott, he just wanted Rod to get the car rolling. If their mission was to pick up Heather, he wanted Rod to stop yakking and just get to it. Heather had already vowed to run away with them, which Scott thought was just great. In the months prior to their arrival, Scott and Heather had talked on the phone a few times and they had exchanged letters and pictures. Scott had asked her to be his "dark mate." As he waited in the Buick, he imagined Heather's face, anxious to see what she'd look like in person.

On the way down from Kentucky, Rod suggested they would all live with a friend of his in New Orleans. He mentioned something about them living in a mansion on Royal Street and hoped to stay until the start of Mardi Gras. But then, Rod hadn't really made any concrete plans. He had also said something about stopping off at the Convent Alucard, a vampire hangout, where he knew a "prince."

Charity hoped New Orleans would live up to its reputation. She couldn't wait to see it. Dana had friends who went to Goth clubs there, and she heard they could hang with some real vampires. Scott talked about a coven in the French Quarter he planned to drop in on. They were all revved up about getting there.

As Nine Inch Nails blasted from Dana's boom box in the backseat, the teens made fun of Eustis, realizing central Florida was really no different than where they had just come from, back home in Kentucky. Either way, they found themselves sitting in a K Mart parking lot. As Rod moved toward the Buick, Charity laughed. Rod stuck his tongue out at her and slid his thin frame into the crammed front seat, blowing her a kiss.

On the drive down, Charity had informed Rod that she was carrying his child. Now, she hoped he would make good on his promises. Even though she wasn't actually positive she was pregnant, in her heart she believed she was. She wanted Rod to settle down, to stop acting so crazy. She figured a baby would help Rod get away from his fantasy world, away from his talk about killing people.

When he was really high, Rod would say he was immortal and hint he was the *son of Satan*. Of course, Charity knew Rod was bullshitting, but then again, Rod loved tempting death and he bragged about his supernatural powers a lot. A master of illusion, Rod claimed he could astrally project himself to a throne in hell as easily as he could project his image into a mirror. Charity thought it was all hysterically funny.

* * *

Though she hadn't seen him in months, Shannon and Rod had been close friends for years. Shannon still considered him her best friend and was happy to hear from him, glad to have him come visit her. But Shannon was completely shocked when she opened the door to find Rod dressed entirely in black, with black hair down to his waist and long black fingernails. He scared her. Just before Rod moved from Florida to Kentucky, Rod had started to change, had started to wear some Gothic stuff, but still, Rod could easily change back, he was still an all-American kid.

Not anymore. The minute he began to talk, Shannon realized Rod was different. She was afraid to let him and Scott into her house, but Rod needed to wash up and he wanted to use the phone. He had Shannon dial Heather at Jeanine's house and then hand the phone over to him.

As Rod chatted first with Jeanine, then with Heather, Scott rounded up the girls and brought Shannon outside to meet them. At first Scott mumbled something about being kidnapped, explaining that Rod had kidnapped him and had taken his car, claiming that he was "okay with it." Scott said he was "willing to go along with Rod," but Shannon wasn't sure what Scott meant.

Charity seemed spooky, too tall and thin, and her hair was an eerie jet-black. Clearly, Shannon didn't approve of her. As for Dana, this overweight girl with short, frizzy hair and an uneven complexion, she seemed like someone who didn't fit in with this motley crew.

Shannon had only vaguely heard of Murray, Kentucky. Going back in her mind, she tried to remember if Rod had ever called her from there. She knew it was the place Rod spent part of his childhood, but she realized Rod hardly ever mentioned anything about it. Shannon really had no reason to be around this collection of characters.

She thought they were crazy backwoods people. When Charity introduced herself as Rod's wife and said she was pregnant, Shannon didn't believe her.

Shannon felt queasy about letting them into the house, but because Charity said she felt sick, Shannon had no choice. Before she knew it, Shannon was feeding Dana warmed-up soup and letting Scott play Nintendo on her computer. While Dana and Charity went out on the back porch to smoke a cigarette, Rod was busy on the phone. Apparently, Rod agreed to meet Jeanine at midnight and promised Heather he would pick her up after school.

At about six o'clock on Monday, the following day, Rod and his friends showed up unannounced at Shannon's. This time they had car trouble—the Buick had a flat, and they needed help. Shannon felt more comfortable around the girls and gave them an ashtray so they could go talk outside, while Rod was back on the phone with Jeanine and Heather. Shannon heard Rod repeating the directions over to Greentree Lane, and as he spoke, Rod drew a little map.

When he hung up, Rod announced that Heather and Jeanine were going to run away with them. He asked Scott if he was ready to go steal the Wendorfs' car, and Scott nodded in agreement.

"Why are you stealing their car?" Shannon wanted to know.

"Because the Buick isn't really working. There's engine trouble."

"And Jeanine and Heather are in on this?" Shannon wondered.

"Yeah. We're headed to Louisiana," Rod told her, "but first we're gonna kill Heather's parents."

"Why would you do something like that?"

"Because we need the car."

"I can't understand why you'd have to kill somebody to take their car, Rod."

But Rod was adamant. He was going to kill the Wendorfs and Shannon was told to keep quiet about it. She didn't believe a word Rod said anyway, so there was no chance she would repeat it. She saw Rod's arms and chest were covered with marks all up and down, like he'd been cutting himself, and she quizzed him about it, but Rod said he liked to cut himself, that he did it because he was bored.

Shannon was disgusted. When Scott and the girls waltzed back into the kitchen, she noticed they had weird cuts too. Scott had some on his neck. Scott pulled a Swiss army knife from his pocket and was about to show her, but Shannon didn't care to see any more. She wanted the knife put away.

"We could use this to kill 'em," Rod said, grinning, holding up a butcher knife from Shannon's kitchen.

"Yeah," Scott said.

"But, you know, that's not the way I'd really wanna kill somebody," Rod said. "You wanna know how I'd do it, Shannon?"

"No, I don't care to hear it."

As Rod pulled some razor blades from his trench coat pocket, Shannon's protests were mocked. Rod pulled a blade across his forearm and let the blood ooze into his mouth. Shannon gasped, but the incision turned out to be so small, there was hardly any blood to wince about.

Within seconds, Rod seemed spontaneously healed, and before she knew it, Rod was swinging from her dishwasher and kitchen counter, building up a rhythm with his body like an acrobat. Shannon kept insisting that she didn't want to hear any more details, but Rod was bragging now, and he just wouldn't stop.

"I'm gonna decapitate them people," Rod hissed. "I wish they had a dishwasher like this, then I could just spring up on 'em."

"Shut up," Shannon shrieked.

But no one else in the room seemed to care. Scott looked preoccupied, staring out at the pool behind Shannon's house. Charity looked a bit grossed out, but she kept her mouth shut.

"Can I go?" Dana asked, finally breaking the silence. "I wanna do something to 'em."

"Yeah, I might need help," Rod told her, "if Scott's not gonna do it."

"I'm there, man," Scott assured him, "and Shannon, you wanna know how I'm gonna do it?"

But Shannon wouldn't listen. She politely moved toward her front door and told the people to leave her house. She asked them nicely.

"We're *ghosts*, Shannon, we're *undead*. You never even saw us here," Rod taunted.

"It's a *game*, Shannon," Scott said, laughing. "You ever play the Masquerade?"

The preppy girl smiled at him unknowingly.

"You should play it sometime," Scott insisted, baring his teeth, "'cause we're gonna have some fun tonight."

PART ONE

THE
SEDUCTION

chapter one

Roderick said he had been asleep for five centuries, that he had been tired of the great adventure called life, but, cursed with immortality, he had grown restless. Somehow, he found himself clawing his way from the depths of the earth, back to the mortal universe and a thing called society. Suddenly, he found himself staring in a mirror, shaving part of the hair on his head, and putting on the grunge dress of a teen at the end of the twentieth century.

In the 1400s, he would confide, Roderick had known the power and privilege of the aristocracy in France. Naturally, the idea of living among the bourgeoisie disgusted him; Roderick had the strongest dislike for peasants. He wondered if he had made the right choice, allowing himself to dwell among the lower classes in a strange, transient place known as Florida, where people wore white and played games in the sun.

During the five hundred years of his slumber, Roderick claimed, he had become accustomed to being a spirit, to calling on "the Elders" in a vast darkness. Roderick loved to roam his phantom cities, the ancient worlds of the Arabians, the Egyptians, the Greeks. But now, Roderick had decided to rematerialize in the flesh. He had decided it was time for Rod to emerge.

Guised as the ultimate rebel, he would cloak himself as an American teen. Roderick, used to being one of the most idolized entities in the world, regarded himself as an equal to God and felt it was fitting for him to choose America. Because of their sins, their greed and corruption, ugly Americans threatened to destroy the planet. Called upon by Lucifer, Rod decided he had to take matters into his own hands. He decided to collect himself an army of American youth.

At first, Heather Wendorf didn't know what to make of him, this Rod Ferrell character. Before they were introduced, she had heard stories around Eustis that Roderick was supposedly a *vampire*—some of her girlfriends had talked about that. Of course, Heather was curious, but she was too busy with her artwork and piano lessons; besides, she was interested in the boys who played on the football team.

When Rod first approached her, the guy seemed odd. Even though he was only sixteen, he was some kind of egomaniac. He seemed to have a need to conquer the universe. Rod had an arrogant way about him that never made sense, especially to Heather. She was the type who enjoyed a rather upscale existence without ever having to brag about it. She was without an ego.

Heather didn't know when she started to become attracted to him, but Rod seemed more sensitive than other guys. She found his voice appealing. She thought she understood his talk about the end of the world. He spoke of mass destruction and was well versed about people like Saddam Hussein, who he claimed was the fourth Antichrist. The guy seemed to be light-years ahead of her. She was becoming smitten.

Physically, Heather found Rod unappealing. He had a long, narrow nose and pale skin, but there was something very sensual about him. In part, it was his flowing black hair, shoulder-length and silky, which was usually tied back into a ponytail. And there was something about the way he expressed his emotions that grabbed her. Rod was enchanting, with his wisdom about good and evil, with his proclamations that he was a fallen angel . . .

Rod was, without a doubt, the embodiment of insanity, but yet, there was something vampiric about him. Perhaps it was his piercing eyes, his long nails, his paper-thin body; whatever the reason, Heather felt he cast off some kind of mystical eroticism. At first, Heather thought it was because she had been reading too much Anne Rice; she didn't really know why she found herself becoming attracted to the idea of drinking human blood.

Rod had turned her on to *The Big Book of Death*, a tome that explored different ways of dying, which Heather needed because she intended to wipe herself out before the year 2000. Heather made no more pretenses about religion. She didn't believe Christ could save her. The only thing she seemed driven by was death, and the grim world Rod offered. When he spoke, it was as if he cast a spell over her. She wanted to die. She wanted to be undead. The word *vampire* didn't matter. Heather didn't care what Rod was.

She knew Rod wasn't any Dracula or strange prince from Transylvania.

Rod filled her void. He was an ancient soul, a space traveler who could come into her dreams and help her transcend time. That's all Heather cared about. She didn't want to be a mortal teenager, trapped in a cookie-cutter existence.

"Lest mortals destroy themselves with their own hate and greed," Rod insisted, "I have been cast on this land. I am the devil's child, walking with earthly feet."

"What do you mean?" Heather asked. "Are you saying you worship the devil?"

"Don't say that," he howled, "that's blasphemy, and if you even think it, then none of us can be released from hell."

Rod would tell Heather these things, yet his manner would be very casual. When they first met, the two of them would just be sitting off by themselves, looking very normal, hanging out in the Eustis High cafeteria. Until she hooked up with Rod, Heather had been somewhat of a loner; she hadn't found too many people she felt connected to.

But then, Rod seemed worthy of her time. He was a newcomer to town, someone who quickly gathered friends, and Heather dropped whatever few buddies she had, so she could absorb him. Before she knew it, she and Rod were becoming inseparable.

"What if you and I were deemed rulers of the world?" Rod asked half-jokingly.

"I don't know, Rod," Heather teased, "I've always wondered when that might happen."

"Do you think you would fit my purposes?"

"Perfectly."

"I'm not mortal," Rod said, poking her in the side.

"Okay," she said, smiling, "you will be given a chance to prove that."

But Rod would just start laughing whenever Heather expected a real answer. After school, it had become her habit to agree to meet him at the cemetery. It was a place where time seemed to stand still and Heather liked it that way. She preferred being a part of Rod's world, even if it was just *pretend*. She thought it was fantastic, the way Rod would comment about the "brutal barbarism" around them. He found the naked and horrible realities of life in the United States to be unbearable—the ugly American golfers, the petty little tourists—they were quite a shocking difference from the elite world he had been used to, living as a gentleman in France.

All the while, Heather's parents were under the impression she was staying after school to watch her sister, Jeni, during cheerleading practice. The Wendorfs trusted their daughter, they never questioned her, so Heather had herself a foolproof setup. After a couple of hours with Rod, she would bounce over behind the bleachers and meet her mom for a ride home with Jeni.

As time moved on, even though Heather's parents noticed some minor changes in her appearance—there were some new ear piercings, there were some black Gothic outfits—the Wendorfs never hounded her about it. Heather was an artist. She needed to expand her individuality.

Of course, Rick Wendorf would have preferred Heather to be another cheerleader, like Jeni, but then his wife always stressed the importance of creativity. Ruth Wendorf encouraged Heather to explore her inner self. If Heather was into New Age, Ruth thought there was nothing wrong with that. Things like healing crystals, or the belief in prophecy, just couldn't be dismissed.

*   *   *

During their cemetery talks, Rod had taken his time about confiding things to his fledgling. He was leery about telling Heather anything, but eventually began talking about his assumption of God-forms. Through the power of imagination, Rod explained, he could re-create himself into the shape of any god. Eventually, Rod promised, he could teach Heather to meditate on simple symbols so she could penetrate their secret meanings and rise on the planes. Rod vowed he would help Heather take her first astral journey, but first she would have to learn to use spiritual energy, she would have to build up her astral body.

Heather cherished this notion. She so wanted to escape the mundane, she'd go home and lock herself in her room to practice meditation with candles. At times, she'd work with various spells, trying to test Rod's authenticity, but she was unable to travel without his guidance. Of course, Heather had never actually experienced Rod's astral projection.

But Rod wanted Heather to be patient. He said she wasn't ready to leave normal consciousness just yet. Rod called Heather a prophet who could "sense spirits" that were not physically present. Having the cemetery right across from Eustis High School was a blessing, he said, because it gave him a chance to teach her the principles of "spirit meditation."

Of course, the first time Heather witnessed Rod in a trance state, she was scared to death because Rod became violent, tearing at his own flesh with his teeth. But after a minute, everything became calm.

To Heather, Rod's consciousness seemed delusional but majestic. She would listen to him ramble about the Hundred Years' War, about the peasants' revolution, about life in fifteenth-century France. He would rant about his "union with the Lord," when he was a boy adorned in magnificent brocades of silk, and would describe himself as a creature similar, in spirit, to Joan of Arc.

Rod claimed he had visions of Heather being burned at the stake. He told her they had both been reincarnated, had been brought back from a life together centuries before, and Heather started to believe him. She started to think she had been "chosen" to live forever.

chapter two

Heather's quest for depth was filled with Rod's sense of eternal darkness. As he described for her the splendor of the earth in the dawn of dawns, his vision of an orb of darkness with a crimson glow behind, Heather contemplated the glory of a place where darkness meant inner peace. Rod could take her there, he said, but it wouldn't be anything like she expected.

Rod always spoke in riddles. With the promise of revealing secret desires, Rod always seemed to be on the verge of doing something demonic. He was somewhat sinister, which excited her imagination. Half the time, Heather didn't know what Rod was capable of. Rod would speak of the savage noises in the wind, yet the two of them would be sitting at the shores of a lake where all seemed silent. Sometimes Rod would point to significant stars, as if he had actually been to these other galaxies. Heather knew

Rod suffered from madness, and she thought it magnificent that he could share it with her.

More than once, Rod tried to get Heather to release her subconscious desires, but that was where she held back. As it was, her enthusiasm about Rod was overwhelming to her. Heather found Rod occupying most of her time, even though it was Jeanine who was supposedly Rod's girlfriend. Naturally, Jeanine resented that Rod and Heather were so tight, but part of the problem was logistic. Jeanine attended school in Leesburg, a good twenty minutes away. Of course, Jeanine trusted Heather like a sister. She knew Heather would never do anything like that behind her back.

As the weeks progressed, Rod was slowly getting Heather to acknowledge part of her dark nature. Without understanding why, Heather began to feel the presence of forces that appalled her. Under Rod's tutelage, she believed she could recognize the existence of her ancestral appetite. In essence, Rod convinced her that she could attain a certain state of mind to perform miracles, that she could evoke, through ceremony and incantation, a medium that would allow her subconsciousness to actually rise and *appear*.

Though Heather longed to have Rod's power, the only thing she truly felt was an evil presence taking over. When she would try to project herself into Rod's dreamworld, she felt frustrated. She would fantasize about lavishly dressed ladies walking down medieval streets in Paris, but her vision of the city came mostly from the little she had learned in French class. Rod would laugh whenever Heather tried to name the grand boulevards or ancient cathedrals in French. Her accent was all wrong, her geography was completely off, and at times, when they were alone in the cemetery, Heather would get so tongue-twisted trying to mimic Rod, she'd wish she never bothered studying French or any foreign customs.

At times, she hated Rod for all his worldliness. He could project himself and describe the beautiful things and fine people of Europe, yet here she was, sheltered under the clumps of Spanish moss that hung around her in Eustis. Heather felt bad that she had never really been anywhere beyond Disney World. She hated that she had no fantastic childhood memories that could compare to Rod's phenomenal history.

When she questioned how it was possible that she might be a chosen one, especially since Heather had tried, but could never conjure any recollection of past lives, Rod would assure her that, with time, her early memories would be restored. Heather would press him about how long she'd have to wait, but Rod would never say. Sometimes Heather would try to argue, insisting that vampires did not exist:

"Where's the proof, Rod?"

"You think too much, Heather."

"You're the one who taught me."

"Just remember, the only power that exists is within you. If you want proof, you only need to look inside yourself."

"No, Rod. I want you to give me some answers."

But he didn't trust her enough yet. He refused to say who Heather's ancestors were. She had become obsessed with the idea of being immortal, she hoped that someday she would have her answers, but meanwhile she was sick of hearing Rod hint about his "forbidden knowledge."

To gain Rod's favor, Heather started to cloak herself in darkness, making a black trench coat and combat boots a part of her new uniform. For a while, she resisted dyeing her golden hair, but eventually Heather started to shift hair colors—she went from cherry red to purple and finally to black. Rod didn't seem to care either way. If she wanted to put on Gothic clothes just for show, that was fine. But it was Heather's soul Rod was interested in.

"You know," he told her, "dressing like a vampire doesn't make you one."

"I know that. I'm not trying to look like one."

"Not that you don't look good in black."

Rod was right. Heather did look good in black, and that was probably why her parents hardly questioned her new wardrobe. Heather's appearance was a bit rebellious, especially for a fourteen-year-old in a conservative place like Eustis, but, as bright and gifted a student as Heather was, her parents didn't see any harm in it. Heather's grades were still excellent.

Of course Ruth wanted Heather to find a nice, clean-cut boyfriend someday—but since Heather didn't seem to be boy crazy, Ruth didn't see the need to rush that. Ruth never really asked Heather about the people she hung around with at school because she knew Heather had all the best values. Heather knew right from wrong, and for Ruth, that was enough.

As a tease, Rod began telling Heather he could smell her blood—so sweet, not the vile blood of vampires . . . He constantly referred to her as his "fledgling," and Heather seemed to enjoy it. Though she'd tell herself she was not a vampire, though she thought she could never kill living beings, the more she'd listen to Rod, the more she started to feel like a monster. As she worried about it, Heather's conscience caused her to feel more remote.

Indeed, in the time that she was closest to Rod, the fall of her sophomore year at Eustis, Heather had become aloof around her family and at school. With Rod's encouragement, she was more deliberately dabbling in witchcraft, but that made her feel nothing, really. It was Rod who was all dark and powerful, and it seemed only he could penetrate her inner sanctum. Rod was able to speak to Heather without words.

She knew she was developing a blood lust for him, and Heather was afraid Rod had control of her mind. It seemed her thoughts were increasingly of him, of his blood coursing through her veins, of his young face that sometimes appeared infinitely old.

And then there was always the hounding question of his being truly immortal. The more Heather pondered things, the more she wanted to shift away from the physical world, into the delirium Rod had created for her. Her family life seemed impossible, her days at school, unreasonable. But if Heather didn't seem to grasp her life, she didn't seem ready to clutch death either. Often, she wanted to go back to the way she was before she met Rod.

But whenever Heather closed her eyes, her head would fill with visions. Out of nowhere, she would see flashes of blood on her fingers—on her hands—her face.

chapter three

As they walked down Orange Avenue, past the pleasant drivers and polite people, Rod would talk with Heather about sacrifice. He established that killing did not break nature's rules.

As he spoke, leading Heather through thick strands of Spanish moss, she saw herself moving through giant cobwebs. There was something surreal about being around Rod. Sometimes she felt like Dorothy in *The Wizard of Oz*, standing on the edge of the black-and-white world, as if she was living in the part of the film that matched up with Pink Floyd's *Dark Side of the Moon*.

To passersby, the two of them were an unearthly sight, these pencil-thin figures dressed in solid black. They stood out against the lush Florida colors, so much so, they seemed to dwarf the single-family houses, the antique shops, and the magnolia trees that surrounded Eustis High.

When Rod and Heather weren't in class, they were spending hours and hours in the Greenwood Cemetery, in a spot they referred to as the "birthplace." It was a magical mystery place, where the pavement melted into grass and the moss dripped onto tombstones. In the quietness of the birthplace, the rest of the world dissolved. Even during those rare times when Jeanine would join them, Heather felt peculiarly alone with Rod. It was as if he had an unending, all-encompassing presence.

On weeknights, when she wasn't allowed to go into town, Heather would take long walks in the woods around her house, happy to be out in the darkness alone. She'd think about the ordinary world of her sister—the Eustis High School football team, the boys who wore shirts and ties to church on Sundays. All that was like a dream to her now.

She'd developed a code to talk on the phone with Jeanine without her parents being able to pick up on what she meant, which was important because Heather was becoming obsessed with death and planned to test Rod's theories out. Heather was always trying to establish what was real, and she knew that Jeanine could help her figure out which of Rod's claims were sheer madness, and which were possible. They thought it was especially crazy when Rod would refer back to 85,000 B.C. and wondered if recorded time even went back that far. Not that she didn't think Rod qualified as a Neanderthal.

When they actually considered Rod's claims that he was this "primitive being" roaming the earth eternally, the two girls would just split their sides. They loved retelling his stories and would laugh wildly as they recapped Rod's notion that Jeanine was an ancient queen, that Heather was some kind of prophet. Rod's mind seemed so crazed—he would jump back and forth between prehistoric and futuristic without any transition whatsoever. Of course, a lot of what he said didn't make any sense, but they didn't care. His world was a hell of a lot more interesting than most of the stupid movies they'd watch.

If Jeanine doubted Rod, she made it a point never to express that directly to Heather. Heather was looking for someone to poke holes in Rod's stories, but Jeanine had a wild imagination herself, and besides, she was half in love with Rod. Jeanine would never contradict him.

As November approached and the weather got cooler, Heather's world turned more gray and gloomy. Her mind was increasingly filled with thoughts of death, but she told Jeanine she liked it that way. Jeanine started to worry about Heather and tried to get her girlfriend to join the Episcopal Church, but Heather wanted nothing to do with official religion.

Heather liked that she didn't fit the norm. She was well aware that she was different, and in case she needed any reminders, all she had to do was talk to her sister, Jeni, the proud cheerleader. Heather loved her older sister more than anything, but she wouldn't have traded places with Jeni for all the world.

Heather always saw Jeni's world as inadequate. Sure, Jeni was popular, she always had a boyfriend, but Jeni's life was superficial, at least in Heather's eyes. To Heather, Jeni's life was boring. It was no big deal that Jeni had won first runner-up in the Miss Eustis beauty contest. Heather was glad for Jeni, but that was never a title Heather coveted. Heather thought beauty pageants were ridiculous, and she couldn't understand why any self-respecting young woman would want to parade around in a bathing suit, just to win a cheap rhinestone crown.

Heather considered that kind of thing commonplace, way beneath her. She aspired to leave the shallow world of Eustis, and since she was too young to leave physically, she'd leave mentally. Heather entered the realm of the supernatural. She lived in a world of shadows, where trolls and fairies appeared from behind streetlamps, where vampires and ghouls were more than just Halloween tricks. Heather lived in an imaginary world, but to her, it was perfectly real.

Heather felt that with enough practice, she might wield powers that would allow her to rise above the ignorant heartlessness of the human race. She was more spiritually at home with the idea of being a high priestess. She wanted to be someone who could shepherd human spirits. She wanted to believe Rod when he told her that she came from a higher plane.

As a little kid, Heather liked to dwell on the mysteries of the unexplained. She would talk to her mother and ask questions about people who had near-death experiences or encounters with aliens. She'd see these people on TV and fully believe their stories. As a kid, she'd raise questions about strange gods, about the demons and angels she could feel around her. Heather asked Ruth about reincarnation, but her mother could never provide answers. Ruth would only say that she believed she had guardian angels. Sometimes, she would tell Heather of her strange dreams, psychic dreams that Heather loved to hear about. In one dream Ruth had, she climbed stairs and met God in heaven. That was a dream about the alpha and omega that Heather asked her mom to tell repeatedly.

Of course, Heather found it astonishing and distressing that Rod would try to invoke evil as a means to gather people's souls; she always thought angels would be a pre-

ferred choice for soul-catching. Baffled, she would watch
Rod recite the Lord's Prayer backward, holding the Holy
Bible in one hand and an upside-down cross in the other.
Having covered his groundwork, Rod would visualize evil
in human form and talk to the "evil figure" in what
seemed to be a struggle for his life. Heather couldn't
understand how Rod could make her feel so good, make
her laugh so much, yet attach all his power to being evil.
He was a tormented soul, it seemed to her.

Rod was determined to convince Heather that evil
ruled the realm of the eternal, and as a way to prove this,
he talked her into reading the Necronomicon, a book supposedly written in the eighth century by a "mad Arab." This
little black book with a pentagram on the cover described
the "Ancient Ones," beings from a dead civilization
before the existence of Mesopotamia. They were supposedly eternal entities who were keeping watch on the gates
of hell. Basically, it was a sorcerer's handbook listing
incantations, exorcisms, and bindings, just a stupid paper-
back that Rod picked up in a Waldenbooks bookstore.
Heather didn't place much faith in it.

The book claimed to contain the essences of all spirits—of the dead, of the unborn—and purportedly it
could reveal the power and secret knowledge of the
Ancient Ones, if one could decipher the thing. Unfortunately, Heather was unable to find a way to pass through
the "seven gates" and the "seven colors" that the book
outlined. She was unsuccessful when she tried to step up
the "ladder of lights" to the gates of hell.

Heather found no truth in this book Rod held in such
high regard, but eventually, when she and Rod performed
a blood-bonding ritual out of a witch's handbook one
November night, she mysteriously felt more connected,

less insane about bloodletting. When Rod used phrases like the "secret tides of blood," Heather wasn't sure exactly what Rod meant, especially since they were smoking weed and she was hallucinating somewhat, but the two of them had mixed their sacred body fluids, and Heather felt that she had taken, at least, one tiny step toward personal redemption.

Around Rod, Heather was in a battle with her soul. Rod spoke of his elders as though they were gods who walked in heaven and hell, and these gods seemed to outrage Heather's spirit. She was not looking for demons or vampires who threatened to drain her mortal blood; she was looking for spiritual communion, for an affirmation that her belief in higher powers might justify her odd human existence. The problem was, the answers Rod seemed to hint at weren't really answers at all. He seemed to be teasing her with puzzles and empty promises. There was nothing real about him.

Heather started to believe Roderick was a *vampire*. He could go through transformations that made him seem like he had existed from the beginning of time. Rod walked the earth as an average teenager with a typical dysfunctional family, surviving largely on McDonald's cheeseburgers and Marlboros, yet he didn't seem to belong in that type of setting. Deep down, Heather felt she was so much like him, she couldn't help delving further into Rod's soul.

When she got into spiritual conversations with Rod, Heather sometimes felt like she stood at the threshold of chaos. The more she entered his inner world, the more she realized Rod was grimmer than anything she had ever imagined. Pain and suffering seemed to be the only things that made up his universe, yet, at times, he could create such joy, such freedom out of darkness, it was unnatural. Rod's philosophies were so compelling. There were moments when he would mock himself and his vampiric world. There were times when Rod seemed like a vampire caricature.

Roderick was some kind of cosmic jester at the center of the universe. He was a contradiction of everything about the human condition, playing the part of a typical American teen, yet exhibiting a blood lust so mighty, it could absorb Heather to the point of physical intoxication. She had finally gotten to where she would allow him to slice her a little, so he could drink from her arm.

During school hours, Heather would watch Rod and his buddies crack jokes in the hallways. They'd make fun of certain teachers, pull practical stunts, they were such immature boys, so *normal*. One of Rod's pals decorated Heather's locker with a Barbie doll hanging from a noose. Of course she was mad about it at first, but then she found it endearing, in a creepy sort of way.

Heather wondered why Rod never invited any of his guy friends over to the Greenwood birthplace, but she didn't dare ask him about it. Rod was the type no one asked questions of.

chapter four

When Rod brought Jeanine to see the altar he had in his room, he spoke to the wandering demon in the air and kneeled to the ground, reciting an incantation beginning at the North and to the East. He was calling to the ghost of the gates. Watching Rod perform, Jeanine thought he seemed to emulate Louis, the character from *Interview with the Vampire*.

Rod wanted her to think his blood wasn't human, but she just couldn't. When he stood up and grabbed a razor from the altar and sliced his forearm, the red line appeared so quickly, Jeanine started shaking. Rod was asking that she drink, that she sanctify her soul. Jeanine had her buddy Eric with her. She figured he'd protect her, but instead, Eric seemed to be mesmerized by Rod. Here was a guy who seemed to have a good head on his shoulders, yet Eric was so utterly willing to comply with Rod's request.

Jeanine felt butterflies in her stomach. She wasn't squeamish about the blood, she and Heather had been cutting themselves for some weeks now, but she hated getting involved in a blood ritual without really knowing how Rod protected himself. Even though she knew Heather drank from Rod, she couldn't help worrying about AIDS.

Hoping to buy some time, Jeanine slipped under Rod's blanket. She wanted the two guys to leave her alone, but Rod grew insistent.

He took his finger, quickly sliced the tip, and smeared the blood between his own lips. Then Rod bent over and kissed Jeanine softly. As she let herself taste Rod's tongue, Jeanine told herself it was no big deal. Eric had assured her that she couldn't get AIDS unless she had cold sores or open cuts in her mouth. Eric had also cut himself and had shared Rod's blood. Jeanine decided it was just easier to go along with things.

Rod seemed to know what he was doing. He was methodical about bloodletting; it was almost like he was a priest giving Communion. In the background, he had *Anti-Christ Superstar* playing, he had the curtains drawn, the incense burning, and soft candlelight glowing. It was a freaky scene, even though it was broad daylight outside, and Jeanine couldn't believe she and Eric had just come from their Episcopal church service, only a few blocks from Rod's house.

It was Sunday afternoon. They had walked over to pick Rod up because Eric had plans to meet Heather down by the lake nearby, and Jeanine wanted to join them. As it was, Rod was scheduled to move back to Kentucky that week. Jeanine was looking for any excuse to see him.

Of course, Rod's mom had threatened to move him away from Eustis so many times, Rod had become flippant about it. He acted like it wasn't happening, so Jeanine wasn't sure if Rod was really leaving. Jeanine hoped he was just threatening, especially since her birthday and Thanksgiving were practically around the corner. But the minute she walked into the house, Jeanine realized Rod wasn't kidding this time.

Jeanine was tearful when confronted with all the moving boxes. Rod promised he'd always love her, that she would live in his soul forever; he vowed to return to see her often, but Jeanine knew better. She knew things would soon be over between them, and in her heart, she wondered if she ever really cared about Rod. It seemed Heather was closer to him. Even though Jeanine could still sense his presence when she slept at night, even though she often dreamt about Rod, she wasn't sure she ever truly loved him.

Jeanine was still curled up daydreaming when all of a sudden Rod joined her on his bed, cutting himself again, this time with an X-Acto knife. Jeanine felt like she was someone else when she wrapped herself around his arm and allowed herself to suck. It was as if she was on the ceiling looking down at the scene, she did not recognize herself. Eric was busy taking it all in, chanting some spell Rod had handed him, and then, out of nowhere, Rod's mother burst through the door.

Needless to say, all hell broke loose.

Sondra accused Rod of performing ritual sex, of being a devil worshiper. She ranted and opened the drapes and turned off the music. Rod tried to calm her with his explanation about "spontaneous cutting," but his mother refused to hear it.

When she saw red on the sheets, she knocked over the incense and holy water trying to tear down Rod's altar. Then she flew toward Rod, grabbing him off the bed by his hair and screaming orders for Jeanine and Eric to get out of her house. Sondra threatened to call the police if either one of them ever stepped foot on her property again, but Rod paid her no attention. Instead, he gave Jeanine a knowing smile, as though everything would be just fine.

"Don't worry about my mom," he said as he escorted his friends to the door, "she's just mad because I refuse to sire her."

"She wants to *cross over?*" Jeanine asked, in sheer disbelief.

"Yeah, she wants to be sired," Rod said. "Don't you find that quite amusing?"

Jeanine started to smile. She found it unbelievable that Rod's mother wanted to "cross over," to be made into a vampire. Jeanine figured Rod was just kidding. Sondra's shrieks had been quite loud, his mom seemed pretty upset when she saw the blood.

Of course, the thought of Sondra blood-bonding was chilling. Jeanine asked if Sondra was crazy, but all Rod would say was that he'd seen her levitate, that he believed her soul was possessed.

Jeanine started to think that Rod and his mom were lunatics, but she didn't really want to believe that. When Rod promised he'd see her by the lake in a half hour, Jeanine just shrugged. She suggested he page her if there was any problem.

After he closed their front door, Rod hardly wasted a moment. He turned on his mother, pulled out his dagger, and held it next to her throat. He pledged to drain her if she didn't leave him and his friends alone, and he made Sondra cry. Happy with himself, Rod threw on his trench coat.

He told Sondra he could never really hurt her and

waltzed over to his room to study his dark image in the mirror. He surveyed Sondra's damage, and spent a few moments restoring a few candles to the altar. When his mother pounced back in, ripping the sheets off the bed, forbidding Rod to leave the house, Rod just mocked her. He pushed Sondra to the side and headed toward the door. He told her to get a life.

"I hate you, I wish you were never born," Sondra screamed at the top of her lungs. But Rod just grinned. Sondra continued her tirade, claiming that Rod ruined her life, that he killed all her babies. But Rod went about his business like she wasn't even there. He collected his pouch of pharmaceuticals, ducked in the bathroom and grabbed a few new razor blades, then gulped the last of his drink from the coffee table.

Sondra picked up a kitchen knife, Rod vaguely recalled, but he rushed at her and grabbed it away, pushing his mother back through the doorway. She was still screaming that she wished he was dead, screaming so hard that she never saw Rod's dagger coming. Rod seemed to just miss Sondra's face. The dagger landed a few inches away from her, stuck solid in the doorframe. With a grimace, Rod warned her that he wouldn't miss the next time.

Heather was already waiting by the dock when Jeanine and Eric got to the lakeshore. More than she'd ever admit, she seemed terrified of losing Rod. When Jeanine told her about Sondra's crazy behavior, Heather felt sick. She hated Sondra. She always thought Sondra was weird. A dull pain had begun in her chest. Rod's spirit gnawed at her.

When she heard more details about the bizarre scene with Sondra, Heather felt sorry for Jeanine. At least Heather had made a new friend in Eric, so she wasn't going to feel so totally deserted. Jeanine, on the other hand, was going to be left flat.

For the past week, Heather hadn't really been around Rod that much. She had been distracted by Eric, who was teaching her a few things about paganism and the worship of Mother Earth, teaching her about spell casting and karma and the wiccan rule called "three-fold." Heather found she was loving it. She was even thinking about adopting a craft name. Heather was happy to have been introduced to Eric, Jeanine's blue-eyed, sixteen-year-old pal, who had a sweet personality and a great smile.

Eric really seemed to know about things like higher powers, about the history behind witchcraft, and instead of hanging out in the cemetery, she and Eric had found their own secret spot by an oak tree next to Lake Eustis. Calling on all the wonders of nature surrounding them, she and Eric had performed a binding spell, and it was obviously working. They were crazy about each other.

The only problem with Eric, he seemed to be a control freak who just didn't want Heather around other guys. Eric said he was trying to bring her through a psychic housecleaning, using wiccan rituals to try to rid her of her evil deities, but from Heather's perspective, Eric was just jealous of her close friendship with Rod. Heather felt that Eric was trying to rein her in.

Heather viewed Eric as a bit of a hypocrite, because around Rod, he acted like he believed in the immortal, but in truth, Eric really didn't have his mind made up. Around Heather, he acted like he honestly believed her claims that she transported herself back to Egypt and other ancient places. Heather would claim she walked around the Minoan civilization of Crete, and Eric imagined that perhaps, he could learn to time travel as well.

When Heather admitted she had this feeling she had once lived in the ancient city of Memphis on the Nile, that she had been trapped inside one of the three great Pyramids two thousand years ago, Eric thought it was amazing. But as time progressed and he questioned Heather, she didn't seem to know much about hieroglyphics or ancient Egyptian customs. Finally, Eric let the matter drop. He decided Heather was a lost soul. She needed help, and Eric hoped through earth magic, he could move her energy away from darkness into the light.

But no matter what Eric did to assure her that he loved her—leaving notes in her window and giving her flowers and good-luck charms—Heather wasn't satisfied. To Heather, Eustis and the surrounding towns all seemed like variations of TV's Mayberry. Even the sweetness of her new boyfriend couldn't change that. Heather hated the sleepy quietness of it all. She told Eric that she would will herself out of Florida by using the prayers and spells of the undead.

Eric tried to understand her. Through Jeanine, Eric knew that Heather was an outcast at her school, that people made fun of her weird Gothic clothes, that some kids called her a witch. He knew Heather wasn't really evil, that she wasn't a devil worshiper, but even Jeanine said Heather had changed a lot in the past months.

All Heather wanted to wear was dark purple or shades of black, and she started showing up in black fishnets and weird jewelry covered with serpents and dragons. Heather was consumed by this vampire stuff, and it was really bothering her boyfriend.

Of course, the more Jeanine and Eric tried to question her, the more Heather's blood was swelling in her veins. She hungered for Rod's presence, for him to give her the powers that he had. She regretted that Jeanine and Eric were turning against her and felt they had something to do with Rod's distant behavior.

Before he left for Kentucky, Heather needed to talk to Rod. She would try calling him late at night, but they could never talk openly with Sondra lurking in the background. As it was, Rod said Sondra was giving him trouble. As soon as he moved to Kentucky, he promised Heather, he planned to make his way back to Lake County.

After her conversations with Rod, Heather would dream about biting into jugular veins, about draining poor souls. Some nights, she'd see visions of blood gushing, of blood running down her throat, and she'd wake up feeling exhilarated, anxious to report her sensations to Rod. But then curiously, when she'd be in a walking state, she'd feel vulnerable, like a dark spirit was playing a trick on her. It was as if she had no control of her own thinking.

chapter five

Even with Rod moving off to Kentucky, Heather hadn't given up on her belief in the "Ancients." She felt Rod was an eternal figure, and that her soul was entwined with his. Of course Rod's departure didn't stop Heather from living in a fantasy world, from seeing little shadow people, tiny supernatural beings who would follow her around. After Rod moved away, Eric got tired of trying to argue with Heather and decided to break things off.

With Heather increasingly hearing "voices" and Rod only calling occasionally, Heather clung to Jeanine, insisting that her girlfriend spend the night so she could catch a glimpse of these moving "shadows." It frightened Heather when she'd hear someone knocking at the door but no one would be out there in the darkness. Rod told Heather these were the incubus and succubus, evil spirits that would have sexual intercourse with her in her dreams. He warned her not to allow the incubus into her bed. When Jeanine stayed over, however, she heard no knocking, witnessed no spirits in the room. She figured Heather was just imagining things, trying to get Rod to call from Kentucky more often.

Either that, or Heather was in some kind of mental limbo, because one minute she'd make fun of Rod's claims that he had turned her into a halfling—she'd say he called her a "vampile" and would just start cracking up over it—then the next minute, she would talk about Rod as if he were going to be her "sire." Heather would say she wanted him to be her "maker," almost as if he was a god. Even though Jeanine didn't believe in "vampiles," she decided to placate Heather, and the two girls got into the practice of feeding off each other on weekends, telling their parents that the various scars on their arms were scrapes, cuts, or cat scratches.

Rod called here and there, pledging to appear to them out of a blue blaze. He promised Jeanine he would astrally project himself, and in fact he did materialize out of nowhere the night of Jeanine's fifteenth birthday. It was after nine o'clock at night, November 25, 1995, when Jeanine was having a bonfire party in her backyard. It was really just a few girls sitting around telling ghost stories, roasting marshmallows, and eating junk food, then all of a sudden, Rod stepped out from the shadows.

Of course Rod was a welcomed guest—the girls were ecstatic to see him. His skin looked especially pale under the moonlight, and Jeanine's other girlfriends were impressed. Jeanine hinted that he had "flown" to see her because he missed her so much. And it was true, Rod hadn't been gone from Eustis long. He had only left for Kentucky a few weeks prior.

Sitting around the fire, Rod talked about preparing for

his six hundredth birthday—there would be a grand ball for him in the next century, perhaps in Paris, perhaps in New Orleans. The fire illuminated Rod's face as he spoke, and he had a faraway expression as though he could see the future, as though he were already at this ball, surrounded by his legions at some wild party.

As Heather listened to him, she felt she was having an out-of-body experience. She'd see herself as part of Rod's family, sitting as the queen of a huge vampire coven, watching over Rod's "minions." Heather called these phenomena "flying dreams." Sometimes she'd feel the ground underneath her melting away, like she was on a roller coaster floating up and down. Sometimes, she'd feel like she was going to die, like her mortal body was being left behind. Around Rod, Heather lived in the air. Only with conscious effort could she bring herself back to earth.

"*You're still mine, I've made you,*" Heather would hear Rod say. Yet he never spoke those words. It was just a telepathic message.

Without a doubt, Rod had this aura about him. He was a dominating figure who could control people's minds. Besides Jeanine and Heather, he had developed a number of groupies who wanted him to remain in Lake County. They were Goth types, people who were into the occult and black magic; a couple of them were Marilyn Manson fans, but they certainly weren't psychos. Two of them, Bob and John, who were buddies of Heather's from Eustis High, claimed to fly places with Rod and share his psychic powers. Both these guys drank blood, but Rod refused to allow either one of them to "cross over" with him. Rod had no particular desire to gain them as followers. People like Bob and John were playing around with black magic for cheap thrills. They flaunted their vampiric ways and tried to *scare* people into believing they were preternatural. Bob actually went to the trouble of getting his teeth filed. Bob was a hard-core occultist who bragged about going down to Club Z in Orlando on Goth nights. But in Rod's eyes, Bob and his clan were little punks. Rod tolerated them but told Heather he would never offer them his embrace.

"An immortal body is a prison," Rod would tell Heather. "People don't realize what it is."

"I do. I know it's a prison," she would insist, "I'm *already* in a prison, Rod."

But Rod wasn't certain Heather was ready for the embrace. The night of Jeanine's bonfire, when Rod refused to perform the crossover once again, Heather pulled him back into the woods, pierced her neck, and let Rod drink fully. When the two of them returned to the fire, Jeanine noticed Heather was sheet white. She ran into the house to get a bandage for Heather and also brought out half of a ham sandwich. Heather needed to eat some real food. It looked like she was going to pass out.

To Rod, it seemed like he had gone over this with Heather a thousand times. He reminded Heather her sense of vampires and witches was only a picture-book version of things. If she wanted immortality, she'd have to learn more. She had to know what she was trying to get herself into. Rod did not come out and say Heather would be a demon if she followed him, but he did tell her she would be doomed to watch everything and everyone around her die. She would be entombed in a youthful body just as he was, feeling nothing but self-love, which brought unimaginable pain. He told Heather that all those around her would become creatures whose lives would have no meaning.

But she couldn't believe that.

chapter six

The subject didn't come up too often between them, but Jeni had a gut feeling something was wrong with her sister, and the night she decided to peek in on Heather, her sister was sitting on the bed scratching at herself with a razor blade. Heather said she was going to create her own scar-type tattoo, it was a form of body art and just a way for her to feel less depressed. Jeni tried to reason with Heather; she couldn't understand what her little sister was so upset about. Heather spoke in riddles about her "family" with Rod. She seemed unjustifiably distraught that Rod had moved away.

Jeni mentioned the personal ad she had seen in the *Lake Sentinel*; she believed Heather was using the name "Zoey" and was seeking vampire kindred. After making some jokes about it, Jeni got Heather to open up a bit. She admitted the ad was hers, but she wanted Jeni to know that it had nothing to do with Rod or Jeanine. When pressed further, Heather told Jeni to mind her own business, threatening to report Jeni's drinking to their parents.

Jeni left the room in a huff, and the next thing Heather knew, her mother was knocking at the door, asking if everything was all right. Heather quickly rolled down her sleeve and told her mom to come in, that she was just getting ready for bed.

Ruth was quite flustered; she had obviously been told about the razor blade. When Ruth asked Heather to lift up her shirt, her daughter refused. Heather promised that she wasn't hurting herself. Ruth suggested counseling, but Heather balked at the notion that she might need professional help.

When Ruth mentioned Jeni's name, Heather flew into a rage. Heather couldn't understand why she was being picked on when it was Jeni who stayed out all night, who caused so much turmoil in the house. Jeni was the one involved with beer drinking and lazy boyfriends, yet she seemed to get away with it.

Ruth decided to believe Heather. She couldn't stand the thought that her baby was mutilating herself, and Ruth *was* having more trouble controlling Jeni. In fact, Jeni had just totaled her brand-new red Saturn and had violated her curfew three nights in a row. Ruth and Rick's perfect cheerleader had turned into a wild girl, staying out drinking until all hours in the morning.

During the later part of 1995, with all the discipline of the household focused on Jeni, it was easy for Heather to spend a lot of time hidden away in her room. In her mind, Heather felt she had become practically nonexistent. She thought of herself as little more than a shadow in the Wendorf house.

Over the phone, Rod suggested Heather move to Kentucky, but from what Rod described, Murray didn't sound like the place for her. Heather wanted to see the world. She wanted to travel to Paris and Egypt, to physically experience these places for real. No longer content to imagine these foreign lands, Heather told Rod she had her heart set on seeking kindred spirits around the world.

Rod vowed to come get her. He just needed a little time.

But when the pitch of Rod's voice got more serious, Heather grew more hesitant. She mentioned the possibility of the police tracking her down, and Rod assured her that was no problem. He hinted that he had control of the cops in Eustis, that there were kindred among them. Rod was certain he could get around any petty authority figures. They were merely an inconvenience, that was all. Rod told Heather he would return to Eustis as soon as possible, that this time, he would come by car and would carry the supplies necessary for them to flee the country. They would head to Mexico, Rod said, but he wanted to round up his coven first.

Heather just listened and went along with the plan. It all sounded so stupid, but she enjoyed playing mind games with Rod, she loved building him up and making him her dark prince. From one perspective, she was hoping Rod would really have the guts to come get her so she could leave Eustis for good. But in truth, she had come to doubt Rod's word. Confused, she had begun to be altogether depressed, doubting her reason for living. After the brief appearance at Jeanine's bonfire party, Rod never returned to Lake County. When Heather asked him to astrally project himself for just a few hours, Rod's answers were vague and irritating. He claimed he had business to attend to in Arizona, that he had "children" who were being killed by a rival vampire clan there.

"You know, Rod, if you're planning on kidnapping me, you're gonna have to kill my parents," she teased. "Because if they're alive, they'll never let me go."

"Don't worry about your parents," he said, "I'll take care of them when the time comes."

"What do you mean?" she wondered, frightened by Rod's tone.

"They can always be tied up. Just don't think about it, Zoey. They're not going to stand in your way."

PART TWO

FROM
THE NORTH

chapter seven

Upon his arrival, Rod had a few vampire covens to contend with in Murray. He learned that the strongest vampire, Jaden, known as the Prince of the City, was interested in becoming his sire. Jaden claimed to be someone before whom Rod was required to bow down. Of course, things didn't work out that way.

Rival clans posed no threat to Roderick, who was used to dealing with competition from self-styled vampires. He knew they were just punk Goths who thought they were immortal, who hung out at vampire clubs down in Nashville. Rod considered them a bunch of local nerds who shed McDonald's and Wal-Mart uniforms to don cat's-eye contact lenses and prosthetic fangs.

But he discovered Jaden was different. Rod decided he had to take Jaden a little more seriously, since numerous kids at Calloway High School were reporting they'd seen Jaden levitate and fly.

No newcomer to Murray, Rod was greeted by his old elementary-school buddies, Matt Goodman and Scott Anderson. The three of them started spending all their time together, and Rod intended to take them into his coven, to ready them for an eternal existence. In truth, his young friends were inspired by Rod's teachings. They knew he had appropriated much of his philosophy from Aleister Crowley, but even beyond that, Rod's time in Florida seemed to have afforded him a worldly vision.

Roderick took great pleasure in rattling their brains, in turning polite chitchat into magical conversations. Rod's imaginary world seemed so real, he could convince them that a beautiful girl suddenly looked like a hag. Scott and Matt believed Rod could turn himself into a nine-foot demon, he was such a wizard at coaxing people. His childhood friends, as it happened, had become his willing targets.

"He did a lot of book buying," Matt recalled. "He'd come up with some wild stuff. He always told me he'd been up at the college library doing research on folklore. I knew he was drinking blood and he was a physical vampire. But I didn't think he was an undead creature."

Rod didn't want to scare Matt, he didn't want Scott to run off, so he decided to take his time acquainting his friends with the sorcery of the undead. He wanted to rope them in slowly, and at first, he never mentioned anything about making a pact with the devil. When Rod would teach the guys his martial arts skills, for example, when the three of them would spar with machetes, Rod never whispered a word about his dark army.

Rod put them through a grueling process, and Matt, in

particular, was good at mimicking him. Scott had some formal martial arts training already, so the three of them were becoming a united force. Rod made them believe the whole world was against them; around Rod, Matt and Scott felt like they needed skills for survival.

In private, each of them shared his own peculiar memories of a tortured childhood; they reinforced the notion that not one of them had been dealt a fair hand. Matt, for example, said he had been placed in a black box in elementary school, a traumatic experience that left him feeling outcast from society. Scott was a misfit with a troubled home life. He had been sent away to foster care, then bounced back into the Anderson household, only to run away again. Rod himself had been shuffled back and forth across the country so many times, no one could keep track anymore, and then there was the allegation that Rod had been sexually molested as a child. Rod would never give specifics about that.

The three of them had grown callous to most human sensibilities. Of course, Scott and Matt thought it funny when Rod bragged about being a killer. Rod would identify himself with people like Jack the Ripper and Jeffrey Dahmer, even claiming to keep certain body parts hidden in graveyards, but then, Rod talked that kind of rubbish all the time. His buddies were used to hearing him speak of killing cops, of killing his siblings, but neither Scott nor Matt gave it any thought.

Still, Rod's sense of reality would swing back and forth. He certainly had a vivid imagination. He seemed much older than his chronological age, and much of what he said did seem plausible, even if he did tend to be dreaming up his own universe. Nonetheless, Matt made up his mind not to believe Rod. He developed major doubts when, for instance, Rod quoted from the Bible, mixing and matching Holy Scripture with principles of witchcraft.

Rod was busy coming up with his own religion that didn't quite make sense to Matt. And after a while, Rod's understanding of good and evil seemed largely unintelligible. In fact, Matt had become so confused by Rod, he had to develop his own techniques for dismissing him. Matt wanted to keep Rod as a friend; they both enjoyed playing fantasy games, things like Dungeons & Dragons and imaginary combat—but that was about as far as Matt wanted to go.

"Rod wanted to be able to take a tree's life force and suck it into his body," Matt explained. "He wanted to summon enough magic to suck in all living life forces so that he could become so powerful that he might end the existence of the world."

Under the pretense of teaching them a few tricks with swords and knives, Rod hoped he was slowly creating a blood lust that would make Matt and Scott his loyal followers. Out in the woods, the boys would pretend to be battling against pure evil, they would imagine demons and gods being blown into oblivion while Rod would chant from magic books. The guys had a lot of fun with it. They liked the world of pretend.

"Your quest for immortality will never be satiated," Matt would tell Rod, "if you refer to being half-devil. If your point is to destroy the entire world, God will destroy you."

"All these people who worship the beast, what they worship is themselves," Rod would argue. "The Beast is man. Man has 666 calculated in his human makeup. The beast must be destroyed."

"That's not what the Bible says."

"It is, if you look at the miraculous signs, if you look at

the fire that has come down on earth," Rod would insist. "If you look at the fires in the Middle East, look at the burning rain forests, you'll realize I'm correct."

No matter how much Matt quoted the Bible and reminded him of the Christian doctrines they grew up with, he couldn't convince Rod that existence on earth wasn't a living hell.

"Vengeance is not yours," Matt argued, "you can't do that, you can't kill people. If you serve the lord of vengeance, you're going to be brought down."

"I don't care what God you worship," Rod hissed. "I'll destroy him in your mind. Why must you obey your God? Where is the reward? Man is waging a war that will bring fire and demons across the whole earth. Man will be enslaved by his own demons unless someone steps in."

"Why do you worship evil?"

"Because that is the only thing that has pure existence. There is no righteousness, no justice in the world. God is evil himself."

Rod was tired of feeling persecuted, sick of trying to fit in with a hypocritical society. He had adopted a personality that brought fear into the minds of others, and that pleased him. Rod claimed he could annihilate his enemies by pulling the life force from their souls. He spent hours and days trying to convince Matt to share in his powers, to join him on the "dark side," but unlike Scott, Matt wouldn't give in.

Rod preached about the many realms of eternal existence and the ways to defy time and space, to defy the laws of physics. Matt would resist Rod's wacky thoughts, but Scott seemed to believe him. Scott was a follower, a quiet type who basked in Rod's weird perceptions of life and death.

Rod asserted that the realm of death was controlled by a fallen angel and used riddles to suggest that he was soon to be unchained, that he was that angel awaiting his place on a throne in hell, and even though Matt warned Scott, Scott went along with Rod. He was willing to submit his will to Rod in order to be embraced.

"Society wouldn't accept Rod, he was shunned," Matt confided, "and Rod got to the point where he wanted ultimate power. As a vampire, as an immortal, he could go out and kill people and prove them wrong. Nobody could stop him, he was practically a god. But I didn't want that power, even if there was a way to get it, because it could damn my soul for eternity."

Having successfully pulled Scott into his dark world, Rod determined that Jaden Murphy could prove to be a useful pawn, and through the grapevine, he set up an informal meeting with Jaden in the Old Salem Cemetery. Of course, as soon as the two of them sat down on Rod's favorite tombstone, the young men bonded. Rod realized he and Jaden had a lot in common.

For starters, they both acknowledged the supernatural within them; they had experience dealing with ghosts and witches, with past lives and undead souls. At the very least, even if Jaden wasn't immortal, Rod decided, he certainly was convincing. And in the quiet of the graveyard, the two of them began to confide in each other. However, when Jaden refused to give specifics about his sire in England, Rod thought it was odd. Still, Rod wasn't going to be too quick to judge. He needed Jaden on his side and really didn't care if Jaden was for real.

Jaden listened as Rod claimed he had been sent to earth to challenge God, stating that he would reveal his prophecy by the year 2000, when he would be reunited with humans and thus end his eternal torment. To that end, he needed Jaden to help him adopt a vampiric family in Kentucky, and Jaden agreed it was necessary. He was only too happy to oblige, slicing himself and offering Rod his arm.

"You realize, we can't die," Rod sighed, "but of course, I have found a great respect for death."

Jaden nodded, cleaning his knife and placing it back in his black leather sheath.

"I find it strenuous to kill mortals," Rod said. "I often drain animals to spare human lives."

"Yes, I find draining humans to be distasteful," Jaden agreed. "Are you sure you're able to make human sacrifices?"

As they philosophized about immortality, Rod and Jaden knew they could not escape from their blood appetite, from the torture and shame they suffered while gratifying it, even if they had to feed off birds and vermin. As the two teens conversed and shared tales of blood lust, Rod learned that Jaden had only been crossed over two years prior. Of course Rod was furious that Jaden had been "made" without the approval of the Elders and blasted Jaden for pretending to be "full vampire," commanding Jaden to produce this cursed "sire" from England. Jaden claimed that wasn't possible.

When Rod discovered that Jaden considered himself a Christian and claimed to use his immortal gifts to serve the forces of light, Rod realized that Jaden was no vampire at all. Under the circumstances, Rod found it a perversion to allow Jaden to remain the leader of the coven, and to himself, he vowed to clean up the sorry state of affairs.

Jaden, disturbed by Rod's satanic principles, knew Rod was trouble and realized he'd have to win him over somehow. In Jaden's view, Rod's ideas about Satan had nothing to do with bloodletting. For Jaden, drinking blood was just an alternative method for spiritual communion, not a twisted way to cross people over in the name of evil. Jaden hinted that he would visit Lake County to identify the locations of Rod's "vampiles," but Rod insisted that his coven in Florida were "children of the millennia" who submitted to his authority, and his authority only. He warned Jaden to stay away from Florida, claiming his "vampiles" had perfected the art of killing and had been taught to destroy all rivals.

As he spoke of his coven in Eustis, Rod bragged that he had trained them to sacrifice without afterthought. Rod argued with Jaden about breaking the commandments of the "Ancients," reminding Jaden that it was he who had embraced them, who had felt the blood spill from their warm human flesh. Only Rod could guide them to the eternal.

When Jaden balked at Rod's ruthlessness, Rod insisted that he possessed the essence of Satan's spirit, that he and his "childer" were Satan's vagrant flock. Rod could not understand how Jaden could claim to be undead, yet fail to guide others in the practice of darkness.

Despite their differences about the gift of eternal life, Rod had beckoned Jaden, had decided to use him, and was determined that they become kindred spirits. After a few weeks of prodding, Rod found himself allowing Jaden to sire him, just to keep peace. As soon as his name became known in the coven, Rod seemed to be viewed as a god. Almost through osmosis, Rod had developed some strange hold among kindred. By drinking from the bottle mixed with everyone's blood, Rod was given an implied higher blessing.

But if, indeed, Rod was a true immortal, Jaden thought it ironic that Rod had grown up there in Murray as part of the mortal society. Jaden scoffed at Rod's elementary-school buddies, calling Matt and Scott "nerds" who had no business dabbling in vampirism, but then, Jaden believed there were no such things as coincidences. Rod seemed to have a bigger picture in mind, and Jaden was too smart to ignore Rod's power. Already, Jaden's coven seemed to want to follow Roderick.

Rod assured Jaden that Murray was destined to be his permanent haven, describing visions of roaming vampires who maintained covens in the sprawling lake resort territory nearby. And Jaden learned not to question Rod about these things. He noticed that from the time Rod arrived in western Kentucky, strange things started happening in Murray.

There were reports of animals hanging from trees. There were rumors about witch's covens meeting to cast demons from graveyards. Bizarre markings had been found along the highways in Calloway County—Jaden started to think all of it was somehow linked to Rod. And Jaden found he was becoming drawn in by Rod himself, constantly meeting with Roderick in the Old Salem Cemetery to "feed" and perform rituals.

"I'm anxious to have other vampires join me," Rod boasted, "so I can teach them about the world beyond."

"Well, if I'm here to serve the force of darkness," Jaden argued, "then I'm not doing a very good job of it, because I still feel human emotions. I still feel love."

Rod confessed to Jaden, that, unfortunately, his own sense of love was fleeting, at best. With his new girlfriend, Charity, for example, Rod said he only lived for the moment, feeling no sense of commitment or real caring.

In the first days of their courtship, Charity formulated the impression that Rod didn't feel anything human at all. Rod was jaded, it was like he came from a different planet, and it made Charity want to convince him otherwise. She desperately wanted Rod to become serious about her and was conjuring images of the two of them surrounded by a couple of kids and the obligatory white picket fence.

Charity, silly girl, was instantly head over heels for Rod. She was the typical fifteen-year-old with a big crush and a great sex drive, and more than anything, she wanted Rod to lose track of everyone else, especially his "girlfriends" in Florida, Jeanine and Heather, whom she'd heard so much about. Whenever Rod spoke of these two girls, Charity would just cringe. She knew they called Rod at odd hours and it really annoyed her. But Rod promised he was only being a good friend, that if either girl had romantic interests, she would be wasting her breath.

Indeed, Rod claimed undying love for Charity, but no amount of love would have taken him away from his vampiles. Charity was a terrific lover, but Rod never gave up his lust for blood rituals and sacrifices. As soon as he'd leave Charity's bed, Rod would meet up with his coven and "feed." Whenever she'd get cozy with him, sharing her vision of domestic bliss, Rod would cancel those thoughts with visions of death. Rod spoke of the immortality he wanted her to share. He confided he had a secret cave where the "chosen" would dwell.

In their moments alone, Rod seemed to contain the sensitivity of the entire human race. Charity believed him to be an eternal spirit and wanted to be near him at all costs, even if it meant following him out to some cave in the darkness of the Land Between the Lakes.

"The first night we talked, Rod told me he was part of a black mass when he was a kid," Charity confided. "He said that these old men had sacrificed an animal and dripped the blood all over him. It was really weird. He was crying about it."

But Charity didn't want to dwell on Rod's past—she herself had been molested by a distant relative—none of that mattered, now that they had found each other. She would emphasize to Rod that unless they lived in the present, they did not live at all. She wanted to tell him that she didn't believe in vampires, but she felt she couldn't.

Rod, meanwhile, was doing his own background checks and was absolutely irate when he learned that, all along, Charity had been hiding things from him. His new girlfriend was pretending to be Miss Goody Two-Shoes when, in fact, she was one of them. Not that it came as any great surprise that Charity had already been crossed over by one of the Murray coven leaders. Rod just didn't like the idea that she was so deceptive.

"Charity, there's something you're not telling me," Rod blurted. "I've been talking to people and asking around about you."

"Yeah, well, what do you want to know?"

"Do you know anyone by the name of Father?"

Charity's eyebrows raised, but she sat silent.

"Never mind, don't answer that. I already know."

chapter eight

When Rod was invited to join the Victorian Age Masquerade Performing Society, a group of improvisational actors who developed their skills by using the role-playing game Vampire: The Masquerade, Rod was amused. The first meeting was impromptu, just a short gaming session on the campus of Murray State University; the people were friends of Jaden's, and Rod teased Jaden about hanging around a bunch of vampire wanna-bes. Rod laughed when he learned that these "performers" walked around campus wearing sunglasses day and night. As if they were movie stars, Rod thought, what a joke.

For Rod, this bizarre masquerade seemed to be an open invitation to feed, a perfect venue for new blood. But Jaden warned him not to think of those possibilities. These college kids were into self-expression, things like body piercing, tattooing, costumes, and makeup. They did not participate in bloodletting; they were mock vampires and weren't ready to be embraced.

Full-blown masquerade sessions lasted from sundown to sunup. At times as many as seventeen members would perform, integrating their natural talent with the directives from a role-playing book. Before anyone could begin to play Masquerade, he had to be instructed in vampire "traditions" and was asked to choose from the variety of distinct vampire characters the book described. James Yohe was the game master, the storyteller, who had come up with a role-playing "constitution."

A tall, good-looking, dark-haired guy, James was the one who set the scene, and he reminded performers that no alcohol or drug use was permitted, that no weapons or harmful physical contact would be allowed. James was good at taking charge of the performance. He could mesmerize the players into believing they were actors on a soundstage.

On Rod's first gaming night, the backdrop James created was a dismal and decaying city, a wasteland where the characters lurked among rusting factories and toxic spills. The "crypt" in James's basement was their first meeting place, and the players were directed to follow him there, to his shared rental house just off the campus, down on Olive Street. Players seemed to like the crypt because it was safer there, they could be less inhibited and really flow with their characters. Free use of imagination was essential, James told them, but Rod noticed Jaden was a bit too serious about the role-playing, that Jaden revered all the phony pomp and circumstance.

When Rod was asked to pull a character sheet from a game book and choose his attributes, he decided to play a bon vivant, someone who wanted to enjoy life while it lasted. A hedonist, a sensualist, a party animal, that was the personality archetype that suited him. Jaden characterized himself as a rebel, as an iconoclast, seeking to destroy the widely accepted ideas of American society. His character's desire was to have the freedom to shirk authority and the status quo.

Besides Jaden, Rod, and James, only two characters were joining them that night: Missy, who played a martyr, someone who desired self-sacrifice, who endured long-lasting suffering, and Shy, who chose to be a caregiver, someone who would keep the others steady and centered. The players were then assigned a quest that matched their character traits, filling out the game sheets by rolling dice to determine points in virtue, knowledge, discipline, talents, and skills.

Rod's character wound up with the lowest blood pool and the lowest combat capabilities. Jaden, the rebel, wound up with high scores in almost everything, above all, in intimidation. Missy's high rolls were in manipulation and linguistics. Shy's strengths were in magic and charisma, but her physical stamina was almost nil.

With all traits determined, the game started, and James handed out props: a few pairs of prosthetic fangs; some sharp, clawlike finger ornaments; a red-dye kit for people to paint blood and various scars; some photographs of their "lost orphan children." And of course, there were elaborate maps that James had painstakingly sketched out.

Depending on the roll of dice, characters would find themselves dueling in the woods, lost in the cemetery—the plot elements would be provided by James along the way—but all of it was imaginary. Fistfights were had, battles were waged, vampires were killed with wooden stakes.

All these struggles for control provided entertainment for the performers, and James acted like a god, orchestrating every player's next move.

The main object was to provoke distrust, debate, and intrigue among the characters, who, as drinkers of blood, were tainted by evil. For a vampire character to "win," he or she had to defeat the monster within by exerting restraint, by nurturing the impulses of human virtue. If a character performed highly throughout his or her quest, the vampire might escape his curse and become mortal once again.

Rod noted that the Gothic aspect provided the ambience for these mortals; the performers were drawn to the menacing flavor of gargoyles and the remote, gloomy medieval settings that the game conjured. To that end, James had created his crypt in such a way to suggest the horror and mystery of the damned. The walls were black, the curtains bloodred. On the ceiling, plaster and clay had been used to produce an effect of ribbed vaulting and pointed arches. It was a seemingly decadent place, where the punk rock and industrial music could entirely drown out the realities of the suburban homes surrounding them.

"Thou shall only sire another with the permission of thine Elder," James began, speaking with dramatic emphasis. "If thou creates another without thine Elder's leave, both thou and thy progeny shall be slain."

Of course, Rod resisted the desire to inform James about the fallacies of this live-action game, but still, it irked him that vampires were described as hunters, not as immortal rulers. Rod realized that this Masquerade was nothing more than a Gothic-punk vision. It was yet another distorted way for teens to take the universe to the extreme. As the game progressed, the players seemed to revel in notions that their government was degenerate, that their culture was bankrupt, and Rod felt their torment. He knew this was the reason he had been awakened from his long slumber. These young mortals were roaming the earth with no reason to exist. They were ready for immortality.

As the characters began their quests, they were able to choose their own social distinctions. For the most part, they would be distinguished by how many generations they were removed from Cain, the first known killer. James took the position of "Prince," the only vampire free to create progeny, the only one who had the authority to call a blood hunt.

Jaden thought that was cute. At some point, he fully intended to introduce James into his vampiric coven, but Jaden felt James wasn't quite ready to unite the carnal and the spiritual. Jaden wanted the time to be right, and for the moment, the game would have to be enough. Jaden always believed that the night would come for the bloodletting to begin, that the Masquerade would cease to be an imitation of vampiric life for dear James. But Jaden didn't want James or his players to feel pushed. That would just spoil everything.

"We have been a thousand places and seen a thousand things," Jaden told Shy's character. "We have always lived among our kind, and our meeting here tonight is a meeting destined to happen a thousand times more unless you can help me gain access to the city's most influential mortal."

"I can lead you to his mansion," Shy claimed, "but only if I know what road you choose."

"Of course, I choose the road of revenge," Jaden said. "The man I seek has broken his blood bond and has begun hunting vampires. I desire that I will come to him in his sleep so I can steal knowledge from him. I vow that he will know the passion of my blood appetite."

"I will not walk that road with you," Shy told him. "Unless I am forced. I cannot be led to visit a vampire slayer."

"We shall see," Jaden said, rolling the dice to determine whether Shy's physical strength would withstand his desire.

Since Jaden's roll gave him no immediate answer, James encouraged Shy to find a way out of the wilderness, to collaborate with Missy and mingle among strangers in the city as a means to escape Jaden's character. Jaden craved blood, and James predicted an Armageddon unless Shy and Missy—both members of the "Camarilla clan"—could extinguish Jaden and Rod's clan, the Sabbat. As James gave an order to Missy to seduce Rod, he realized she looked quite appealing in her tattered satin dress. Missy's eyes seemed to dance in the candlelight as she spoke an incantation for a love spell. She was sent out to tempt the so-called Sabbat, and James felt he was falling in love with her. Missy was a compelling vixen.

James ordered Rod to make a fireball. He needed Rod to create a diversion so that Missy and Shy could flee Jaden's clutches, but Rod failed in his dice throw and was unable to help them. When it was Shy's turn, she rolled successfully and created an energy ball that brought havoc down among them. Shy earned a second roll, one that allowed her to become invisible, thus Shy's presence was reduced to the sensation of a body tingling in the room. She waited in stealth to thwart Missy, who was designated her next attacker.

Rod noticed that toward the end, Jaden had become completely engulfed by the role play. When it was his turn

again, Rod decided to shock Jaden back to reality by biting his lips, but Jaden, in return, wrapped Rod into a pas-
sionate kiss, sucking Rod's lip until it bled. For Rod, who
felt the feverish excitement of another man's touch, the
masquerade ceased to be an act. Jaden seemed to have the
strongest imagination of any of them, and he was able to
produce in Rod a feeling of sensual attraction.

Rod had been ready for a night of killing, for the taste
of Jaden's blood, but now, as he pondered Jaden's full lips
and the impact of Jaden's breath, Rod viewed his friend
with a new lust. Swirling his velvet cloak and flashing his
canine teeth, Jaden seemed most endearing. But Rod had
to stop his thoughts. He didn't want to think of Jaden as
anything more than a brother.

chapter nine

"**M**urray is a big circle, but it's like a black hole," Shy would later say. "It sucks you in and never lets you go. At first it's great, you've got all these friends and everybody seems to be real. Everything is so different because it's a college town, it's run by young kids. Everybody seems to be cool and you love it. But then it starts getting tense."

After the holidays, when 1996 rolled around, things had become complicated for a number of the young people in Murray, among them, nineteen-year-old James Yohe. He was trying to keep his mind on his college studies, was still running the live-action game, and had even become an amateur playwright, but his personal life was getting in the way of his achievements.

Over Christmas, he had become engaged to Missy, and just days after Missy moved in, Shy and her dad showed up to report that she was pregnant, that Shy would take a test to prove James was the father. James decided to live up to his responsibilities and let the girl stay with them until the baby's birth, giving up his king-size water bed. Obviously, Missy hated having Shy around and refused to believe James was the father. There was incessant arguing, and Shy would often spend nights elsewhere as a result.

"We weren't very formal, it was crazy," Shy confided. "We were family and enemies all wrapped up in one. That's another thing that happens in Murray. You hate each other, you love each other, if someone needs a place to live, you make amends."

Jaden had now become a fixture at the Yohe house as well, still participating in the Masquerade, but mostly hanging around watching B horror flicks and entertaining his girlfriend, Ashley. Rod also appeared often; he hated being around his mother and loathed going to school, so the Yohe house was a perfect getaway. As for the Masquerade, James had taken the game to new levels, creating vampire scavenger hunts on the college campus and out beyond, to the "Vampyre Hotel" hidden deep in the woods in the Land Between the Lakes.

With practice, James had become quite adept at keeping a complex story line going among his cast of characters, and Jaden seemed to be really impressed. Both Jaden and James had warned Rod to stay away from the young kids joining in the new games, but Rod was somehow taking the Masquerade too seriously, telling Jaden he planned to embrace certain players, especially the young twins, Cindy and Cynthia, girls who had become enthralled with the idea of crossing over.

Of course, James always had his suspicions about Rod—the guy acted weird—and some people flat out believed Rod was a real vampire. But then, Rod would never confirm it.

"Do you think you have eternal life?" James finally asked.

"No," Rod insisted. "It's just a game. You, of all people, should know that."

"Then why does everybody want to create such a mystery around you?"

"Look, if I get cut, I bleed. If I get shot, I die. I'm just like everyone else."

"Then why do you always talk like you're supernatural?"

"Because all these people are forcing me to prove things," Rod told him. "Some of these little teenyboppers ask me to bring them death, they want to be undead. But I can't offer that. All I have is my body, my blood."

As usual, James would get nowhere when he talked to Rod. James was bored with the cryptic messages, with the hints of eternity. He decided he had real responsibilities to worry about—between Shy moving back and forth, between his difficulties at work and school—and he stopped concerning himself with Rod's exploits. If people wanted to suck Rod's blood, if they wanted to "feed" from Rod or Jaden or whomever, James didn't feel it was his place to interfere. As long as nobody cut themselves in his home, James was cool with it.

"My whole thing is Goth. A lot of people mix up the idea of Gothic and vampires," James clarified, "but to me, Gothic is more about the Victorian age, about decorum, not about vampirism.

"There were rumors about Rod and Jaden being vampires, about bloodletting, and them making their own sect," James recalled, "and I thought it was primarily teenage curiosity. It seemed to be a new thing that had popped up, and I mean, some people experiment. I hadn't heard of any incidents as far as people dying from it, per se."

The fact that James didn't associate himself with vampirism really didn't matter, however, because with all the lies flying around town, with all the chaos in the Yohe household, rumor had it that James was one of the chosen "sires." Of course, the truth was that James had refused to cross over, that he was not even really speaking to Jaden because of it, and even though he let Jaden hang around the crypt, James found he had trouble being civil to Jaden. James thought Jaden, the most outspoken of the group, was abusing the vampire game. James believed both Jaden and Rod were violating the rules by trying to slice players during role play. Jaden entirely denied it.

He told James to confront Rod on the issue, expressing his own struggles with Rod, who was increasingly taking drugs and losing touch with reality. For Jaden, it was Rod who had become a frightening character. The two had become involved in a tug-of-war over Ashley, Jaden's girlfriend, who insisted that Rod was stalking her. Ashley complained that Rod would appear in the strangest places, that he was following her every move. Of course, Rod refused to admit it, but Ashley's claims still created tension between them.

With all the internal struggle, with all the rumors about murder and bloodshed and LSD use in the crypt, the young people at the Yohe house were feeling more and more out of control. Jaden suspected Rod was using LSD to enhance the role-playing for certain female players. Jaden had come across some tabs of acid hidden in the crypt and had scolded Rod, who admitted to stashing the drug, but swore it was only for his personal use.

Not that Rod needed to use drugs to lure new players or female followers. In fact, he had so many wanna-bes around, he had more girls hanging on him than he knew what to do with. Besides Charity, his on-again, off-again girlfriend, there was Shy, his frequent sex partner, there were Jeanine and Heather, both of whom wanted to come visit, and there were his new fledglings, girls still in junior high school whom Rod would sometimes meet at the Old Salem Cemetery.

Then above all, there was his mother, Sondra, who mocked Rod for being into devil worship, yet seemed to be more of Rod's friend and follower than she was his mom. When it came right down to it, Sondra was no different than Rod's other groupies. Even though she had no evidence that anything was actually going on between them, Shy felt Rod and his mom acted more like they were boyfriend and girlfriend.

"The way Sondra looks sometimes, she acts more like Rod's lover than his mother," Shy confided. "It's almost like she's flirting. It's hard to explain. It was her body language, but that was the only way she knew how to act around a man. That's why Rod thought his mom was hitting on all of his friends."

So, life among mortals was a soap opera—really—but none of it mattered to Rod. He didn't need people. He didn't care about their petty accusations and insignificant lives. He had the dark vastness of the universe. He had Lucifer's realm to contend with. Rod's life was magical. He couldn't be bothered with the humiliating vulnerability of little teenagers. Rod was good at using people and then disentangling himself when it suited him. He never worried about shattering someone's heart or disorienting someone's mind.

Whatever the moment required was the emotion Rod could produce. His purpose was to perpetuate his following, and to that end, he found Shy to be an excellent contact. For Rod, it was convenient to pull at her heartstrings, to use her to help him gather up his troops.

A beautiful redhead with a petite frame and compelling green eyes, Shy had no problem attracting young men. A number of junior high boys felt she was their "spirit guide," and they would join her at the Old Salem Cemetery to talk to Rod, wondering whether he *was* indeed a true immortal. Of course, Shy always built Rod up. She would promise these boys that Rod could open up the gates of heaven and hell, but when they would first meet Rod, they weren't so easily convinced.

Rod looked like a normal skinny teenager, even when, with his hair hanging wild in the wind, he would hang upside down from a tombstone, reading from his book of shadows. Rod would do things to freak people out—swallow matches, even claim he could shoot fire from his fingertips—but later, a lot of the younger kids would get into fights over his supposed "powers." Some believed Rod was a walking spirit, others made fun of the whole prospect of him being a mystical creature.

"You might not believe me, but Rod is a demon," claimed Robert, one of his devoted followers. "I have seen Rod turn into a nine-foot-tall man with a sword. He's got vampire in him. It's like somebody sent him here to help us remember things, because when you look at Rod, he gives you part of his aura, part of his thoughts, and the next night you dream of stuff that you didn't even think about before." Robert would insist that Rod was "the missing link to everything."

But if Rod was a link, he must have been an evil one,

because everyone around him seemed to be experiencing nothing but bad tidings. In his followers, Rod perpetuated thoughts of grief, of self-loathing. He made his "soldiers" feel there was no good thing on earth, telling his fledglings they could not seek comfort in each other until they destroyed mankind.

"There was a lot of spiritual energy in this area," Shy recalled, "but then everybody was starting to get real crazy. It was said there was going to be a war between the chosen and the children of God."

Shy believed in all magic, and though she never allowed Rod to fully embrace her, she did think Rod had a spirit that had energized her supernatural capabilities. He was a "dark person" who could take control of people's minds, and in the early part of 1996, when Rod mentioned that he had cast a spell on Shy, claiming he had unleashed the elfin side of her, that he had turned her into a fairy, Shy believed him.

For weeks, Shy practiced walking in shadows and astral projection. She became a witch and studied candle spells and white magic. She molded herself into Rod's image of what an elfin fairy should be, and she felt closer and closer to Rod, but nonetheless, she didn't rate as his number one girl. Indeed, when Shy decided to confront Rod, insisting that he choose between her and Charity, her whole plan backfired. Rod used Shy's white witchcraft against her and said he was tired of hearing her talk about angels and winged creatures. Shy had become a pest. He wanted her out of his life.

"Rod wanted power," Shy confided. "He started talking about his realm, about how he couldn't be with me because I was a fairy, because I was good. He said that if I didn't leave, horrible things were going to happen to me."

Ignoring his admonishment, determined to pull Rod

away from Charity altogether, Shy continued to work her love incantations and earthen magic on Rod. She moved out of the Yohe house and built a harvest altar in her new apartment so she could start a coven, holding meetings and celebrations on pagan holidays, hoping to lure Rod by the power of concentration.

It took months of devoted energy, but it paid off, because that summer, while Charity was away in South Dakota visiting her mom, Shy had managed to nab Rod. With Charity gone, Rod seemed to be in favor of getting married. He claimed he truly loved Shy, and in a moment of passion, he agreed to get engaged.

The summer of '96 was a happy time for Shy. The "war" she had anticipated had never materialized, she felt safe with Rod at her side, and she was excited about having a baby. The number of Rod's followers had grown, so Shy felt like a queen among mortals. She would walk through the Land Between the Lakes, where a deserted, crumbling building had become Rod's secret meeting place, and she would act like a high priestess, calling to the four corners of the world, casting spells on evil spirits and holding séances.

Best of all, her private life with Rod had become somewhat domestic. With her social security and welfare money, she had managed to set up a makeshift home, and when they were by themselves, Shy would call Rod silly names like Bunny Foot and would tease and laugh while she imagined her baby's nursery, making plans for Rod to adopt the baby as soon as possible. Initially Rod was so sensitive, so sweet about her pregnancy. Shy felt that Rod would be the perfect father, especially since James didn't seem to give a damn.

With Rod, Shy felt she had found "the one." She felt they were really good for each other, especially since they had a child on the way. For one thing, Rod seemed less obsessive about death, he had grown up quite a bit since he had rid himself of kids like Matt and Scott, and most important, he had stopped taking LSD. Rod would have whiskey now and then, and he still smoked pot, but that was it.

Shy felt he was finally on the right track. Even though he was only sixteen, Rod appeared to be happy to take on the responsibility of fatherhood; it seemed to stabilize him.

And Shy didn't feel the need to worry about things like parental consent. She hated Rod's mother and figured they'd have to live together "in sin" for quite some time before Sondra would ever break down to give Rod her blessing. In the meantime, Shy had to share Rod's time with Sondra, who would call every night insisting that her son return home.

In Shy's view, even though she was three years older than Rod, he was by far the most intelligent, the most knowledgeable guy she had ever known, yet at the same time, because he seemed so easily manipulated, Shy wanted to mother and protect him. Shy took great pleasure in being the stronger of the two, pretending to lead Rod around by the nose. It was funny, the way Rod never argued about it. He didn't care if Shy needed to act like a big shot, as long as she was paying all the bills.

However, Shy's bliss didn't last long. With her baby boy about to be born, clearly things were becoming twisted between the two of them. Rod was starting to get mad about the way Shy tried to exert her authority. She had given him a bad name among certain followers, and Rod couldn't tolerate that. Shy had taken him for granted, and keeping it to himself, he decided he wouldn't marry her, that he would dump her the minute Charity returned from out west.

Indeed, a lot of people hated Shy, she was baggage for

Rod. Neither Jaden nor James could stand her, they bad-mouthed the girl every chance they had. And Rod had gotten to the point where he felt sick at the sight of her, especially in the moments when she tried to show people that he was under her thumb. As she and Rod began to fight more often, Rod started to make mention of her murder. He would tell others that he wanted her dead. Yet, no matter how much he would kick Shy down, Rod couldn't seem to get rid of her.

"When we went to look for my wedding dress," Shy boasted, "I took Rod into JCPenney's on a dog leash. The saleslady asked me if he was potty trained, and I thought he was so cute. I tied him to the chair while I went to try my dress on."

Obviously, Shy never bought the dress. In fact, she never even got jilted at the altar, because the minute they left Penney's, Rod called Shy a whore and threatened to kill her newborn child. She claimed he threatened to *sacrifice* the baby boy unless she packed up and moved out of town. But in reality, Rod wanted Shy to disappear because he had a new force to contend with—Jaden's sire, the mysterious guy from England, had come back to Murray to take control of his "childer."

Shy must not have taken Rod's problems too seriously, because within days of his threats, she decided to stand by Rod's side. Having shifted the responsibility of raising her baby to her mother, leaving him across the state line at her mother's home in Tennessee, Shy returned to Murray where she moved into a trailer park with some of her coven members. Certain that Rod and Jaden were about to have a showdown, Shy decided to mount an attack with her coven, hoping to prevent bloodshed.

Shy wasn't worried about her baby. He was safer being

out of Kentucky, and besides, Shy wasn't feeling like the motherly type. A wisp of a girl who, days after the delivery, didn't look like she had given birth to a baby at all, Shy was a kid herself. She was unwilling to sit at home doing nothing all day and night, and anyway, she knew her mom was lonely and bored. The baby was better off . . .

"I hope you've got your group ready, because we're going to have a war," Shy told Rod, having made a special visit to see him at the Vampyre Hotel.

Obviously, Shy was hoping for a reconciliation. She offered to join forces with Rod, making up horror stories about the "sire" from England, and Rod finally agreed to stick around for her. Shy needed protection. She talked him into going back with her to her trailer so she could show him the place where someone had tried to light a fire. She was sure Jaden's sire was about to burn everyone up.

"Consider it done," Rod told her, "the realm will protect you. You'll be okay."

"No, I won't, because we're already blackballed," she insisted, "and I know something's going to happen. We just got to concentrate on keeping us alive."

"Well, most of these mortals are dealing with a dark force they don't understand," Rod said, "the Elders don't like it."

"I'm being chased by shadow figures," Shy told him. "I can feel them, I can see their auras."

Rod assured Shy that there was nothing to be afraid of. He had his blade, and he was on her side. Rod claimed he had already killed Jaden's sire, she recalled, and pulled out his knife with dried blood on it, bragging that he had just made the "sacrifice." Shy just laughed and wanted to know where the blood really came from, and Rod told her he had killed some Goths in Nashville, that he had drained a few humans in preparation for his battle.

Shy didn't like the sound of it. Rod's story seemed too believable. He was giving too many details and she started to get scared. She wanted her old Rod back, she wanted them to go off and join a traveling theater troupe together, but Rod wouldn't even consider it. He made it clear that he would kill anyone who stood in the way of his confrontation with Jaden's sire.

Shy figured the blood she saw on the knife was from an animal. She knew Rod was dabbling in black magic with his followers, that there had been talk of animal sacrifices up at the Vampyre Hotel. Rod was now back with Charity, who he claimed was his "dark bride," and Shy worried that Charity was having an evil effect on Rod. No matter how much she tried to warn him about her, Rod just laughed. Charity was an innocent, he insisted, she was the chosen bride because she was so pure.

Although Shy had never met Charity, from what she'd heard around town, Charity was a scary person who was capable of hurting people. Of course, Shy couldn't get through to Rod. Rod was so embroiled with Charity, the girl was playing along with the vampire game. According to Rod's followers, Charity planned on having the starring role in Rod's life, willing to go along with his wishes in her desire for immortality.

Shy just wanted Charity to go away. She wished the girl had stayed with her mom out in South Dakota. She told Rod that she had proof that Charity was a sleep-around, that Charity didn't really love him, and Rod wanted to see it. When Shy offered to bring Rod to visit a couple of Charity's other "boyfriends," naming two guys specifically, Rod suddenly listened. In his heart, he knew Charity wasn't always faithful, and now Shy was riling him up.

"I'm obsessed with you," Shy finally admitted, grasping at straws to win Rod's affection.

"In real life," he asked, smirking, "or in some made-up dreamworld?"

"I think it's real, Rod."

"Why?" he asked. "Why would you want to do a stupid thing like that?"

"Because you're a vampire pretending to be a mortal pretending to be a vampire," she said, laughing, "and I love you. I always will."

But in the end, Rod and Shy had two different agendas. Charity later confided that after Rod checked out Shy's stories, he wound up giving beatings to both of Charity's "boyfriends." Rod did get back together with Shy for a bit, but he was just biding his time. Within days, when Rod started talking about splitting up again, it came as a total shock to Shy. She couldn't comprehend that they weren't going to be married. She thought they were made for each other. It was because of Rod that she had given up her child, she said, hysterical because now, her mother refused to give the baby back.

Rod tried to explain that he viewed Shy as an antidote to evil, that she was in his way. He had work to do; he was just getting his army started. Shy begged and pleaded, reminding him she could call on multiple gods, that she could enlist the help of fairies and even vampires, but her words fell on deaf ears. Rod had no need for Shy's amateur witchcraft. Rod still slept with Shy on occasion, just because he was sadistic and demented and liked playing with her mind, but after a while, when he told Shy his dreams—when he mentioned his fantasy of slicing her from ear to ear—Shy finally got the picture.

One morning, Rod had her so frightened, she ran to the bathroom to check whether she had gauze bandages in the trailer, worried that he would actually slit her throat. That's when Shy realized that her elfin magic wasn't enough. She tried to protect herself, she tried to keep herself from allowing Rod to walk all over her, but none of her spells kept Rod away. Rod would come and go as he pleased.

When she came home one day to find half of the windows of her trailer busted out, Shy's coven members insisted she get rid of Rod or move out. Shy knew that Rod had set her up, that she had to break things off with him, but still, she held on to the belief that his spirit would always be with her.

"When we broke up, we had this joke that we'd meet again in Hardee's in three hundred years," she reminisced. "It's true that we have been together in past lives, that our souls have been connected."

chapter ten

"**Y**ou're grounded," Sondra was shrieking. "You didn't call me, you didn't let me know where you was at, so you can just go lock yourself in your room."

Rod was used to it. He didn't answer, he just walked over to the fridge, grabbed a Coke and a couple of cookies, and started to dial a phone number.

"You look at me when I'm talking to you, young man," she demanded, slamming the phone down. "Where've you been? Who were you with, you little liar? You answer me, Rod, or your CD player is going to go out the window, and I mean it."

"I stayed with Charity," he told her, his eyes rolling, "and why do you care? You weren't even home last night. You were out with Kyle."

"**Do**n't you worry about where I was at," she said, grimacing. "You're a little slimeball. You think I don't know what you were doing? You're playin' with little girls, and if you don't watch out, you're going to be in jail for the rest of your life."

"Oh, shut up, Mom."

"No, you shut up. And you're going to quit cutting school or I'm going to report you as a runaway and call the police."

"They hate me at school. Why can't you get that through your head? I'm not going back there."

Sondra had been having trouble dealing with her son, almost from the day of his birth. Roderick, her only child, was born with the umbilical cord wrapped around his neck. He was almost stillborn, and Sondra believed it had somehow affected the kid's brain. Sondra was divorced from his father when Rod was just a few months old, so Rod never knew his dad. As far as authority figures go, he had Sondra's parents, Harrell and Rosetta Gibson, but whenever Sondra felt like undermining them, she'd tell Rod he didn't have to pay attention to their requests. Sondra didn't want her son to suffer the same unhappy childhood she had gone through. To anyone who would listen, she described her parents as "mentally and emotionally abusive" types, insisting that they were strict Pentecostal fundamentalists who made her existence a living hell.

"They were part of a very, very strict religion," Sondra complained. "They had a very strict dress code, short hair for a man, long hair for a woman, no makeup for women. You were not allowed to go to the movies or go to dances, you were not supposed to go to the beach. Basically, you were supposed to go to their church services and that was it."

Because of all of the turmoil between her and her parents, Sondra had quit school at age sixteen. She felt persecuted and misunderstood by the system so she really didn't feel right about forcing Rod to attend. When she was Rod's age, Sondra was a misfit. Even though she was pretty, with a cute button nose and wide-set gray eyes, nobody paid any real attention to her. At age seventeen, she got pregnant, was married and divorced, and was being accused of being an "unfit mother" by her father.

In truth, after Rod's birth, Sondra did feel unfit. She was outcast from the teen society at school, she hated going to church, and because she was different, she never held a "real" job in her life. At the most, Sondra would keep a job at a fast-food restaurant for a few weeks and then quit.

Sondra had been married twice, but her marriages only lasted for a couple months. In between husbands, Sondra had been a professional dancer, a street prostitute, and a welfare recipient. But she mostly survived by leaning on her parents, who pretended they didn't know about her drinking and pot smoking, who denied that their youngest daughter was living in the fast track.

Sondra was always immature, and she used her "baby talk" to get her way whenever she needed to. With Rod, she had taken the role of friend, which she thought was a better way to have a relationship with her son. In her view, Sondra tried to be a good mother by making sure Rod kept a neat room. But, having the mentality of a little girl herself, Sondra was unable to really guide him.

From the moment they had moved back to Murray, Sondra was worried about Rod's troubles at Calloway High. He was a transfer student, and apparently the local kids didn't accept him. She knew Rod stood out because of his dark clothes and satanic practices. She was aware that none of the teachers liked him, that he was on the verge of being expelled for a number of things, mainly his truancy. Rod had been cited for little things, like wearing jeans with holes cut too high in the thighs. He had spent time in detention for smoking cigarettes on school grounds. He was a behavioral problem in class; in particular, he used foul language in front of two teachers, who had reported him, Mr. Pigg and Mrs. Stonecipher, both of whom he had a field day making fun of in class.

The assistant principal, Dennis Fisher, found he was having weekly meetings with Rod, who denied any involvement in cult-type activities, even though other kids had alleged Rod Ferrell was into witchcraft. At one point, it was determined that Rod would attend an alternative school rather than be suspended from the public school system.

"We talked a lot about Rod's behavior," Fisher recalled, "and best I can remember, he was just a troubled kid that maybe just didn't like authority. He didn't like people telling him what to do and didn't have much direction. I can remember some of the excuses he would give for some of his actions. He would blame it on his home life.

"We had heard about some of the students involved in the occult and some of the students drinking blood," Fisher confided. "I remember seeing Rod's arm where it looked like razor marks on it, and I remember him telling me that they had done it, tasting blood. He didn't mention any names, but said they had tasted each other's blood, and I thought that maybe he was suicidal and I was worried."

Fisher didn't want one of his kids committing suicide. He didn't like that Rod was hurting himself, and he counseled Rod to stop his involvement with the occult. He warned Rod that self-destructive behavior could lead to much more harm, but Rod just sat there without listening.

Fisher tried to advise Rod that dabbling in the occult could lead to serious problems, but Rod twisted Fisher's words around. He thought the assistant principal was pointing fingers for no good reason. Rod would promise Mr. Fisher that he could "beat the system," but Fisher would remind Rod that the jails were full of people who thought the same thing.

"You know, seeing those types of marks on your arms, you could hit a vein one day," Fisher finally told Rod. "Something bad could happen."

Dennis Fisher tried to make a difference. Out of the one thousand students he was in charge of disciplining at Calloway High, the assistant principal spent a considerable amount of time with Roderick Ferrell in his office. But Rod would use Fisher's counseling as an excuse to go home and complain to Sondra, to gain sympathy from his mom about being picked on at school.

"People at school didn't like the way Rod looked," Sondra explained. "I was angry about it, because I thought the way he dressed was perfectly fine. I don't have any objections to a trench coat and combat boots. He could have sat in school and done his work and been perfectly fine. Because I remember when I went to Murray High School, that I dressed strangely, and I guess you could say I was treated exactly the same way. They did not want me in the school at all. I had a hard time finding friends."

But eventually, Sondra realized that Rod's problems went far beyond his style of dress. When he was suspended from school in May of '96, Sondra Gibson went down to have a chat with Dennis Fisher. At first, she was in denial about her son's involvement in the occult and devil worship, but then, after her meeting with Fisher, she had second thoughts about Rod's weird behavior. Within a week of their meeting, she called Fisher back to report that she had become afraid of her son.

Apparently, Rod had come home to find that Sondra had changed his room, that she had thrown out all his black sheets and curtains and replaced them with a yellow floral pattern, and he flew into an absolute rage. The boy physically went after her with a knife.

"Listen, lady, if you're afraid to stay in the house with your own son," Fisher told her over the phone, "you need to call the sheriff and let the sheriff come, because we can't do anything for you."

"Well, I was hoping you could talk to Rod, that maybe it would help," Sondra begged, "because I'm afraid he's going to hurt me."

"I'm sorry, Miss Gibson, I can't help you. You need to call the sheriff if you're afraid to stay in the house."

Eventually, Rod and his mom attended an "expulsion hearing," and Rod was kicked out of school. He would not be allowed to attend Calloway High for at least one semester, and there was no guarantee that he would ever be allowed to come back.

"We went in front of the school board and I signed the papers," Sondra recalled. "I told them that I thought it was okay for him to go ahead and sign out of school. What we had talked about was, he would get a job and then get his GED later."

But of course, Rod never got a job. Instead, his violent behavior escalated, as did his drug use. At the suggestion of Dennis Fisher, Sondra took Rod to see a counselor at a place called Western Kentucky Mental Health, but it wasn't of any use. Rod was assigned to write an essay about drugs, and he refused to comply. After one brief session, he told his mother that the counselor he met with was just "stupid."

"Rod said it was just a waste of his time," Sondra confided, "and from what I saw, 'cause I talked to the counselor for a few minutes, it *was* just a waste. As far as I'm concerned, it didn't do anything."

In the summer of '96 Sondra Gibson filed a Beyond Parental Control report on Rod Ferrell, having gone down to the Administrative Office of the Courts in Calloway County. She told the court-designated worker, Janeann Turner, that Rod had been involved with drugs in Florida, that she suspected he still abused drugs—that she smelled marijuana in the house—and she felt Rod was involved in a satanic cult.

Sondra complained to Ms. Turner about her son's threats, reporting that Rod had stated several times that he was going to kill her, that he was injuring himself by cutting his arm. She told the court official that she had attempted to ground Rod for his behavior but he would ignore her. She said her son often stayed out all night, completely ignoring curfew, and she called her son "verbally abusive."

A report was filed with the court, and Ms. Turner scheduled a meeting for Rod and Sondra to return to see her that week, but the two never showed.

In early August, Sondra contacted the Murray Police Department about Rod's leaving home without permission. In the interim, Rod had met with Janeann Turner— he signed an agreement with the juvenile court system and had agreed to see a mental health worker. But then he missed his appointments. Rod had also promised to report home on time, but Sondra confirmed that Rod usually stayed out with his friends all night.

As usual, Sondra called the police to cancel the runaway report she had filed the previous day. There was a good reason for his disappearance. Rod had a big fight with his girlfriend, she said. Now that Rod had returned home, Sondra had forgiven him. All was well, she promised.

In mid-August, Ms. Turner followed up with a phone call to Sondra, only to discover that Rod had missed yet another mental health appointment. By late August, Sondra had called Ms. Turner again, this time to report that Rod had broken up with his girlfriend and was "coming in wild." Sondra said he was being "very verbally abusive" to her, and Turner scheduled a "diversion conference," requiring Rod and his mother to come into her office. But of course, the day of the scheduled meeting, Sondra called to say Rod "couldn't make it."

When Ms. Turner rescheduled Rod's appointment into mid-September, Sondra and Rod did appear, and this time, Sondra reported that Rod's verbal abuse continued and she accused him of abusing LSD. Sondra told the court official that Rod was "carrying around an occult book" that she didn't like. Sondra blamed the combination of the book and the LSD for causing Rod's "self-inflicting wounds."

"He was starting to go out more, and he was starting to be more uncontrollable," Sondra confided. "It was mainly the drugs. They was really bad."

The social worker suggested that Rod be sent away to Charter, a rehab place where he could receive the appropriate care for his drug problem, but Sondra didn't like that idea. She wanted to keep Roderick at home with her. She insisted "some really terrible things happen to children in those kinds of hospitals."

Sondra hoped she and her parents could save Rod, but by November of that year, her son's problems had gotten so bad, she felt she had to leave the matter in the hands of the law. Sondra called Ms. Turner to report that Rod was "doing something destructive in his bedroom." She filed a Habitual Runaway complaint and was finally ready to press charges against her son.

Based on Rod's failure to comply with the court's "diversion agreement," it was determined that Sondra Gibson's complaint would become an official petition, that Sondra would have to sign a "promise to appear." There was a court order for Rod to go before a juvenile judge to determine what disciplinary action should be taken.

chapter eleven

"On one occasion prior to my son leaving in May, Sondra kissed my son against his will," Penny Murphy wrote in a sworn affidavit submitted in Calloway County. She was writing on behalf of her fourteen-year-old son, Jamie, who had come into contact with Sondra throughout the summer of '96. Jamie and his brother Jaden had spent a lot of time hanging out with Rod Ferrell, who, that summer, had moved into a tiny subsidized apartment with his mom. Penny Murphy was mortified when she found out about Sondra's vile letters and conduct and decided to have the thirty-five-year-old woman thrown in jail.

"Subsequently on May 17, 1996, Sondra mailed a letter to my son, a copy of which is attached hereto," Penny Murphy's affidavit stated, "which suggests that she desires to have sexual intercourse with my son. In the letter, she acknowledges that she knows he is 'very young.'"

Penny Murphy was flabbergasted when she learned that Sondra Gibson had built some kind of pictorial shrine celebrating Jamie. When she questioned her eldest son, Jaden, about it, he talked Jamie into turning over Sondra's sick "love" letters.

"On June 23, 1996, Sondra mailed my son another letter," the affidavit continued. "In this letter, she solicits my son to permit her to sodomize him and to have sexual intercourse with him."

Penny Murphy's complaint stated that Sondra Gibson had even sent Jamie a key to her home, asking that Jamie come live with her. Penny told officials that in the letters Sondra made "satanic references" and spoke of "becoming a vampire and being his bride."

Sondra Gibson would eventually be summoned to appear in a Calloway County court on criminal misconduct charges. Two pornographic letters would be entered into evidence, which would ultimately cause her to serve jail time. The first started off innocently enough, with Sondra referring to her job as receptionist, bragging to Jamie about her computer skills. Sondra casually mentioned Rod, who had recently been expelled from Calloway High, telling Jamie that Rod occupied most of his time with Charity, though he still kept his long-distance friendship with Jeanine and other girls in Florida. She hinted about moving back to Florida herself, fantasizing about life on the beach, and promised to take a few pictures of herself on her next trip down there. She suggested that Jamie have some pictures taken, asking that he send some new photos so she could show them to Rod.

In her letter, Sondra offered to buy Jamie a necklace "so you can wear it and know that you're thought about and missed a lot." She didn't want him to go to so many parties or have so much fun that he might ignore her. "Just try not to forget who still cares about you," she insisted, reminding him about what he meant to her. She told Jamie how sexy she thought he was and went on about how much she missed him.

"You may be very young, but <u>you are fine</u>," she confided. She wished he was eighteen so she could have "wild sex" with him every night. She hoped her words wouldn't offend Jamie.

"I think about being french kissed and fucked by you all the time," Sondra wrote. "I hope it doesn't upset you by my feeling that way."

Telling Jamie that she wanted to be his friend, she hoped she'd receive a written response from the boy. When she didn't, she decided to write him a second note. Complaining about how much heartache he was causing her, Sondra wanted to make sure they were still friends. She wanted him to know that she dreamed about him every night, that she couldn't wait for him to return. "I long to be near you, for your embrace, yes Jamie, to become a Vampire," Sondra confessed, "a part of the family, immortal and truly yours forever."

Sondra assured Jamie that he shouldn't be afraid of sex. She didn't want him to be scared of being with her, she didn't want him to be put off by her vast sexual experience. She promised that she would never hurt him or make him feel uncomfortable in any way. "I know guys talk and you've probably been told by Jaden and them that I'm wild and a slut," she wrote, insisting that Jamie ignore the rumors, insisting that she hadn't had sex with anyone in months. Sondra vowed that her thoughts were only of Jamie, that he was the only guy for her. She wanted Jamie to spend the night "two or three times," telling him, "I dream of you crossing me over while you're getting off."

Sondra wanted Jamie to keep her apartment key. She invited him to feel free to move in with her. She felt Jamie's dad would probably give Jamie permission to sleep over, and she wanted the boy to think of her apartment as his home too. If there was anything in particular he wanted to keep there, Sondra offered, she would empty out a drawer and make some space in her closet.

She urged him to come to Murray for the Fourth of July, inviting Jaden as well. Before Sondra signed off, she promised to wait for him for eternity. Jamie would later admit he was disgusted when she elaborated on her fantasy:

"I'll wear my blue denim sundress and we could kiss for awhile, then while we're kissing," she suggested, "I'll unzip your pants and go down and lick you and suck you until your just about to get off in my mouth, then I'll pull my dress up and move my panties over and guide you inside me."

On November 12, 1996, Sondra Gibson was charged with "soliciting rape" and "soliciting sodomy." She had signed an Affidavit of Indigency, stating she was on food stamps, owned no personal property, and had no steady job, thus she was appointed a public defender, Dennis Lortie of Murray. Mr. Lortie later petitioned the court to reduce the felony charges against his client to misdemeanors; however, the charges were not amended. When Sondra's lawyer filed a motion to dismiss the case, that motion was also denied, and Sondra Gibson was scheduled to have her day in court.

chapter twelve

"Rod's problem was that he didn't listen to the laws," Jaden confided. "I accepted him into my heart, as well as my life, I gave him the gift of the embrace, but he didn't understand it. He didn't respect life. You're supposed to respect your sire, but he would constantly break our laws."

When Rod found out his mom was soliciting Jamie, he considered telling Jaden about it, but at the time, he and Jaden were hardly speaking. Back in August, Rod had filed an assault complaint against Jaden (aka Steven Murphy), and Jaden had been thrown into jail. Jaden Steven Murphy was released on $500 bond and in September 1996 was sentenced to serve six months in the county jail as well as attend six sessions of counseling. It was all because of Rod's sworn affidavit, which reported the following assault:

My name is Roderick J. Ferrell. I am sixteen years old. I live at 906 Broad Apt. F-6 in Murray. I have no phone.

On Thursday, 8-28-96, at approx 11:50 pm, I was at home with my mom, Sondra Gibson, when Steve Murphy and Mike stopped by. We talked for awhile then Mike and I went downstairs to smoke a cigarette. About the time I finished my cigarette, Steve came down. We talked for awhile then he asked what I had to do with Cory Duncan messing with his girlfriend. I said "nothing" and he said "Don't lie to me."

He grabbed me by my throat and slammed my head into a brick wall. He began choking me and said "Don't fuck with me." He kept choking me and cursing me when I looked away from him. I was about to pass out when he released me. As I was walking back upstairs, he said "now you know I'm superior and you're under me."

My mom and I have had problems with Steven in the past. I believe he will try to hurt me if he has the chance.

                              Further, the affiant sayest not.
                                            Rod J. Ferrell

In addition to the jail time and counseling, Jaden Steven Murphy had been ordered to have "no contact" with Rod Ferrell for two years, but when his proof of counseling was presented to the judge, Jaden was released on probation after just a short jail stint, and as far as Rod was concerned, things would eventually be mended between him and Jaden. Their fight was just stupid anyway—and of course when Sondra's salacious letters had surfaced, it gave Rod further reason to reunite with Jaden. With the common goal of undermining Sondra's unwanted sentiments, the two decided to meet in a tucked-away rural cemetery and have a chat.

"Sondra was constantly talking to me about how sexy Jamie was and how adultlike he was and how she wanted him," Jaden recalled with disgust, "and she'd tell Rod the same stuff, and Rod would come back and tell me about it.

"Rod thought it was pretty fucked up, because Jamie was a virgin at the time, and Sondra sent him a key to her apartment. Rod fucking hated his mom because of it. He wanted her dead. He even proposed the idea of killing her to me."

Before their big fight in August, before the court system had become involved, Jaden had spent many nights with Rod and Sondra at their apartment, and for a while, Sondra seemed really cool. Sondra was finally living on her own, happy to have gotten away from her parents, and to have Rod to herself. The apartment was tiny, but it was hers to do with as she pleased, and she loved having Rod and his buddies hanging around. She let them have the run of the place.

Sondra even encouraged Rod to do the decorating because she thought it would bring her son closer to her. She allowed him to spray-paint pentagrams on the floors, to build altars in the bedrooms. Initially, Rod thought his mom was into vampirism as a spoof, but when he realized she was serious about being embraced, he hated her for becoming so involved.

In fact, it was Sondra who forced him to sign an affidavit against Jaden, Rod claimed, believing that his mother was jealous of Rod and Jaden's tight relationship. Rod went on to call Sondra "another wanna-be." His mom looked ridiculous with her jet-black hair and her Goth attire, and Jaden agreed. Now, the only thing on Rod's mind was how to get rid of her. Sondra was making a fool of herself, Rod said, confiding that she was constantly throwing herself at his male followers, that it wasn't just Jamie she was after, that Sondra's list included even Jaden. Of course, Jaden wasn't the least surprised, but Rod was completely ashamed of her.

As far as Jaden was concerned, the whole thing was laughable at first. The idea of Sondra being a vampire seemed pretty funny, and in fact, Jaden would often tease Rod about it. But then things had become serious after Jaden's mom had filed her complaint. For Rod, Sondra's open sexual invitations to Jamie had become the final straw. He wanted to leave Murray. He had homicidal ideas about Sondra and was afraid he might carry them out.

In stealth, when he met with Jaden to figure out a game plan, the two of them decided to ignore the law so they could join forces against Sondra. More than anything, they wanted to keep her out of their "family." The two young men discussed the "laws" of the undead; Rod acknowledged Jaden as his sire, promising his unending loyalty, and Jaden decided to forgive Rod. In the still quiet of the deserted rural cemetery, the two blood-bonded. They realized they needed to stick together to keep Sondra and any other adults from interfering with their vampiric world.

"I'm so sick of her shit," Rod complained. "She has no power over me, and I'm sick of her telling me what I can and can't do."

"Man, I understand how you feel," Jaden agreed, "but what can we really do about it right now? We've got the restraining order, so I can't even be seen with you."

"No, but you can go see Sondra and threaten her so she'll mind her own business."

"What for? So I can give her the power to throw my ass in jail again?"

"Let's just kill her," Rod blurted.

"Look, man, we're not gonna fuckin' kill her. That would ruin everything. We'd get all kinds of shit from people playing the game, and it would break our coven up. It would end our way of life."

"Well, I'm gonna kill her anyway, and I'm gonna kill my grandfather too," Rod insisted. "I hate that sick bastard. I want that motherfucker dead."

"I know how you feel, man, but it's not gonna happen," Jaden said, laughing, "because then Sondra wouldn't be around to marry Jamie. And your grandpa needs to give the bride away, right? I already talked to Jamie about it, and he says he's ready to embrace her as his dark mate."

"Cut the bullshit, man."

"Well, if you want your mom to get over my little brother, why don't you make her pull that stupid crap off the wall. I mean, that shit is sick, man. It needs to come down."

Unlike Jaden, Rod didn't find any humor in the situation. Rod didn't think the shrine was funny, especially since Sondra had Jamie's pictures surrounded by incense and flowers. Most days, since Sondra didn't work, she would sit around for hours just staring at that wall. Rod knew if he tore the pictures up, Sondra would go ballistic.

Rod just wanted to get away from it all. He felt it necessary to pick up and leave town. He said he had just been down in Lake County for his mom's birthday, that he had reacquainted himself with his group of fledglings and wanted to move back there. Roderick promised Jaden that there was "an army waiting" for them and asked him to move to Eustis. However, Jaden didn't seem too crazy about the idea.

"We're looked upon as being real ancient and power-ful," Rod vowed, "there are people down there who will follow us."

Rod tried to make Eustis seem appealing, he did every-thing but beg and plead, but ultimately, Jaden wasn't interested. Jaden had just graduated from high school and planned to attend Murray State. He wanted to get his col-lege degree in drama and then begin his acting career, perhaps even try his luck in Hollywood. Jaden wasn't about to leave Murray to chase after a bunch of Rod's groupies in yet another hick town. He told Rod not to worry about Sondra. If she wanted to think she was immortal, Jaden thought it was no big deal. They could just placate her, Jaden said, so she would keep her mouth shut if she ever saw them together.

But Rod wasn't so sure they'd be able to get around her.

chapter thirteen

In the heat of the summer, when Rod went to visit the Gibson house, showing up with bruises from a fight with Jaden Murphy, Harrell was furious. Rod claimed he was okay, but Harrell discovered Sondra had taken the kid to the hospital. When she told him that Jaden almost broke Rod's neck, Harrell forbid his grandson to spend any more time with such a bad influence, but Rod just laughed.

"Rod could come here and sit and talk very normally," Harrell said, "but then that Murphy kid would come around, and he'd be a completely different person. Right down from where the Murphy kid lived at, they were sacrificing animals, I can tell you that."

"I'm not going to take you over there anymore," Harrell threatened Rod, scolding him. "You're getting into some stuff that you can't get out of."

But Rod insisted on going over to see Jaden, even if it meant more trouble with the law.

"I can't get out of it, Grandpa," Rod insisted, "they'll kill me if I do."

"Rod, there's nothing under the sun you can't get out of."

"I'm a vampire. I can't die unless someone cuts my head off."

"You've done gone off the deep end, boy."

"What has happened, in the last few years Satan has taken over all the power. God has no more power on earth."

"Rod, that's just not right. That's not true at all."

"The Bible even says Satan's got the power and you Christian people can do nothing," Rod insisted. "You can't defend yourselves."

"Nobody controls Rod," Jaden later confided, "Rod does what the hell he wants to do.

"We'd go out, we'd have a good time, and it didn't matter what his mom fucking told him. It didn't matter. She just had this thing against me. She accused me of casting a spell over her and sodomizing her one night."

It was true that Sondra made all kinds of allegations, Jaden said. She even claimed that Jaden had sodomized her while Rod watched, which both Jaden and Rod vehemently denied. Sondra would later deny ever making this claim, but in any event she was a troublemaker, her own father would attest to that. Sondra had been involved in witchcraft and drugs for most of her adult life; her boyfriends were either pimps or pushers, and everyone around her became used to her lies, to her fantasy dreamworld that she developed from her belief in the occult.

Rod's grandfather Harrell would advise the boy to get on his knees and pray, telling Rod, "You need to go back to church," insisting that "there's no law against being good." Rod would act like he was interested, he'd profess that he liked church services, but Harrell knew that the boy was lying. Much of the time, Rod seemed high on drugs; Rod was a mess, and Harrell blamed Sondra for it.

"She'd expose herself in front of Rod like a little teenage girl out on the beach with a little bikini on," Harrell recalled. "If my mother would have done that in front of me, my mother would have ended up on the road back then."

Harrell didn't approve of his daughter's lifestyle in any way. He wanted her to live by the codes in the Bible, and he couldn't stand her defiance. When Rod was young, Sondra refused to take care of her child. She threw all the responsibility of Rod on her parents while she ran around with her drug-dealer friends. When Harrell would fight with her about it, Harrell said, Sondra would threaten to have someone in her "drug group" kill him. Harrell seemed unable to control Sondra, and his wife, Rosetta, seemed equally powerless.

"When Rod was a baby," Harrell recalled, "Sondra would not take care of him. My wife would work, and she'd come home and take care of Rod like it was her own baby. Sondra would never take care of Rod."

Harrell and Rosetta spent a lifetime reprimanding Sondra, but nonetheless, it became their responsibility to raise Rod. Because of Harrell, the family moved back and forth. Being a traveling salesman, Harrell was able to jump between Kentucky and Florida, taking Sondra and Rod with him, which made it difficult for Rod to feel he belonged anywhere. Rod never had a teacher or neighbor to look up to, he was never grounded, and all his life, he would defy authority. He enjoyed mistreating older people; it was something he'd learned to do at a young age.

"I would try to talk to Rod, to teach him," Harrell said, "but Sondra would say, 'Rod. You don't have to listen to Grandpa, he's not your daddy.' So I had a limit of what I could do with him. I tried to be an example to him, but Sondra, all her life, resented me trying to be a father to him."

Instead of teaching Rod things like sports or helping with his homework, Sondra was busy showing the kid how to make love potions. She was intrigued by tarot cards and witchcraft, and she subjected Rod to whatever fantasy world she could. Just to make Harrell angry, she would encourage Rod to disobey him, and Rod did, in fact, take exception to his grandparents' rules, even though he knew they were only telling him to do things for his own good.

"When we moved to Florida," Harrell continued, "Sondra took up with this fellow, David, he was into witchcraft. I don't know what in the world he was. He claimed to be a shaman priest."

To get a rise out of Harrell, Sondra would involve Rod in little candle spells. Sometimes she would play games like Dungeons & Dragons and would then make the play world seem real, allowing Rod to "playact" as a character to avoid dealing with his grandparents' demands.

"Rod and I played a board game with dice and characters," Sondra recalled. "Over the weekend we usually played it. You pick out a character, and then you choose different types of things the character has. Rod liked to be a king or a warrior, types like that. But then we stopped playing because my parents thought the game was of the devil."

As Rod grew up, he discovered his actions had no consequences in the Gibson house. Once he became a teenager, things really escalated. Rod discovered he could get away with just about anything. When Sondra first discovered Rod bloodletting with Jeanine and Matt in his bedroom, for instance, she did nothing to punish him, and neither did his grandparents.

Instead, Sondra went to her boyfriend, Kyle, to ask for advice, but Kyle seemed to think it was "just a teenage thing," that Rod would "get over it." So Sondra let the matter drop.

Once the family moved to Murray, Rod would confide to Harrell about his experimentation with drugs, explaining it was because he was being picked on by the "rich kids" and feeling like an outsider in the Murray school system. Well aware that Harrell already disapproved of his long hair and black fingernails, Rod even spoke about the bloodletting, always hoping to shock his grandfather as much as possible. He loved seeing the old man cringe. Rod was most happy when he could make Harrell feel morbid.

"If you cut yourself and you take somebody else's blood," Harrell warned, "you're in danger of getting diseases and God only knows what will happen to you."

"Well, people do it as a blood oath," Rod said, "a lot of different groups do it."

"You shouldn't do it at all, nobody should. And if you cut yourself, no matter what, you should use a real good instrument and use alcohol if you get cut. Don't kill yourself by playing stupid."

chapter fourteen

"Bloodletting can be a sexual act, vampires are very sensual," Jaden explained. "The embrace, whether it be male on male, female on female, is sexual. It's the taking of one's fluid into your body, the joining of souls and spirits that have walked the earth for thousands of years."

"I want you to kill me," Rod pleaded, having tracked Jaden down at the cemetery. "This is my final hour. I'm ready to die."

Rod stood before Jaden and his coven with his legs crossed and his arms stretched out. He was doing an impression of Jesus Christ, hanging from an imaginary cross in the middle of the Old Salem Cemetery, and Jaden thought Rod made a good martyr.

"Why in the hell should we kill you?" Jaden howled. "Because that's what you want? Why would we give you the release?"

Rod stood silent.

"You're going to suffer, just like the rest of us," Jaden said, sneering.

"If you don't kill me, I'm going to lose it," Rod said. "I'll go on a rampage and kill every mortal that stands in my way."

Things were coming full circle. Rod was claiming to be the Antichrist, and he vowed to "take out" Jaden's entire coven unless Jaden pulled his sword to prepare for a duel. Rod wanted Jaden to slice his head off. As he stood begging for death, Jaden mocked him. Rod was living in a pathetic little dreamworld, believing he came from the "land of the dead," insisting that Murray was just a "bloody battleground" where he had been sent to unite evil spirits until all hell broke loose.

It was peculiar that Rod felt so strongly about the mysticism surrounding Murray, especially when, on the surface, the place was just another Kentucky farm town, just a country village with "good home cookin'" signs adrift in a sea of white church steeples. At the center, a quaint town square with an old stone courthouse was surrounded by craft and antique shops. Murray certainly wasn't the kind of town that could be construed as mystical. If anything, it was too all-American. If it weren't for the college, there would be nothing but white bread, bowling, and gospel singing.

But Rod never saw Murray that way. He never paid attention to the physical world around him, which he claimed was just "an illusion created by mortals so they could feel safe." Standing in front of the group, Rod began shaking, he looked like he was going into a trance state, and spoke of angels falling from the sky, of wars and different killings. He wanted to take Jaden on a "spirit walk" and claimed a demon was passing through his body.

"I know everything about you," Rod told Jaden. "I know how old you are, and I know why you were sent to me."

Rod claimed Jaden was two thousand years old, that they had had their first meeting in their dreams, centuries before they physically appeared in Murray. Rod said he'd been calling to Jaden for five hundred years, claiming it had taken that long to walk from Jaden's dreams into his physical life. When Jaden realized Rod was going crazy, he knew he had to stay levelheaded. He told Rod he refused to pay homage to a demon and ordered Rod to leave the cemetery.

Rod was screaming at Jaden about his ancient memories, insisting that the two of them would walk the earth forever. He was breaking down in tears in front of the whole group, shrieking, "Kill me, just kill me," but Jaden just found the whole performance pitiful.

"You've betrayed us, and you are now forever banned from these gatherings," Jaden said, his voice calm. "Now leave quietly or I will be forced to have you escorted off these grounds."

"Our childer will be calling to you in your dreams," Rod shrieked, looking back at Jaden through the spikes on the cemetery gate. "You can't escape me, because I'll always come back. In your dreams, I will be your most powerful vision. I will blot out your landscape, and all you will know is my image."

"Get a grip, you sick motherfucker," Jaden yelled, "this is not the Masquerade anymore. You can't kill and expect to get away with it."

chapter fifteen

"I realized Rod was going over the edge when I watched him kill the cat, when he slammed it into a tree," Jaden confided. "That just blew my mind, that he did that. Because then I knew just how little respect he had for life."

On that note, Jaden ended his relationship with Rod. The two had been plotting an escape from Murray and had gathered coven members to discuss the possibility of moving to Baton Rouge. Then, in the middle of the meeting, Rod and Jaden had gone off into the woods by themselves, and Rod picked up a stray kitten, taunting the tiny creature with an evil grin.

"He just picked it up and was petting it, and I started petting it," Jaden recalled. "And then I took a couple of steps back and was sitting there talking to him, and he's still petting the cat. And then he just threw it. Smacked it right into a tree."

* * *

Having been ousted from Jaden's coven, Rod decided to declare war. He was making Molotov cocktails in his bedroom and planning to blow up the Old Salem Cemetery with the help of his buddy Peter Reynolds.

"At that time, I called the police," Sondra admitted. "It was Rod's idea to make some bombs and he was talking dumb, saying he was going to blow up certain areas of Murray. He and his friend Peter were making bombs in the house and I told them to get out."

In October of 1996, the Murray city police visited Sondra's apartment and wrote up a report. Unfortunately, they discovered there wasn't any real evidence to collect. The authorities told her there wasn't much they could do. They snapped a few photographs of Rod's room and left, advising Sondra to track her son down.

As a precaution, Calloway County sheriff Stan Scott decided to have his men stake out the Old Salem Cemetery that night, just in case there was trouble. The deputies hovered in the dank bushes for a couple of hours, hoping to spy bizarre people in capes and fangs, but the cemetery remained still.

Sheriff Scott and his men were used to getting complaints from Sondra. According to the sheriff, she'd call his office at all hours to report apparitions in her bedroom, to report a bloody goat's head in her blankets. When the deputies would arrive, however, they wouldn't find anything to support her claims. The goat head, for example, was actually a mounted steer head, just an old hunting trophy someone had placed in Sondra's bed as a prank.

"We'd been told about all kinds of weird stuff going on in that apartment," Sheriff Scott confided. "We'd also been told that Rod and some of his friends would go in the woods behind the apartment and from what some of those kids were telling us, that was where a lot of the mutilations of dogs and cats took place.

"Some of the kids told us that Ferrell liked to kill cats," the sheriff said with chagrin, "that he'd swing them around and break their necks. We even had reports that apparently Rod had buried animals in the ground after he had kicked their heads off. Something about he would take a dog and bury it in the ground and leave its head sticking up, or bury it alive."

Rod's involvement in these particular incidents was never proven, but Rod and Sondra caused a lot of grief for the authorities in Murray. The everyday townsfolk had become scared of the two of them. Sheriff Scott would cringe when he'd see them walking the streets of Murray like two ghouls, wearing black costumes with beige face paint and heavy chains. Even worse, they seemed to be gaining a following. The Murray Police Department was having more complaints about Goth people who seemed to be popping up in the town. The straitlaced locals were sure these scary kids were into witchcraft. People wanted them arrested for loitering, for making noise, just anything to get them off their quiet streets.

"When you meet this kid, you're not going to believe he's only sixteen," one of the deputies warned Sheriff Scott. "This kid doesn't seem to be a sixteen-year-old. You're going to think you're talking to somebody in their twenties."

Rod Ferrell had been called in to Sheriff Stan Scott's office the first week in November 1996. A probable cause for "cruelty to animals" and "criminal trespassing" was filed by Officer Warren Hopkins regarding a break-in at the Calloway County Humane Society.

An animal control officer reported that two puppies had been killed, their limbs separated, and authorities learned of Rod Ferrell's alleged involvement through their Crime Stoppers telephone line.

Matt Goodman placed the call, claiming that Rod and his friend Frankie Brittin committed the act. Matt could only offer hearsay, but he told authorities that Frankie was bragging about the animal sacrifices.

"Mr. Goodman made mention that he knew Rod and Frankie had been down at the animal shelter," Officer Dennis McDaniel noted. "He also made mention that he had seen Rod Ferrell kick and slam a beagle into a tree once before."

Ten Polaroid shots were taken of the mutilated puppies. The photos were shown to Frankie Brittin, who denied his involvement but said he had heard about it from Charity Kessee, who was supposedly yapping about the puppies in the Murray High cafeteria. When the police pulled Charity out of class, however, she just looked at the pictures with disdain. She had no knowledge of the incident, she said, and felt certain Rod was incapable of doing such a thing. Charity thought it was horrible that they were accusing Rod. Her boyfriend was an animal lover.

But Shy told officials a different story. Shy had recently spoken with Mr. Ferrell, she reported, and Rod had made some statement about "doing something at the animal shelter with his knife."

Since the time she stopped dating him in late July, Shy told the police, Rod had gone through a vast transformation. Rod started getting really weird after he dyed his hair black. He started dressing like Marilyn Manson, wearing bodysuits and painting his nails black. Sometimes Rod would wear eyeliner, Shy told them, boring the officers with the minute details of Rod's attire. Shy said she didn't know why Rod had gone from being "a sweet, quiet little boy" to being "more demonic and demented."

"He would do his face paint like Gothic makeup and would do his hair in these ponytail braids, sort of like a billion ponytail holders," she told them, "so that he could hurt somebody with it when he flipped his hair around."

Shy alleged that Rod was abusing all kinds of drugs, LSD, pot, and handfuls of unnamed pills, including Prozac, but ultimately, her statement amounted to a bunch of fluff. She told officials that Rod killed one of her cats, but she couldn't get anyone from the trailer park to substantiate her claim. Her statement was not enough to convict Rod of any crime.

chapter sixteen

"Charity was young and impressionable," Ashley recalled. "Rod told her he loved her, he told her he cared about her. He told her he wanted her, that he'd do anything for her, and she was just fourteen. She fell for it. She thought, you know, that he was the love of her life. He loved her, and she did everything he said."

As Jaden's girlfriend, Ashley got a close-up view of Rod's love life. She saw the girls come and go, she knew Charity was being manipulated, that she herself was some object of Rod's twisted desire. At one point, Rod threatened to kill Ashley if she didn't turn over her "power."

"The intention with the vampire game was to have fun," Ashley explained. "The other intentions were, we were a family. It was a place to belong, it was a place where you could go and be loved and not be judged for who you were. You could be yourself.

"It was a spiritual thing," Ashley said, referring to bloodletting. "You were able to have a piece of your friend with you forever. That's how I saw it. I think that's what it was to most people. But I think, with Rod, he just lost touch with reality."

If Rod was actually taking lives, if he was hurting animals and talking about human sacrifices, then Ashley wanted no part of him. She complained bitterly about Rod following her around, and when Jaden reunited with Rod for a brief while, Ashley was furious. A preppy girl who came from the "right side of the tracks," Ashley was engaged to Jaden, she loved him, but now she was having second thoughts.

With the vampire game suddenly turning *real*, Ashley knew she wasn't making the proper life choice. Doing her own soul-searching at the time that Rod came back in the picture, she made it clear to Jaden that she did not want to associate with either of them unless the blood rituals stopped. She later offered a different version of the events that led to Jaden's arrest.

"We tried to stay away from him," she recalled, "and then Rod started threatening. He tried to hurt Jaden, Rod tried to beat him with a baseball bat, tried to stab him. Jaden went to jail because he was defending me. He didn't hurt Rod, but he choked him, and because it was an assault on a minor, Jaden had to go to jail for it."

After Jaden was locked up, Ashley said, Rod cornered her and threatened to kill her, to smear her guts around so people could see them. Ashley was ready for the fight of her life. Since she felt she had already lost, she didn't care if she lived. She told Rod she was willing to die, but he just laughed at her like she was crazy. He claimed he was joking, that he could never really harm a woman.

"Rod had told us he'd killed other people," she confessed. "He said he'd killed other people and kept their body parts, but he would never let us see them. In a way, I could see Rod doing something like that. He just said it and laughed about it. Like it was funny that he could hurt people.

"Whatever, Rod. Have your fun," Ashley finally told him.

"I will," he said with a playful tone, "I will feed off mortals and animals and whatever else crosses my path."

"Okay, Rod, play your sick little games."

"It's my fate. Whether you like it or not, I'm a killer"—he smiled—"and I can have you whenever I want."

Rod would speak of his unbearable pain, of the demons he could feel peeling the skin off his body. His wild imaginings took him away from his waking life, and he loved to carry others along with him. He'd make people feel like they were sitting around a campfire, where ghosts and spirits abounded, ready to unleash their immortal souls.

Rod would tell stories about demons serving him up as a meal, sawing his head off for their main course, then chopping his heart out of his chest for dessert. He'd describe seeing his flesh sizzling in a skillet. But when he would threaten people about chopping them up into "bite-sized bits" and cooking them up like they were animal meat, that made coven members queasy. Of course Jaden would just laugh, he always thought Rod was hysterically funny, but Ashley would shake her head in disgust. She had gotten beyond the novelty of immortality. She didn't want to spirit-walk, she just wanted Jaden back the way he was when she met him. Jaden was an actor. He had talent and might go places. She didn't like seeing him wasting his efforts on Rod's evil games. She wished she had a wand that would make Rod disappear.

Charity, on the other hand, was all too eager to hang around Rod. Ashley tried to warn the girl to keep her distance, that Rod could only bring trouble to her down the road, but Charity thought Ashley was being too rough on him. Charity understood Rod's pain, she empathized with his torment.

Being raised an only child by a dad who was often gone at work, Charity felt alone in the world. She felt that darkness beckoned her, and was exploring things like voodoo and the Scottish druid culture. She had become interested in the sacrificial use of blood. She wondered if evil had gripped her soul; it was something that repulsed her, yet she desired it. She longed to know the darker half of life, to be dead, yet alive, to be everything and nothing all at once.

Before she allowed Rod to embrace her, Charity had walked many nights hand in hand with him, letting Rod lead her through the utter darkness of the Land Between the Lakes. She had slept nights feeling only his touch under the cold black sky, and she started to believe that without Rod, life had no meaning. Rod seemed to be offering her the ultimate ride.

Of course, at times, Charity's affections would waver. Whenever they would argue, Charity would find other "boy toys" to occupy herself with. She couldn't understand why she cheated on Rod, but then, Rod was so possessive and controlling, she sometimes felt forced to sleep with other guys, just to remind herself that she was her own person with a free will. It wasn't that she loved any of these people, she'd tell Rod. It was just that she wasn't ready for a total commitment. She was too young for that.

Rod would say he didn't really care who Charity went out with, he knew her eyes were filled with lust for him.

That was all that mattered. They shared each other's blood, they had become "one," Rod said. There was "no way out" for her.

"Now and forever let us stay in love and as love," he wrote in countless letters, "and at every minute of every hour, know that I love you."

When Rod and Charity were in bed together, she experienced some kind of chemical reaction, her body always seemed hotter than fire, and her mind would drift into an unknown realm. Rod would tell her that their love bonded them to each other more than the angels were bonded to God. She was the only sweet thing in this cruel life, he'd whisper, the only human who was worthy.

Charity was his queen. He would flood her mind with images of their eternal embracement, of their rapture, of their sweet kisses, telling her that the "fires of heaven and hell" could not keep him away from her. Rod promised she would be seated next to him eternally and she loved the romantic illusion. Rod was changing her life; he was adding to her world. He was an immortal full of humanistic feelings. She could let herself go with him and feel completely connected. Rod appealed to her subconscious. He gave her dark side a context. Charity felt she was tapping into a part of herself that she never knew existed.

Rod would tell her that he lived with her in her dreams, that he was coming into her house at night just to stare at her while she slept. When he reached in his pocket and showed her the key to her home, having produced it like he was some kind of magician, Charity couldn't believe it. It seemed horrible that he was sneaking in on her, but at the same time, it was spectacular and romantic.

"Where'd you get that?" she wanted to know, pointing at the brass key that looked so much like her daddy's.

"It's not for you to ask," Rod said. "Just put your arms around me and know that I will carry you away when the time is right."

"But I don't want to leave Murray, I like it here. I can't leave my dad and my friends."

"You have already let your body die," he reminded her, "and soon, you will leave the weakness of mortal desires behind. You will feel no need to hold on to your silly childhood playgrounds. You will be flying over the fields of your youth, watching them from the air in amazement."

Charity sometimes believed that Rod could give her eternal life. She even felt like a vampire, like she needed to suck blood in order to subsist. She had the overwhelming feeling that Rod knew something that she didn't and would ask Rod stupid questions, like why she didn't need a coffin, but he would just laugh at her. When Charity would complain about being visited by "dark lords" in her dreams, Rod would become angry. He made it clear that he was her sire, the only "lord" she should permit into her dreams.

"Do I have to take a little drink to keep you in line?" he asked, biting playfully at her neck.

"Maybe you do."

When Rod would suck on her, that would really draw Charity in. Even though he offered no answers, she believed she would learn her fate, in time.

Rod loved to perpetuate the mystery of his ancient existence, to encourage his girlfriend to search for darkness as a state of mind. He was sexy and desirable, he was a loving, caring preternatural being who could go to incredible depths of pain and offer a sense of beauty out of misery. Charity thought he had a beautiful dark side. She was intrigued by his triumph over death.

Rod would tell Charity that she was undead, that she

was still moving, still on earth, still passing through time, but she was living on the outside of the universe. She did not have to play by mortal rules. Rod didn't want her to play silly Masquerade games or to become involved with the fake characters who only knew about immortality from storybooks. Charity was larger-than-life, he would tell her, she was his eternal mate.

Rod was deviant, but he was a bit of a Prince Charming as well. He encouraged Charity to express her sexual freedom without feeling uncomfortable or weird, and their relationship became one of domination and submission. Their sex life flourished in an atmosphere of wonderful, mischievous discovery, and Charity loved it. Rod was like a four-dimensional character, there was so much going on with him, he was outrageous, especially in bed. He was a dream lover who could be a perfect gentleman one minute, then turn into a freak the next.

Their blood exchanges seemed to heighten their "sacred bond," and with each blood kiss, Charity felt she was flirting with death. She liked the idea. Rod was erotic, his whole vampire mentality allowed her to give in to her pain, to explore her sensitivities, to carry deep spiritual messages through body contact.

Rod reached her somehow. In his presence, she didn't feel like an outcast anymore. She loved to spend time with him, she saw a lot of herself in Rod, although occasionally, Rod would go too far and press for utter control. Charity would struggle and question the truth of Rod's motives, but invariably, Rod would win their power exchange. Charity would always wind up the submissive victim. On one level, it became a bondage relationship, and Charity would feel locked in. Though it frightened her, she couldn't resist the excitement, the thrill of giving in to evil.

chapter seventeen

Rod,

Hey baby, what's up? Not much here, except writing and loving you! OK, sorry about the phone being busy. It wasn't that I didn't want to see you this weekend, cause I did, but Dana wouldn't go over there. I tried to get her to go Saturday morning, but she doesn't like you. Oh well.

Why have you been so paranoid this week? Tell me the truth——did you kill those animals or have anything to do with it? Ever since they started questioning you, you have been acting weird. I'm not trying to say you did it, but it has just made me curious.

Anyway, sorry I didn't come over any time this weekend. Gotta go.

I love you, Charity

Charity had been prompted to write the note after thinking about a little black kitten that used to hang around Rod's house. It was just a stray cat that Rod would feed occasionally, and with all the rumors flying around town, she realized the kitty wasn't scratching at Rod's front door anymore. She wondered what happened to it. She thought it strange that the kitten just disappeared, especially since Rod seemed to love the fluffy critter.

"Hey, Rod, where's that little black cat?" she finally asked, thinking that perhaps Rod had given the kitten away to the kids down the block.

"Oh, the neighbors put duct tape around its mouth and lodged it right up against a wall."

"What? And you watched them do that? Where's the cat now?"

"It eventually died."

Charity started yelling, she became hysterical thinking that Rod could smile about such a horrible thing, but he told her he had no control over the neighbor kids. He insisted she stop worrying about it and reminded her that people were cruel.

"Close your eyes and relax," Rod whispered. "You are with me, and you're safe. Nothing dare touch you or anything you love as long as I'm here. I'm gonna make your every desire come true, baby. I'm not going to let anybody hurt you."

It was one of the many lines Rod handed Charity. He would tell her of his lust, of his desperate need for her. He claimed he was reaching out to her from his dark abyss, from his memories of past lives with her, where he was her dark knight in armor, he was her protection against weak mortal minds.

When he was alone in bed with Charity, Rod would

show his vulnerable side. In bed, he wanted Charity to drown his grief with her lips. He wanted her to take him away from his sorrowful place where the living world was "truly gone." He explained that without Charity, there were "no more golden sunsets." Rod claimed that all he saw was darkness, even in the light of day.

"He told me he was five hundred years old," Charity confided. "He would talk back and forth with Scott, and they would both act like they lived in England in past lives. They would insinuate it."

From the time Jaden had gone to jail, Rod and Scott had become inseparable. At some point, Rod had crossed Scott over, and together, they had the whole routine down. Scott would secretly tell Charity that being immortal was painful, that he was sick of making new friends every century, only to have to remove them from his thoughts.

Scott described the "pain of leaving people behind" and claimed his soul was "older than any immortal." Charity laughed at Scott's enthusiasm. She could tell Scott knew nothing about immortality, but she didn't want to discourage Scott's fantasy world. Scott was such a lost soul. He needed "family." She herself never professed to grow fangs or have yellow eyes, and she found it amusing when Scott would assert such insane things. She never saw his eyes turn yellow, she never saw long canine teeth, but Scott did draw funky designs on his arms, and occasionally he would walk around with black eyeliner on. He liked to copy Rod.

Of course Charity never made open fun of him; she felt compassion for Scott. She could sense Scott's pain. He seemed to be sending telepathic messages to her, and she felt his presence, especially when she turned her attentions to other boys. Scott had a big crush on her, she knew, but that seemed to be okay with Rod.

Charity figured it was only fair. Since Rod constantly accused her of being a "jealous bitch," it was only right that she get all the guys she could; she loved to drive Rod crazy. It was a way to pay him back for hanging all over Shy and Ashley. Besides, if Rod was going to waste half of his time with Scott, then it was only natural for Scott to be hoping for a little fling.

Of course, Rod had the theory that all females were weak, that they all fell prey to lies and deception, and he knew Charity was a big flirt. He claimed he didn't see anything wrong with that, but then, she noticed how fickle Rod would become the minute she wasn't available.

"He wouldn't let me go anywhere by myself," she recalled. "He was scared some of the guys would rape me. He'd get really protective of me. He'd follow me around and I wouldn't know he was there."

Rod just wanted all her attention, and it bugged her that he would sneak up on her and threaten to break up whenever he caught her talking to another guy. He seemed to pick fights with her for absolutely no reason and was willing to do just about anything to cause a drama with Charity. She found herself proclaiming her love over and over, just to keep Rod steady.

What baffled her was Rod's insistence that she was his dark mate. If they were destined to be together for all time, if they were truly soul mates, it didn't make sense that Rod would constantly claim to feel so empty and lost, that he would be putting feelers out for other women.

On the one hand, he would tell her she fulfilled all his needs, yet the moment she wasn't at his side, he was off chasing other skirts, making promises over the phone to

his "girls" in Florida. Rod was trying to pull the old double standard on her, and Charity wasn't about to let him
get away with it, even if he was immortal.

To Charity, it seemed Rod thrived on pain. He loved creating scenes, and their fights became more frequent. She
was constantly confirming that she loved him, that he meant
more to her than her parents or anyone else in her family,
but it didn't seem to faze him. Charity would beg Rod to
stay true, saying she had become afraid that he would find
someone to replace her, but he did nothing to allay her fears.
Secretly, Charity was trying to get pregnant, figuring, under
the circumstances, that would be the best insurance policy.

Of course, when she finally got up the courage to question
Rod again about the lies she was hearing, Rod assured Charity that her friends didn't know what they were talking
about. He was being accused of slaughtering animals, he
said, because he had been "framed" by his former buddy
Frankie. Rod promised her that the police had no evidence,
that he would never be indicted for the crime, that the investigation was bullshit. He admitted that he had been served
some papers, that he had an appointment to appear down at
the sheriff's office, but said it was "just a formality."

"He came in here wearing white theatrical makeup
and had his lips painted red," Sheriff Scott recalled. "His
hair was parted in the middle and it was long, just hanging down, and we got him downstairs and started talking
to him for a total of about fifteen minutes, and he was
very defensive. He started off from the bat, trying to
accuse us of picking on him because of his beliefs."

"You don't have a right to question me," Rod said, getting
huffy. "I can worship any God I want, I can wear whatever
the hell I want, and that doesn't make me a bad person."

"Well, what we have to ask you doesn't have anything to do with your beliefs," the Sheriff said. "We're down here trying to talk to you about a criminal investigation. There were two animals butchered alive, are you familiar with what I'm talking about?"

"I have no knowledge of that," Rod insisted.

"Well, Frankie Brittin is a friend of yours, correct?"

"Correct."

"Well, Matt Goodman signed a statement saying that you and Mr. Brittin broke into the animal shelter."

"You know, if I wanted to kill animals, I wouldn't need to go to any shelter, because the woods around here are full of them. Now, wouldn't I be stupid if I didn't realize that?"

"We have allegations that you were involved in a break-in, Mr. Ferrell, and we need some answers about your whereabouts on the evening of October fourteenth."

"Look, man, I'm so sick of everybody pointing fingers at me. I've had about all I can stand from you people. I didn't do anything to any dogs, I was with my girlfriend, Charity, that whole evening, and if you don't believe me, you can ask her. I don't know why you're so worried about me, when all I do is mind my own business. You all should realize that I've been doing a great job of holding myself in check."

"Why? What's your problem?" the sheriff asked, struck by Rod's ambiguous tone.

"I haven't released myself. If you think I've done anything wrong, you're going to be wasting a lot of your time. Everybody's after me in this town, and I don't know why. They've kicked me out of school, they've misjudged and mistreated me, and it's all because I don't look and act like them. I'm not a little preppy rich kid. I'll never fit in around here. And you know what? I haven't killed anybody, yet."

"Why would you feel it necessary to do that?" the sheriff asked, not expecting an answer, taking Rod's comment with a grain of salt. It was obvious Rod Ferrell was just trying to act tough, and equally clear that Ferrell's comments were warped. He presented himself as an outsider, insisting he couldn't identify with the people of Murray, yet he had been born and raised in the town and certainly had a whole gang of kids at his disposal.

If the sheriff could have jailed Rod Ferrell for any crime, nothing would have pleased him more. The kid was twisted, he was a walking time bomb, and the sheriff was sure Ferrell was behind the troubles that had been mounting among this whole Goth circle. The sheriff wanted to nab Ferrell, but the young man had no criminal record, he was not a juvenile delinquent, and without a confession, there were no grounds for putting him behind bars. According to the files, Ferrell had never been a suspect in any crime or violation whatsoever.

To Stan Scott, Rod was a punk with a big chip on his shoulder and a bad attitude. Of course, the sheriff and his men tried to press Ferrell for answers, but Rod had nothing more to say. Rod was finished playing their game, and if there wasn't any arrest warrant, he wanted to leave.

When the sheriff realized he wasn't going to get anywhere with the boy, he let Rod walk. There was still a pending investigation, the sheriff told him, hinting that Ferrell would have to answer to a judge in open court.

"We were just questioning him about his involvement," Sheriff Scott recalled. "Rod claimed that he didn't know anything about it. He didn't know who did it, he didn't know why they would do it. He just felt we were picking on him because he was different."

chapter eighteen

Charity wasn't sure about Rod. Sometimes when they would drink blood, Rod would make fun of her for cutting herself. That was one thing about Rod—he was always contradicting himself, twisting things around—his victims would somehow believe they were predators. When they would talk about death, Rod would encourage their morbid thoughts, and Charity was no exception. When she told him she wished her mother would die, Rod silently approved. Without ever realizing it, Charity had become rather cruel.

The girl was confused. She wanted to be Rod's queen, she had dyed her hair black and had made vows to run away with him, yet she was scared of Rod. He would hand her pieces of glass and ask her to cut herself, he would shatter ashtrays and lightbulbs and act totally berserk, so naturally, she was finding it hard to feel serious about him. Rod and his friends were spiraling out of control, and she wanted to change him, to make him a more responsible person, but that was an impossible desire.

"At one point, Rod and Scott and a couple other people, I don't remember who it was, they started Rod's living room on fire," she recalled. "They were just messing with fire. They were trying to make it dance and caught the curtains and the couch on fire."

At the time, Charity thought it was funny. She and Rod were in the bedroom when they heard Scott yelling "Fire!" and Rod ran out to the living room with a sheet wrapped around him, laughing hysterically at the burning couch.

"You don't know how to control fire," Rod barked as he doused the flames, "you little dumb ass, you save your practice spells for your house. You can blow your parents up if you want to."

But Scott just laughed. He helped Rod extinguish the fire and barely spoke a word. Scott was a quiet, soft-spoken type. He tried to portray himself as a maniac, he claimed to have visions of hanging himself by a noose, but even with Rod as his mentor, his "Albert Einstein," as he called Rod, Scott just didn't match up. In comparison to Rod, all of Scott's knowledge seemed to be on the comic book level. Rod would quote Shakespeare, he would quote Plato, he would channel their spirits and mutter a bunch of philosophy, but Scott never knew what any of it meant. Scott would go along, but he was just making things up. Scott didn't have enough education to truly understand Rod, no less question him.

Rod would pretend to become an apparition, to revive ancient prophets and bring them back from the dead. He wanted Charity and Scott to believe he could return spirits back to human shape, but in Charity's mind, at least, Rod was only pretending to do the impossible. Nonetheless, Scott would try to get Charity to go along with them, because when she didn't, Rod would become threatening.

"Rod never told me he was going to kill me, other than one day he was mad at me," she recalled. "He took me into the kitchen and had me trapped between the stove and him, and he pulled out the knife drawer and I started screaming, but then he took a pot holder out and hit me upside the head with it."

By always draining her emotions, Rod was able to make Charity feel like she was on a roller-coaster ride. She seemed to be getting drawn in further with each fight and makeup session, but still, a few slices of broken flesh had not become her passage to a magical world. Charity knew Rod was teasing her, that he was using smoke and mirrors to portray this demon character; but, for the sex alone, it was worth it to go along with Rod's strange ideas. In fact, from the minute the two had met, she had given up her association with the "Father" of the rival vampire group in Murray. Rod was so overpowering, she felt it best to appease him.

"His big thing was, he was a control freak," Charity confided. "Rod liked to have people under his power. He liked to know he had power over people. He would tell me things over and over, repeatedly, and after a while, I would want to believe him."

chapter nineteen

Life certainly wasn't boring with Rod around. He would search for telltale signs of past civilizations, looking for evidence of the "cult of the dying god" that had destroyed Roman virtue and would now smash every remnant of American culture. He would gesticulate about the worship of Osiris, "the judge of the dead," who, in an earlier epoch, was responsible for the decay of Egypt. He would describe visions of the return of the god of the lower world, of himself being the "force and fire" behind Osiris.

Whenever possible, Rod would try to take Charity on a paranormal journey. He would bring her out to the woods behind his apartment and share his secret inner landscape, hoping that she would find her place inside his mind. He wanted her to be one of the "many personalities" that dwelled within him, he would explain.

Rod claimed it was only a matter of time before he

would take over the universe. He said that the first act of his reign would be to plunge the world into a huge and ruthless war.

He would talk about taking over the airwaves, about using TV satellites and the Internet to bring on a global catastrophe, and though Charity wanted to consider Rod's talk gibberish, though she wanted to think his mythological chatter was just a facet of his mood swings, Rod would be so deliberate about it. He seemed so coherent, it scared her. Charity would listen, sometimes wondering if Rod suffered from a multiple personality disorder. But Rod never reacted when Charity would hint about it.

He was determined to make Charity see that he had been sent to earth on a mission. At times, she figured it was the LSD talking, but then, she wasn't sure if Rod was still on acid. At times, being around Rod gave her a sick feeling. He would talk so crazy she was sure he was drugged out, and the idea of heavy drugs made her uneasy. She would beg Rod to stay clean, but he would just mock her, telling her she was at a different stage in life, that she didn't have the heightened sensibility to comprehend eternity.

Rod would torment her and call her a "druggie" because she was on Prozac, yet he himself was a sneak and a liar when it came to drugs. She was convinced he was stealing her prescriptions, swallowing her Prozac and Xanax, because pills were always missing when he was around. But Rod would always deny it.

Charity started to get annoyed with Rod. She would get angry at every little thing he did, trying to make their relationship a constant challenge. She knew how to push his buttons, how to get a reaction out of him. She'd insist that she didn't believe in his powers, but then quickly change her tune when he'd threaten to dump her, to sleep around with her girlfriends. Charity knew he could easily do that. Her girlfriends were all enamored with Rod. Some were in the process of being embraced, she was sure. Her friend Cindy had already admitted that she and Rod had a one-night stand, and her other friend Beth seemed so smitten with Rod, Charity felt she had to tolerate Rod's beliefs.

Charity was caught in Rod's web. She felt she needed to keep him, that she couldn't live without his love, so she tolerated his behavior. His threats and lies and crazy notions were all just a part of the package.

When Rod spoke of various methods for global destruction, Charity would sometimes try to argue, but then he'd get really nuts. She said that he'd threaten to chop her head off and burn her body if she didn't shut up, and Charity finally got to the point where she just wouldn't take him seriously about anything.

Rod was so crazy, she felt he needed her. She knew he would go off the deep end without her protection and understanding. She was his life raft, and when Rod claimed he was put on earth to fight the Godhead, she would try to offer him a reality check. He would say it was his obligation to "unleash the secrets and wisdom of the ages" so that mankind would end, and she would just change the subject. She would talk about having kids and going to beauty school, just mundane things like that, trying to divert him.

"I pretty much blew him off," she confided. "I knew better than to ask stupid questions or try to overpower him. When people would tell me Rod was out of control, I'd tell them he wasn't a dog, you know, that I couldn't train him."

Sometimes Rod would use punk rock lyrics to prove

his theories, things like Marilyn Manson's "Hate Anthem" and other Manson messages of destruction and decay. Rod claimed to have proof that the world was nearing an end. He was waiting for mankind to self-destruct, and in the meantime, he had no use for anything but blood, which gave him the ability to "overcome time." After the mortal world was over, Rod promised, he and his collection of wounded angels would rule.

If nothing else, Rod was ambitious. His knowledge and criticism of the abilities of the government, however, were mere rantings. Rod wanted to destroy all world powers, he wanted to clean up the mess of human civilization, but he was utterly ignorant about such things. He would talk about "a nuclear nightmare" as though he were an expert, but much of his knowledge came from news sound bites. Charity would listen to bits and pieces of Rod's predictions, amazed that Rod could infuse certain facts about world leaders, claiming to know these powerful men—and she became afraid to challenge him.

"What questions do you have of me?" Rod asked her. "Where should I start in answering you?"

"Well, I don't know if you have false memories or if these dreams you have are happening in the real world."

"You want logic? You expect me to be logical?" Rod asked in a cynical tone. "But there is no truth in logic. Any genius will tell you that. You think Mozart wrote symphonies using logic? You think Picasso worried about what was logical?"

Charity didn't know what Rod was getting at. He would try to explain his theories to her, but as many times as he would clarify things, she would still wind up feeling confused.

"If people relied on logic, no miracle would ever

occur," Rod said, pointing at the sky as they lay in the woods one night. "What do you see when you look into outer space?"

"I see the stars, it's the Milky Way."

"What you see is galaxies that contain billions of stars. But tell me, what percent of those galaxies do you think you really understand?"

"I don't know. Not much."

"If you think about the speed of light, if you realize stars are light-years away, then you realize how much you fail to perceive," Rod told her. "Ninety-nine percent of the universe is totally ignored by the human brain. Everything you believe to be reality is a complete illusion, Charity. You trust the five senses, you think you can see and hear the truth, but your eyes and ears play tricks on you. You're constantly being fooled."

"What do you mean?"

"It's like watching a film. Think about what happens when you watch a movie, Charity. You see a happy scene, you laugh. You see a sad scene, you cry. But it's not reality, it's just a filmmaker playing with your emotions."

"Yeah."

"So, learn to look at the world like it's a movie theater complex. You don't have to let Hollywood dictate what your reality is, you know. You can decide what movie to walk into."

"What are you talking about?"

"That's the best way I can explain it, baby. Look, if you want to be in a good mood, you go see a comedy, right?"

"But what do movies have to do with me?"

"Once you realize that you choose your own reality, then you're not at the mercy of outside forces. You become all-powerful. You pick your own movie. And you don't do that with a logical mind. Logic has nothing to do with fate."

"But I don't understand," she argued. "If it's fate, then how do I have a choice?"

"You choose your fate."

"So, what you're telling me is, I'm making up my own movie?"

"I'm saying that you wind up being tricked by things that seem real," Rod insisted. "Look, in the past, people thought the world was flat, right? That's a perfect example. People believed that because they'd look out at the horizon. They thought that was where the world ended."

"But they were wrong."

"Exactly."

"But how do I know what you're saying is real?"

"How many times are you deceived by your eyes? Like when your house keys are sitting on the table, right in front of your eyes, but you swear you can't find them. You look all over the entire house, then twenty minutes later you come back and suddenly, there they are."

"What's your point?"

"Your perception goes beyond physical sight. Once you realize that, you can plane walk, you can leave your physical body and enter other realms. All you have to do is concentrate, and you can join me in the eternal universe. You'll start feeling our past lives together. You'll become flooded with thousands of memories of us together."

"Really?"

"It's all in there, Charity. It's waiting for you to tap into it. All you have to do is think about it, and it will come to you."

"But I've tried that," she promised, "and it hasn't worked."

"Did you ever hum a piece of music in your mind, then turn on the radio and there it was?"

"I do that all the time."

"Did you ever think about a friend you haven't seen for months, and suddenly you bump into them at a store?"

"Sure."

"That's your mystical insight, baby, that's your psychic self. It's proof that you can get beyond the five senses."

Charity wanted to believe him. She wanted to join Rod in his other realm. He would tell her that she was already there, but most of the time, she felt like she was talking herself into it. When he drank her blood, she felt somewhat connected to Rod's field of energy, but she wasn't sure she was actually getting in touch with her immortal soul. Rod would tell her not to fight it. He would ask her to acknowledge her destiny, explaining that doubt was a part of the cross over process.

"You've got to test everything for yourself," he would say, "but if you want to know the greatness of your own power, you must let go of your mortal ideals and just leave all your preconceived notions at the gate."

"You assume that I believe the supernatural exists," she would answer, really wanting to tell him that she flat-out didn't believe she was "undead."

"You must seek it," Rod would say. "If you want to end your loneliness and agony, I will be your gatekeeper. I will guide you through the transformation. Once you deny your human nature, you will receive everlasting fulfillment."

chapter twenty

"Rod talked about going on a rampage," Shy recalled. "He said he wanted to kill Jaden and he wanted to kill his mom."

Rod knew his whole coven had turned against him. They had snubbed him at Halloween, and Shy recalled that Rod decided they should all be killed. To Shy, Rod would describe the various methods he planned to use. He would beat James and Jaden to death, he would drain them, hang them upside down, then dismember them.

Shy wasn't considering taking Rod back, she had already become romantically linked with Jaden, but she still cared about Rod. She had a soft spot in her heart for him, she knew he was being outcast, and she'd chitchat with him when she'd see him at local hangouts.

But when Rod would start to rant about killing Jaden, Shy warned him to stay away from her trailer. She was still living in Grogan's Trailer Park with her little coven, and she had plenty of protection, she bragged. She liked Rod, but she couldn't afford to let him come visit her. She never mentioned that she had become an "item" with Jaden—it was just a fling, really, and she didn't want to stir up trouble.

On November 5, 1996, Shy (aka April Doeden) signed an affidavit with law officials in Calloway County to complain of an attack involving Rod Ferrell, Michael Shaeffer, and Jason Jones. According to her statement, Shy said the three young men had come driving up in Jason's car, that Michael got out of the car and had come to her door looking for Jaden, that an altercation had taken place between Rod and Jaden. She reminded authorities that the two boys were still at war, that there was a restraining order for Jaden to keep away from Rod, and reported that Rod was the one who insisted on all of them "talking."

She explained that when Rod and Jaden started to become physical, shoving and pushing each other around her yard, Shy asked her girlfriend Shannon to run inside and dial 911.

Shy told authorities that when she walked behind Jason Jones's car to write down the license plate, the three boys jumped into the Ford Escort and Rod said, "Back up."

"Jason slammed the car in reverse and backed over me," Shy told police. "I was able to jump back, almost out of the way, but the right rear tire ran over my right foot."

Shy reported that she had been taken to an emergency room, that her foot had been x-rayed and did not show any broken bones, but she complained that she was badly bruised. She wanted to press charges.

"Jason Jones knew I was behind his vehicle," she wrote

in her statement, "and he deliberately tried to run over me."

Later that day, the Calloway County sheriff's department took a statement from Jaden Steven Murphy regarding the "trespassing and harassment" incident at Grogan's Trailer Park. Jaden told authorities that Mr. Ferrell was an "unwanted guest" at Shy's home, that Rod had repeatedly been asked to leave, but he refused, and confirmed that Jason Jones, did in fact, run over Shy's foot.

"After the three unwanted guests were told to leave," Jaden wrote in his witness statement, "Mr. Ferrell told residents that he was a nine-foot demon and he wanted someone to kill him to free him of his worldly existence and make him more powerful."

An arrest warrant was served in mid-November 1996, charging Jason Jones with wanton endangerment, a class-D felony. Jason was released on $2,500 bail, provided he had "no contact" with Shy. Nine months later, Shy dropped the charges, and the Calloway District Court allowed Jason Jones to sign a "diversion agreement," which called for a twelve-month probation period, at the end of which the matter would be officially dismissed.

"That was the last time I saw Rod," Shy recalled. "He was standing under my streetlight before they all got in the car and did that crazy shit. Rod was begging Jaden to kill him, and we all thought it was fucking hilarious, because Rod was really trying to scare us but Jaden was making fun of him. Even Rod started laughing, I mean, he just went nuts. He was threatening to take me with him if Jaden didn't chop his head off.

"I was actually trying to stop them from fighting," she confided. "I didn't want Jaden to go to jail. They all thought I was trying to protect Rod, because they thought

I still loved Rod, and I told Jaden I did love him, because I never stop loving people."

Once Rod was gone, Jaden consecrated the trailer park grounds. He was taking certain precautions because he'd heard rumors about dogs and cats hanging from trees in the woods behind Grogan's. Jaden knew that Rod was messing with Satan worship and figured Rod was planning an attack. Of course, it didn't help matters that Jaden's mom was still going forward with the rape and sodomy charges against Sondra. Jaden knew, with that trial date coming up, Rod would find reason to put his black magic into practice.

chapter twenty-one

"How do you feel about interplanet, biocosmic, bioplasmic energy?" Shy asked, poking into the side of her friend Eric.

"What?" Eric asked, mystified. "What the hell are you saying?"

"Hold out your hands."

Eric stretched his hands out and Shy placed hers directly underneath.

"Do you feel it?" she asked. "Do you feel the energy?"

"Yes, I feel the energy."

"Well, good," she said, laughing, "let me try to toss you an energy ball."

"I don't think I'm ready for that."

"Don't you worry," Shy persisted. "You believe in karma?"

"Everything is predestined," Eric said, sheepishly looking down at the rune stones Shy had drawn from his pouch. "You have drawn the blank rune," he said, showing her. "It can pertain to death, and it's a test of faith.

"It's the rune of elemental disruption," Eric continued. "Drawing it indicates that the current events seem to be totally beyond your control."

"That's exactly what I came over here to ask you about. Look at my foot brace." Shy showed Eric. "I'm being thrown into a psychic battle. Rod and his friends just tried to kill me."

Eric was a master at divining rune stones. The sacred symbols of the Teutonic races, rune stones were the center of a system of magic that had been resurrected. By going to Eric, Shy felt she could get a handle on her fate. He had asked her to pull stones from his velvet pouch, he had called to the four corners of the earth, and he could make sense of the symbolic messages, Shy hoped. With a little help from a guidebook, Eric could interpret the ancient runes and offer her sound advice.

It was an art, Eric's ability, and although the casual observer might confuse runic philosophy with the occult, Shy knew better. Of everyone in their circle, Eric made the most sense. He was well read and had certainly done his homework on witchcraft. When it came to wicca, Eric knew what he was talking about, and unlike Rod, Eric was believable when he invoked spirits.

To Shy, Eric's wisdom seemed to go deeper than that of any other sole practitioner of witchcraft. Sharing secrets with him usually led to a catharsis for her. She could always count on Eric for spiritual cleansing. As a dedicated seeker of the meaning of life, he could lead her through her various "symbolic deaths" and offer her a consistent rebirth. With Eric, Shy went into a state of transformation;

she found she could cope with the evil forces around her and realized Rod had been sent to test her.

Of course, when she had told Rod about Eric, Rod just laughed and called the guy a *werewolf*. Rod loved to make fun of people, and to that end, he had labels for everyone: certain people were trolls, others were druids, others were elves—his list was endless. Rod liked to use names to make people laugh, and with Eric, for instance, the *werewolf* label came about because the guy was hairy all over. Eric had a full beard, a mustache, even hairy fingers. Rod was so sophomoric about it, Shy thought. Eric couldn't help it if he looked like a crude primitive.

"I think a bunch of people who have active imaginations and are interested in paranormal phenomenon decided to feed each other's games of let's pretend," Eric said, trying to explain all the chaos surrounding him.

In addition to his witchcraft, Eric practiced shamanism, a belief in good and evil spirits he learned from a "medicine man," a young buddy of his who was a shaman. Like Jaden and Rod, Eric had begun by playing Vampire: The Masquerade, but like everyone else in their role-playing group, Eric felt overly pressured by James Yohe, their pushy game master. Eric wanted creative control of his character and began dabbling in different phenomena as a way to gain it.

"A bunch of arguments developed," Eric recalled, "because James can be rather anal and annoying. He was running the game, but after a while, people just stopped going. James got very strict with the story lines he had planned out. We wanted him to be a little flexible."

Once he walked away from the live-action game, eighteen-year-old Eric studied *Buckland's Complete Book of Witchcraft*, and based on the book's instructions, he managed to create a place where his friends could feel comfortable seeking answers to their religious needs. In his big Victorian home, a rental he shared with a few buddies, Eric built an altar, consecrated his tools, and erected a temple, marking a circle on the floor in the middle of the living room.

Most of Eric's friends confided that the church had failed them miserably; there was no spiritual communion to be found there. For Eric's closest friends, the religious practice of wicca was really thought of as "the craft of the wise." It was a positive force that enabled them to perform rituals and explore their gypsy selves. Being wiccan gave them freedom. They could choose to believe in many gods or could believe in just one. They could choose to protect the earth, or they could control it. It was a personal religion that had no specific set of rules, so any belief was fair game, which was why Eric liked it.

Of course, among most of his college classmates, Eric had to keep his witchcraft secret. As he was among the top students at Murray State, his straitlaced peers would misconstrue his magical efforts, particularly the judgmental super-Christians he hung around. They were the types who thought the church held the only answers. Eric knew they would automatically decide he was up to no good if the word wicca was mentioned.

Just out of curiosity, Eric had participated in blood rituals with Jaden and Rod. It all seemed kind of cute and innocent to him at the time. Being a first-aid instructor and a lifeguard at Murray State, Eric thought he had been quite careful about it. He didn't think of any consequences. He let Jaden cut his arm, made sure the wound wouldn't get infected, and considered it no big deal.

"I gave blood to the Red Cross, I gave blood to my

roommate," Eric said, "so I considered it the same kind of thing. I didn't really believe they actually did it, that they were actually vampires, but then Jaden always said he was. That was one reason I let him cut me a few times. He told a story about how, when he was little, one of his relatives gave him a jar of deer blood and he sat there and happily slurped away."

Jaden was always bragging about his blood lust. He and his group hung out at Hardee's, and right there in public, they dared to recite verses from *The Vampire Bible*. In between handfuls of french fries and hamburgers, Jaden would stop to offer up his life force energy. Dressed in sheer black, sticking out his tongue at strangers, the "local yokels," as he called them, Jaden would beckon to the undead gods. His followers referred to Jaden as the one with "the calling." They would gather around him and feel transformed, body and soul, as they became living vampires.

Jaden proclaimed he and his coven were the only "true" witches and warlocks, so powerful they could create a magical "chamber" amid even the most mundane of settings. Jaden's coven members could visually sight the undead in the Hardee's windows. When Jaden would ask his coven to show off their energy transfer abilities, they claimed to feel the sensations of being touched and stroked by misty vapors. They would describe visions of flying, falling, and traveling through tunnels. This so-called astral universe would carry his group beyond the greasy smells of the fast-food joint, beyond the cheap paper wrappings and hard plastic seats, beyond ordinary flesh.

Whenever Rod would show up, however, all magical conversation would cease. Jaden liked to think of Hardee's as his personal office, his turf, which Rod did not violate. From the time of their physical fight, Rod had been officially exiled from Jaden's form of vampirism. Rod and his spooky girlfriend were no longer a welcome presence in Jaden's inner temple.

In Jaden's eyes, Rod had defiled their most ancient pact. By going to the authorities, he had virtually become prey. Rod had forfeited the right to patronize Hardee's, Jaden told his coven. Jaden wanted Rod destroyed, he would whisper, and he would look over at Rod and smirk.

Rod would sit at the opposite side of the dining room. Usually he would come in by himself, and Jaden couldn't understand it. The restraining order had been Rod's idea, yet he would come into Hardee's and sit there, trying to stare Jaden down.

chapter twenty-two

Charity couldn't stand the way Rod would break up with her every five minutes. She was ready for a permanent situation and had a surprise to tell Rod about—she was almost positive she was pregnant.

Charity and a bunch of her girlfriends had gone to visit Rod on Halloween. They had dressed up as vampires and had gone trick-or-treating over to Rod's, who was absolutely shocked to see them, especially since Charity had Dana and Cindy with her, both of whom Rod disliked.

The girls arrived just as Rod was on his way out. They ran into each other on the stairwell, and when Charity opened her mouth to show off her fangs, when she went to bite Rod, he acted like he wasn't interested in trying to get back together. She thought he was putting on an act—she had heard about his suicide attempts, about how he missed her so much—but he remained strangely aloof.

"I had on a long black dress, with a Gothic-style cape," she recalled. "I was dressed up, with black eye shadow and very dark lipstick, and I don't think he expected to see me on his doorstep. He wouldn't even kiss me until I took my fangs out, which was weird. He wouldn't even look at me with my fangs."

Rod liked to think of Charity as a good girl. She was a churchgoer, a decent student, and had a prissy way about her that he found appealing. Charity had class. She didn't curse and run around drinking, she was the girl of his dreams, and he had proposed marriage to her many times. She had accepted a small gold engagement ring—but then when Rod got to the point when he was stoned all the time, Charity had given the ring back. Tired of his blackouts, of all the acid and pills, she decided to force Rod to choose: either the drugs or her.

"Rod would be on acid or mushrooms and he'd trip out," she confided. "He'd think the chocolate chip cookies were talking to him, or the couch was going to eat him. And no matter what I told him, it would go in one ear and out the other. He'd see dancing macaroni and cheese, he'd just flip me out, and Sondra would just be in the kitchen laughing at him."

Charity couldn't understand why Sondra permitted Rod's drug use. It wasn't like Rod just experimented with drugs occasionally. He was completely out of control, and Charity desperately wanted to straighten him out. Rod would walk seven miles to her house, having tripped on acid along the way, and he'd make her laugh, projecting his voice into her Barbie dolls, turning on her black light and conjuring psychedelic images. By then Rod would get so carried away, he was becoming so out of touch with reality, and more and more paranoid. At times, he would take shelter in her closet, certain Charity's bed was after him. And she was at a loss about what to do with him.

"He wouldn't ever let himself come down," she recalled. "When the drugs started to fade, he took more. He never came out. He was like a walking zombie. It was getting really annoying, because I couldn't tell him anything. He wouldn't understand what I was talking about."

Charity realized that most people were unaware of Rod's severe drug problem. Certainly, his "girlfriends" in Florida had no idea they were spending hours on the phone with someone who was tripping, she was sure. Charity had been around enough to speak to Heather and Jeanine herself. She would say hello to these girls, even though she hated that Rod was so involved with them. Rod's fantasy world with them seemed to be an outgrowth of his drug habit, but Charity refused to fill these girls in. If they wanted Rod so badly, she decided it might be a good idea for him to move back down there.

Charity didn't like the burden of watching him self-destruct. She finally asked for some space and started dating Brian, a churchgoing boy-next-door who treated her like gold.

"Charity said she was sick of the vampire stuff," Cindy recalled. "She was tired of Rod following us around all the time. He was obsessed with her. The whole time they were split up, all Rod talked about was how Charity didn't really love him. He started talking about killing Charity's dad because, as he put it, Charity's dad was keeping them apart."

Charity's affair with Brian only lasted two weeks. She finally had to let Brian go because Rod was always lurking in the shadows, always calling and checking on her, just as a "friend." When Rod discovered that Brian was trying to win Charity back, that he was sending her flowers and "playing house" with her, cooking Charity meals on occasion, Rod decided he would befriend Brian.

Rod claimed he enticed Brian to cross over and join his coven. Rod was good at that—he always seemed to get his way. Brian wasn't the first ex-boyfriend of Charity's that Rod had brainwashed.

In early November, even with all the trouble brewing around Rod, Charity decided it was time to share the news of her pregnancy. She and Rod had officially reunited, and she knew she couldn't wait much longer. She was disappointed, however, when she finally told him. Rod certainly wasn't as happy about it as she was. In fact, he wasn't happy at all.

"The night Charity told Rod she was pregnant, Rod said he was going to jump off the arts building," Cindy confided. "He said the cops were bugging him about the animal shelter, his mom was constantly yelling at him, his grandparents were bugging him about something, and Charity was pregnant with somebody's baby, but he didn't know who the father was."

Rod told Cindy that his life had been hell since he was seven, when he had been molested as part of a "Black Mass." He claimed he did not feel human, that he did not feel any emotions at all, that he was afraid to have another baby, claiming that he already had a baby with Jeanine. To Cindy, he cried about the death of his tiny little infant, who he said had been killed in a car wreck.

When Cindy passed that information along to Charity, little did she know she was repeating another of Rod's made-up stories. Charity took it to heart and became even more afraid to tell her dad about the pregnancy. She decided to spend quality time with Rod, hoping that they could get along better. At least that way, she figured, her dad might be willing to offer them his blessings. As it was, Charity still went to youth group at church, she was still a Girl Scout, and her dad didn't want her spending any time with Rod whatsoever.

Charity hinted that Rod was about to get a job, perhaps in nearby Paducah, but her dad didn't even want to hear it. He had forbidden Rod to come to their home. Charity's dad was a God-fearing man, and in his eyes, Rod was an undesirable character, certainly no match for his pretty little girl.

Of course the last thing Charity wanted to hear about was talk of moving down to Florida, but that was Rod's plan. He intended to form a coven with Jeanine and Heather and was hell-bent on moving these girls in with him and Scott. When Cindy heard about it, she told Charity she was crazy to go along with the idea. Cindy herself had crossed over, and she reminded Charity that she felt no special powers. She thought Rod was a complete fake and advised Charity to move on with her life, to stay away from Rod's pretend world of vampires, dragons, and werewolves, to have the baby on her own.

"It was like when you were a little kid and you play pretend," Cindy explained. "Crossing over was like when little kids say they are blood brothers or sisters with each of them pricking their fingers and putting them together. I went along with it for a time, saying I was a vampire, just playing pretend. But it was just for the fun of it, just something to do."

But Charity wasn't looking for any practical advice. In the weeks before Rod was about to leave Murray, Charity was doing everything she could to appease him. She even let him drag her into some occult ceremonies he was holding in the boiler room of the college stadium.

"Rod believed in many gods and said he worshiped whichever one when he wanted something different," Cindy recalled. "He had an interest in magic and said he needed one more book so he could become a god. I don't know anything about it all, but Rod said stuff about being a pagan. I don't know what went on in Rod's head, but I didn't want to be a part of it."

Just the idea of it, at first, did give Charity the creeps. But then, when she actually crawled down into the boiler room, she was pleasantly surprised to see it was just Scott, Brian, and Dana sitting there passing a candle around. The narrow area was lit up, and on the cement floor, Rod had set up a small altar with holy water and daggers. There was nothing to be frightened of. Really, it was a spiritual communion, and Charity found she liked it better than going to church.

In their first meeting, Rod led them in a meditation where they all concentrated on "glowing ropes" to time-travel, and Charity did feel like she had projected herself with the group. They all experienced the sensation of being on a beach, possibly in Florida, with the wind against their faces, and the sun beating down, burning their skin.

As the winter moved closer and November flew by, Rod's new coven had become pretty close—they were hanging out together at the Vampyre Hotel on weekends, they were spending time at the Old Salem Cemetery during the week, and they were using human blood to bond their souls together. Rod's coven had begun to make contacts in the spirit world and they were having great fun with it, able to ask questions of the "ancients" and draw responses through automatic writing.

Rod was helping the group become versed in the *Necronomicon* and the *Witches Bible*. They had gotten bold enough to practice their spells in the woods behind Hardee's, and sometimes they would perform magic in the middle of the student center on the MSU campus. They were all at the point where they could concentrate just about anywhere. They could make supernatural things happen.

Rod had taught them how to move objects through telekinesis. He had taught them how to make other people their "puppets." He was their master, and with his guidance, he could make them see aliens, he could take their souls on voyages, he could walk into their dreams. Rod and his coven were spending a lot of time communing with spirits and talking to the dead. Trusting Rod as their sire, they would take their blood and mix it in a cup and pass it around to partake. Everyone felt it was safe—they had all been tested for AIDS, they were all clean, and it was okay—as long as they kept their sacred rituals within the "family."

Still, when it came to Rod, Charity would waiver back and forth in her beliefs. Even though he vowed he was off the drugs, he was becoming more and more unrealistic—he claimed he could fly, for example, and was jumping off buildings just to scare her. She felt haunted by his presence, but was too smart to become entirely drawn in.

When Rod started a crusade to take the coven to yet another level—deeming them fallen angels and warriors against God—Charity had a hard time going along with it.

"Rod believed we were prophets," Charity explained. "All he'd ever talk about was the end of the world, and he said we'd all pull through it. I was supposed to be fire, Heather was air, Scott was water, and Rod was void. We were all prophecies, that's what he'd say. I thought he had lost his mind."

Charity began to realize that everything surrounding Rod was bizarre. For one thing, she couldn't understand why her girlfriend Dana had become so glued to him. Dana was kind of a goof, an overweight girl who was unpopular at school, yet somehow, she had become Rod's trusted servant. Charity knew Rod didn't like the girl, but suddenly, when Dana signed the lease to her own apartment, Rod and Scott just about moved in there with her.

Dana's apartment was the hideaway Rod and Scott needed. They were close to making an escape from Kentucky, and they just wanted a little time to pull their strengths together. Though they were never charged with it, Rod and Scott were suspected of having pulled off a burglary wearing ski masks at a nearby Shoney's. Now, they needed to gain access to a decent car. Knowing that Scott's Buick Skylark wouldn't hold up, the two young men were secretly considering knocking off Rod's grandfather. They needed the old man's Jeep.

With a hand-drawn map of the wealthy Wendorf residence in their possession, Rod and Scott were about to leave Murray in the dust.

chapter Twenty-three

"I think we need to separate Scott and Rod," Sondra phoned to warn Mr. Anderson, "because I fear Rod's going to do something really bad."

Mr. Anderson agreed. He didn't want his son under Rod's influence anymore. Their innocent role-playing had gotten way out of hand. Rod was telling Scott that the Andersons weren't his real parents, that Scott was born from Satan, and Scott seemed to half-believe it.

Sondra reported that Rod and Scott had spent $2,000 accepting collect calls from some girls in Florida. She had canceled her phone service and requested that the Andersons ground Scott. She learned that Mr. Anderson had some vague notion about a girl in Florida whom Scott was talking about "taking for a wife," but then, since Scott was only sixteen, since the boy never even had a girlfriend, the idea seemed ludicrous.

Mr. Anderson was sorry about the phone bill, but there was nothing he could do about it. He had no money, no control over his son. He complained that Scott had "run wild" ever since Rod came into the picture.

Apparently, Rod and Scott shared numerous secrets. Rod had made promises to Scott, among them, that Heather would be Scott's "dark mate." Rod said Heather had agreed, as long as Jeanine was willing to run off with them. Rod vowed to take the girls to Cairo and Rome, he promised Heather he would take her to see his castle in Wales.

When Heather would ask about things like passports and money, Rod claimed they needn't worry about such details. Of course, Heather never really believed Rod. She and Jeanine would laugh with each other every time they would hang up the phone with him, yet sometimes Rod seemed so impassioned. He was supposedly preparing to drive down to Eustis. He wasn't sure exactly when, but he needed them to be ready to drop everything at a moment's notice. Heather and Jeanine were used to hearing that. For months, Rod had promised that he'd be down to get them, and then he'd never show up.

"We were supposed to remove Heather from hell," Scott confided. "The way I interpreted it was, we were going to go down to get Heather—you know, take her away from her parents—and then take off to Louisiana or North Carolina, just take off and live together somewhere."

Scott knew Rod could easily tear a person's mind apart. He had watched Rod use mind games to attract followers for various covens. Rod was a great liar, he could look people in the eyes and tell them a story and sound so incredibly real. Scott was sure Heather and Jeanine were under Rod's spell and had no doubt that these girls would accept Rod's commands.

In the beginning, Scott thought he could read between the lines, that he knew the real score, but he himself had fallen prey to Rod's fantasy universe. Rod had quite a position of power, especially with these girls in Florida, and having Scott there in the background to confirm his preternatural claims didn't hurt. Scott became convinced, especially in the weeks before they arrived in Eustis, when the young man had reached a point that he honestly believed in Rod's immortality.

"Rod tried to talk me into it," Scott explained. "What he was doing was consuming the blood of other people so he would, in fact, *become* them. In other words, he was more than one soul. He was trying to achieve his ultimate being by consuming the blood of all animals on earth, of every living being. He saw fit to do it because he read it in the Bible and he found out it really works."

Rod told Scott they needed to rescue Heather, whose parents were "hurting her." Rod would talk to Heather on the phone, sometimes for six hours at a pop, and he felt pressured to get down to Eustis. He claimed he needed to remove Heather from her unhappy household immediately. Scott thought it was strange, because whenever he would ask Heather about her mom or dad, the girl didn't seem to have any major complaints. Still, he was afraid to confront Rod. His mentor was all-knowing, all-powerful, and beyond reproach.

"He could see things differently," Scott recalled. "Rod could understand things because he would consume part of someone's soul. That's where all his intelligence came from. It was very much like he was seeing himself in the mirror, only being six different people at the same time."

As he described the Wendorfs to Scott, Rod made Heather's parents seem like absolute monsters. He said they were snooty rich folks, that they reminded him of the greedy and selfish people of the aristocracy in Europe, that they were the types who cared about nothing but themselves. Rod was annoyed that these people dared to put their own trivial needs ahead of their daughter. In Rod's view, the Wendorfs seemed more concerned with things like fancy restaurants and new cars than their daughter's well-being. In his eyes, they didn't deserve a girl like Heather.

Scott wasn't exactly sure how Rod came up with the theory about the Wendorfs being evil. From what Scott could grasp, Heather lived in a brand-new house on a five-acre lot; she lived in the picture-perfect household. Her parents drove around in expensive vehicles, her dad played golf in country clubs, her mom didn't need to work—the Wendorfs afforded Heather the good life.

Heather never said anything bad about her parents that Scott could recall. In fact, not once could he remember her complaining about them, but of course, he didn't talk to her half as much as Rod did.

Whenever Scott talked to her, Heather seemed so obsessed with death, she didn't have time to talk about anything else. She would incessantly talk about having a hunger for blood, about her desire to be embraced. If anything, she acted like she almost didn't have any parents to worry about. All she wanted was to live with Rod, forever.

"She didn't really go on about her parents that much," Scott said. "She didn't say much about them at all. From what my impression was, they were nice people, you know. Compared to me at that time, they were probably a lot nicer than I was."

Scott was caught up in the Gothic world, he was

obsessed with the Dark Ages, with Ozzy Osbourne's lyrics that described the "army of the devil's children." Scott knew all about Rod's plan to "bring forth hell's army," and at the time, he thought it was a fantastic challenge. He wanted to be in on it and took an oath to serve Rod for eternity.

"Rod wanted to sacrifice souls and bring down most people," Scott confided. "Rod thought he was the prince of demons. He told me he was the third Antichrist, the devil's son.

"He wanted to consume the souls of so many people," Scott explained, "and by killing them, he could send their soul back to its origin, possibly send it straight to hell. The more souls he sent down there, the more possibility that he could open the gates of hell and complete the circle and let the demons release."

Rod told Scott he'd seen all the demons shackled in chains and claimed that if he could unshackle them, he would receive the "gift of the undead" and have "a face-to-face meeting with the Prince of Darkness."

"He wanted to be able to kill without ever having to worry about being killed," Scott recalled. "But, even if he wasn't mortal, even if he was undead, he could still be killed with a stake through the heart or with holy water. There's more than one way to kill a vampire."

Scott believed that Rod was a living creature who was destined to suffer eternal damnation. He believed Rod had the ability to cast death spells, to reanimate the dead so he could drink "the blood of the damned." Poor Scott had crossed the lines between role play and reality. He thought Rod had the forbidden knowledge that led to eternity.

The games they role-played mentioned things such as the "chalice of the dead," and Rod would tell Scott things like that really existed. He pledged to bring Scott to a fountain of blood, to take him to the "forest of tormented souls" and allow him to drink from an eternal evil flow. Scott believed Rod when he claimed he could grant others immortal strengths and superhuman powers. Scott had visions of himself as an "angel of light" able to "slay one hundred thousand men in a single-handed combat." Rod didn't think there was anything crazy about that. He encouraged Scott's fantasies and encouraged his buddy to have "memories" of their past lives together in France. Scott would dream about the two of them in velvet vests, in white, ruffled shirts, and Rod would smile knowingly. He had Scott believing that they were eternal brothers.

To Scott, Rod's plans to destroy all mankind made perfect sense. He wanted to know if Rod intended to bomb the United Nations, and if so, he begged to go along, to share the power and the glory. Scott was so busy living in a world of role-playing games, so caught up in imaginary sword fights and battles, he never questioned Rod's motives. He didn't care why Heather and Jeanine had become Rod's prime targets, that didn't really concern him. Scott was a kid with no direction, and Rod had given him a raison d'être.

Besides, Scott had learned early on not to question Rod. When Rod had first come back into his life, Scott would sometimes try to get straight answers out of his friend about vampires, but Rod would always manage to confuse him. The more Scott would press for specifics, the more perverse Rod's responses would become.

"First of all, if you were the third Antichrist," Scott had argued, "you wouldn't be sitting over here on your butt in the United States. You'd probably be in command of some large army over in the Middle East, packing nuclear weapons."

"Blood is life. It brings strength, power, and peace," Rod would tell him. "We have fangs to suck the life out of all living things. Our powers are of the blackest darkness. The first rule of the vampire is to never question your strengths. Take in my knowledge, and you will overcome all the beasts on earth."

Rod always insinuated that the world was not to be destroyed by his hand, that he and Scott didn't need to worry about Armageddon. Doomsday was already written in the stars. Nostradamus had predicted the "false dust," Rod said, which was an evident sign that the earth was shutting down. Rod insisted the prophet was referring to the smog that cars had created in every city center. He said Nostradamus was right, that the earth had become an unsuitable place for mortals to breed. Their blood had become tainted, Rod told Scott. They were feeding from poisoned fish.

Rod blamed human laziness for the disaster, angry that mankind relied on fossil fuels and thus destroyed the environment. He looked at the world from an ancient perspective, horrified at the pollution modern man had created.

Rod claimed that in 1555, when Nostradamus had published the first part of the Prophecies, he predicted the world's end in 1999. According to Rod, Nostradamus also dabbled in the occult and took his inspiration from black magic; that was how the visionary had successfully forecast the French Revolution, the Holocaust, and the "great battle fought in the sky" that would end all human life. The earth would become even more black, Rod promised, as humanity struggled with larger chemical outpourings, with fires caused by oil-spill disasters.

"There's no way you can be Satan's son," Scott would persist, "or you'd have some sort of power."

"We shall see," Rod would tell him. "Those who doubt my power will struggle for their lives."

"Well, if you're an immortal, then why do you bleed? Why are you flesh and blood, just like everybody?"

"I was born a human but I was possessed by a demon as a child. That was part of the sacrificial ceremony. Then I was brought back to this physical body. I was reincarnated into a human soul, but I'm actually many people. When my soul was taken over by Satan, I became entrapped in this human body."

"Well, you seem normal to me. At least, sometimes."

"I am Satan's child even though I may seem like a mortal."

Whenever Scott would imply that Rod was going overboard, that Rod was going a little bit crazy, that maybe his friend should consider getting some professional help, Rod would smirk with delight.

Rod found it so pretentious and arrogant that Scott would dare think that way. He was becoming frustrated with Scott, who didn't understand the wars, the intrigues, the plagues, that only Rod had lived with for so many centuries. Scott was a new vampire, he hadn't lived through the machinations of world leaders the way Rod had. Scott couldn't keep up, so he would lean on gibberish, speaking in tongues to avoid dealing with the serious issues.

At times, Rod would bring Scott to a nearby toxic waste dump and pontificate about the Western World producing more than it could consume. He became enraged by an American population that allowed the third world to starve, that would look at TV images—scenes of misery from Ethiopia or Bosnia—and do nothing to help. His view was that humanity deserved to be detested, that, as the devil's child, he had been sent to earth to erase all of mankind's wrongs.

Rod looked down upon American teens, whom he viewed with utter disgust. These were the most self-centered creatures walking the planet, he would tell Scott. These were the people who concerned themselves with petty desires, with designer labels and designer ice cream.

Scott couldn't figure out precisely what Rod meant, but he knew Rod hated the world, that he didn't see the earth as a fit place to exist. On occasion, Scott would hear reports that Rod had tried to impale himself, that he had thrown himself on a spiked metal fence, but no matter how many wounds and scars Rod had, he would deny ever trying to kill himself, insisting that there was no way that his blood could drain out.

PART THREE

TO
THE SOUTH

chapter twenty-four

You have created rage within myself to very bitter points of hatred. My soulless remains now crave to destroy you in every way, to drink your kindred soul. You've given me reason, now I give you rebirth through the loss of your soul. Only through this new life that I give to you, shall your crimes be washed away. But all of my hate, rage, and darkness can not stop me from loving you.

Rod Ferrell, untitled journal entry

Dear Journal:
I wouldn't usually tell anyone but there was a time once when I totally lost it. Everyone was on to me, I just went through a break up not too long before, and the midnight air called to me. I went out to go for a small walk up at the end of my street. I walked

by a woodsy field where I hoped snakes would come to poison me.

I see the faces of the people involved in my problems. They float by uttering previous sayings. Sometimes they disturb me, scaring me. I want to turn them off, put them aside.

                                        Heather Wendorf

Dear Heather:

I took the liberty to write you this letter in case you want to call me. As you know I'm 1017 years old, my mortal name is Howard Scott Anderson and my mortal age is 16. I hate my mortal name and I plan on disowning it soon. Oh, Me and Rod are planning on taking you to see the wonders of the world, such as Paris, London, and many more foreign countries. My actual birthplace was Scotland. Sometimes I talk in a Scottish accent. I have a taste for the bagpipes, I like their bonny little tunes.

My actual breed of vampire is called a Dampyre. It means psychic vampire. In other words, I feed off blood and souls of those who I choose to kill. But I haven't killed a person in almost 200 years. I was wondering if you would like to meet me sometime. I can easily arrange it. Maybe someday you'll have the chance to taste of my blood.

As you see, I have cut myself and bled on this paper to show you that you should have no fear of me. As you said, my dear brother Rod has lost all humanity, but I can't because I'm half human, half vampire. I'm a person you have to keep an eye on, because I like to play games with people's minds. You'll probably think I'm sort of a freak. Many have called me that, they've even called me Lucifer at times. I am a sword fighter, a man of deception and hatred but I don't like to lie to people. I show no mercy to men! But you are not human, I take it, so you're safe.

By the way, do you have a boyfriend? Rod told me he didn't know if you did. I'm a loner. With much regret, I've been searching the world over for a vampire, then Rod told me of you, and eased my inner turmoil.

Well, I hope I haven't offended you in any way but I must bid you farewell.

I hope you write me soon, Your friend in darkness.

Scott

Dear Scott:
I know I've already written to you but my life has been getting pretty hard on me and writing always takes me away from reality. My mind has been thinking too much and I've not been able to control what's going on inside me.

I feel isolated and I probably am. But that would be my own fault because I've been inadvertently avoiding people here and there. My souls feels split in two, like two different people, one of them non-aggressive, passive, whom I usually show to most people. Then two is the essence of vengeance, hate, destruction. Purely chaos molded into a hideous monster writhing and tearing the inside of me to ribbons.

She wants out. She wants to show herself and do what she sees fit to do. I do well to trap her inside and not dare free her. Not yet, at least.

Sometimes I see her running circles in me, enraged because she is oppressed from taking matters into her own hands (claws). I often wonder who has a creature in them like mine. You told me of yours. But unlike me, you can express what is going on inside. I have to chain her down. I just await the day when both she and I could be free of each other. I am already screaming inside. The voice echoes and tremors run through my body. I am crying inside. I am laughing insanely, but nothing is a bit funny.

Blood would taste really good right about now, or maybe ice cream. Hey, what am I saying? Blood is good all the time! Why is everyone so wrapped up in this love thing? It's just some word that's an excuse to get the other person on good terms with you. Why am I telling you all this? Oh well, it doesn't matter. This thing called love is my confusion. For some, it's used as cheap amusement. Tell me who love has? I know it's unsafe for me to say it. I might get hurt too much again. I don't want to be sad again. Before, I was happy and laughing, now, I'll become ill and down. I don't want this now. Help!

I'll let you go now. Perhaps I'll write you later again,

                                                    Heather

Dear Heather:
I'll try to send you a picture, if I do, it will be an older one, and then in time, I'll send you a recent picture. By the way, I will come and pick you up when I'm 18 mortal years of age, that should give

you a lot of time to visit and stay in touch with your friends down there. I took it from Rod that you and Jeanine don't trust me. But I don't trust anyone except my younger brother, Rod. Me and Rod only trust ourselves. If I get time, I will visit you soon. Remember, our goal is to destroy the world! Our time is here forever, for we can't die. Our food is the blood of mortals, our pleasure is watching them die.

Oh, I loved the picture you sent, but I'd already seen it in a dream. It hit me like déjà vu when I saw it. It made my heart linger a bit. By the way, me and Rod are friends again. He said he talked to you, but I don't care what he does, that's his business. Pay close attention to what I say.

You spoke of love in your latest letter, and I would like that of you. If you want me as your dark mate, I would be pleased. If it's not money that you want, then tell me what you want, I'll appease you as best I can. Because you sent me that picture, it made me want to hold you and ease your pain.

You hunger for blood. Well, I have many minions. I have more blood than can fill your hunger. I don't know if Rod told you, but I am a virgin. The reason why is because I never could fuck a girl and then just leave her.

Write back soon with your decision ok? I can never lie to a girl, especially one of your kind, it's taboo in my codes. So believe that what I tell you is true. But for now, I must go.

I can help you, you know how that goes,

Scott

Scott:

I was extremely pleased when you and Rod made peace. I know at this time it's sort of a weak truce, but it's overly better than nothing at all. I do have to say that Jeanine and I had a bit to do with it. When all of this started, I felt terrible, for all our plans had been uprooted. I mean, how can only Jeanine, Rod, and I be happy truly? That would only be a trio of us and I so much planned for a quartet. Two is company, three is a crowd, but I believe four is a family, a coven. Be it a small one though, but I don't complain at all.

One thing is, after this incident, I was being used as a tug-of-war between two friends, and I feel I've lost something. I don't think my trust in both you and Rod will ever be what it used to be for a very long time. The thing is, I am a gullible and naive girl. I admit that in full and with that, I can be easily taken advantage of. The good side is my loyalty can be quite strong when given proper reason. I hope you understand what I'm saying.

Being naive and being innocent is a beautiful thing. It gives my eyes a different perspective of my world. When things happen to break my innocence and relinquish my naive self, my worries increase. Please consider that to me, being naive isn't just a part of my characteristics but more of a defense.

I say all this not to be accusing or to sound at all angry, just to inform you on my feelings. I shall tell Rod the same. All is still good.

I had a wonderful dream a while ago. It was most likely wishful thinking. In the start it seemed I was working for some rich woman in a large house. Perhaps I did something wrong but in any case, the woman threw me out. As I walked down the road a while, I noticed a familiar house. When I went inside, Jeanine, Rod, and you were there. It all seemed right. After a while, one of us noticed that two guys had been prowling around outside. Quick as a flash we were outside and with no effort, both you and Rod caught the two of them. It was agreed to drain them, and to my surprise & delight, Rod offered me the first kill.

With one look at his neck I felt something inside me happen. Growing. I didn't know what it was until the guy I was about to feed from grew hysterical. I distinctly felt my fangs growing out. And with every second they grew, my hunger grew stronger. When I couldn't stand it anymore, I went down to open his neck. Unfortunately, when I was about to bite down, my mother came in and woke me up. That was really frustrating, I'm sure you can relate.

The thing is, after this dream was over, I could still feel my fangs with a slight tingle in them. To you, I'm sure this is an everyday thing. But for me, it was a first feel of a new gift. A great awaited gift. For me, it was a reason to wait patiently for more.

P.S. I don't know what you said about love. We shall talk about that in a letter following this one.

All and everything and all—

Heather

chapter twenty-five

Heather had a lot of problems sleeping at night. She'd sit and stare at her posters, her teenage paraphernalia, just wincing under her covers in her cluttered room. Trying to divert herself from screaming out loud, she would imagine her body changing. She would struggle for domination of her own mind, but her brain never cooperated. She was always in mental agony, believing that she had an alternate personality hidden in her system.

Heather's headaches were sometimes so severe, her skin would become tight and her face would take on a faint white color. Uncomfortable in her own skin, Heather would look into the mirror in horror. Under the moonlight, she imagined her physical characteristics merging into a new form—a more animal form capable of inflicting abuse to her body.

Her mental state was so rocky, she would become so

distressed, there were occasions when she would literally drop to the floor crying. Holed up in her room, she would debate over the razor blade lying on her desk. Her desire to feel pain would always win, and she would grab the blade, hoping the physical suffering would distract her. As she would position the edge of the blade on her inner arm, tears would stream down her face. For a split second, Heather would contemplate the repercussions of her action, then she would take a deep breath and slice. She would watch in amazement as her flesh would turn bright red and finally start to scar.

All by herself, Heather would enter her peculiar dream-world, envisioning darkened forms of beasts peering back at her from her window. As her mind raced, she would tell herself that she could seek her fate in the eyes of the mystical creatures that haunted her. She would stare out her window, trying desperately to connect with her monsters, but none of them answered her. Heather often felt invisible. She would rage at the monsters in the woods, only to hear silence.

Throughout the fall of 1996, while talking long distance with Rod and simultaneously wishing she was dead, Heather spent a lot of "alone" time making up these fantasy characters, writing journal entries about the "wild beasts" who were waiting to carry her off into wilderness. Heather despised the teenage pressures of dating and making friends. Not that she had problems finding new boyfriends. After Rod left, Jeremy had become the one special guy in her life, but he didn't seem too serious about commitment. She went out with him and they had fun together, but Jeremy couldn't relate to her world.

Jeanine had similar dating woes. She hated the dating scene, and just for kicks, she was going out with her game master, Bob, a troubled kid with a blood lust. For Jeanine, who liked learning new magic tricks, Bob was someone to waste time with. But even with all the magic and witchcraft, Jeanine's life felt empty. Wiccan people had a spirituality that Jeanine simply didn't have. She would read witches' handbooks and practice spells, but none of it meant anything to her. For Jeanine, the only thing that was enticing was death. Suicide was looking more tempting each day, she wrote in her diary, where she jotted down various methods of killing herself, having taken direction from a manual called *The Big Book of Death*.

Jeanine hated high school, she despised her parents, she wanted Rod back, and more than anything, she missed seeing Heather. Life would be better "out there" Jeanine wrote in numerous poems, alluding to the immortal universe Rod promised. In her letters to Rod, Jeanine often mentioned that she wanted her soul to "leave." Evil had seduced her, she insisted, telling Rod that only his promise of being undead could save her. That was all Jeanine could think about.

In certain letters, Jeanine would grill Rod about Charity, clearly nervous about losing him. She didn't like that Rod was associating with other girls. She hated being separated from him and wanted the long-distance aspect of their relationship to end. In her letters, she asked for assurance that Rod would come back for her, and he would sometimes write back a note proclaiming his love, though he never mentioned a concrete plan for them to get back together.

Jeanine was so desperate to see him, she had even drawn Rod a map of the Wendorf house, explaining that it would be easier for him to retrieve her from there, because the Wendorfs never locked their doors. To impress him, Jeanine made the map rather elaborate, including diagrams of the furnishings in every room and specific instructions about how to get to Heather's window.

During their phone conversations, Rod made vague references to the Wendorfs. He asked Jeanine questions and discovered the Wendorfs were well-off, that they lived on a five-acre plot in a brand-new house with a built-in pool, et cetera. But to Jeanine, he never appeared interested in visiting Heather. He never made any comments about appearing at Heather's window. Rod was saving the map, however, just in case.

Over the phone, Rod would assure Jeanine that Charity meant nothing to him, that she was just another victim who did not believe in the "mind things" that he and Jeanine shared. He convinced Jeanine that she was the only girl who understood his condition, who realized that he had "no choice" when it came to prey, intimating that Charity was merely someone from whom he could feed.

"When I hold you in a gentle embrace," Rod once told Jeanine, "the soft winds of eternity will blow over us, and my thoughts and desires will be only of you to love me the same."

But following her long chats with Rod in the middle of the night, Jeanine would awake in a panic, trembling in tears. Jeanine suffered with a self-induced madness, living in a personal hell that was inspired by her own evil thoughts. In her eyes, Rod was to blame. Rod was pursuing the weakest and most vulnerable parts of her mind. After listening to Rod, Jeanine would walk around Eustis like a zombie, seeing nothing but blank stares and worthless smiles. As her mental suffering increased, all she dreamed of was "watching red blood drain from flesh."

"My parents don't understand why I'm different and

why I try to show it. They don't care," she wrote in her diary. "I am a time bomb waiting to explode."

Jeanine hated Leesburg High. She wanted to be in school with Heather and resented her parents for shifting her out of the Eustis school system at such a critical point in her life. Jeanine wanted to kill herself, she would confide to Heather, and Heather could only empathize with Jeanine's suicidal tendencies.

Both girls obsessed about death and immortality and spent hours communing with spirits in their secret "birthplace" in the cemetery, but that wasn't really helping Jeanine. Even though she sometimes thought she saw Rod's image appear in the cemetery, Jeanine couldn't help feeling she was just imagining him. She wanted Rod to materialize for real.

Rod was her salvation, the only one who held the answers, Jeanine decided. She wanted to be more like him, to escape the modern world and travel to past centuries. Having bought into Rod's gloom-and-doom beliefs, Jeanine had come to feel it was futile to try to change the screwed-up world. As a kid, she had been on a mission, she had been interested in the environment and was on a crusade to end pollution. But Rod changed all that. He made her realize that no one could make an impact on the filth and garbage generated by the hypocritical society that surrounded them. Rod told her the woods were burning, that not even God could save the greedy and ignorant mortals from themselves.

Rod convinced Jeanine that the world was destined to end by the year 2000. Over the phone, he would advise Jeanine to ignore the mixed images of the media, referring to the "worthless chatter" of the information age as being no contest in the face of Armageddon. Newscasts were a brainwashing mechanism, he insisted, cautioning Jeanine to stay away from the news, encouraging her to retreat into her artwork.

A gifted art student, Jeanine would draw pictures of herself in past lives, enclosing these strange images in her letters to Rod. Jeanine started to believe that she actually belonged "back in time," and Rod promised he would take her there, but when Jeanine pressured him to project them both into the Victorian era, Rod would tell her things had become complicated. He would insist that she'd have to wait.

Until Rod's return, Heather and Jeanine decided they would drum up a make-believe past. The two girls pretended to live in a bygone century, walking around their quaint resort town wearing Victorian lace and odd items they picked up in the vintage-clothing shops in nearby Mount Dora. The girls looked like a pair of misfits, and tourists would stare at them as if they were creatures from the underworld. In the tropical heat of Florida, they wore silly things like black velvet hats and black lace gauntlets, seeming all the more bizarre in a tourist town where the general attire consisted of starched white shorts and spiked golf shoes.

Against the backdrop of the all-American resort area of Lake County, where driving ranges and tennis clubs flourished with palm trees and lush flora, Heather and Jeanine looked like a pair of freaks. As an added attraction, Heather had started dying her hair different colors—first it was hot pink, then it was purple; it seemed like every few weeks Heather tried something new. Her parents didn't really approve, but her mom wanted Heather to feel free to explore her artistic self, so she never said anything about it. Ruth Wendorf had no idea that her daughter was in training to become a "vampire." Ruth told her friends that Heather's outfits were "cute."

But as Heather retreated further, relishing a world where death and dying were her only focus, Ruth started to become heavyhearted. Ruth decided that Jeanine was dragging Heather down. Whenever Heather was around Jeanine, both girls would become morbid. When Heather started to cover her room with dead roses and upside-down crosses, Ruth tried to put a stop to it. But Ruth couldn't seem to control her.

Even though Ruth liked Jeanine, she blamed Jeanine for twisting Heather's mind. At a loss about what to do, Heather's mom decided to restrict the amount of time the two girls could spend together, but that didn't seem to help. If anything, Ruth Wendorf's new rule tended to act as a catalyst for Heather, who was hell-bent on running her own life.

Dear Scott:

I've just gotten lonely lately. I don't get to see Jeanine all that often. Every weekend is just not enough to catch up with her. I'm sure Rod has an enormous phone bill because of all the collect calls Jeanine and I have been making. It's like both of us can never talk to him enough, even when there is nothing to really say. But he never cares. He was the one who told us to call collect.

You know, just the other day, I was ready and willing to up and leave it all. Somehow, Jeanine and I convinced Rod to come down. When he couldn't get a ride from any immortals he had to stoop down to ask for help from a human. Her father was a truck driver and he said he would give him a ride to Florida. They got as far as Louisiana and the guy ditched Rod. Fortunately, Rod had some sort of family member in New Orleans.

Last Friday night, Rod called Jeanine and I at my house and we had a very interesting & involved talk for a couple hours. He called up reporting that he was 100 miles north of Eustis. It was funny, cause he called from some house he had just broken into. When he heard the police show up, he split. An hour or two later, he called from Leesburg, which is close to Eustis. Do you know how hard it is for me to get Rod so very close to me and then not to see him?

Lately, I can tell this whole situation is changing me. Things that I used to feel were important I don't care so much about; friends, family, school, and even basic humanity. Last night I had a disturbing dream. I was in a room and in that room was a small child, an infant girl. She was so small I could hold her in one hand. It was like I could hear her thoughts and she could hear mine. I remember I asked her questions, and she said she knew me, that I was an old friend.

Then I don't know why, but I went straight for her little neck. She started to scream and cry, just like a little baby. I know it was just a dream but I can still taste her blood and smell her scent. She smelled like any other infant, just sweet and innocent. This makes me think about things. It makes me ask myself is this what evil is really like? Did I enjoy it? Does this make me a monster? Do I care anymore?

Heather

chapter Twenty-six

"We were talking on the phone with Rod one time," Jeanine recalled, "and he started going off about the floating-head dudes. He said the floating heads were the Ancients, that the Ancients told him that he's supposed to be the king of the world."

"Would you be my queen?" Rod asked Jeanine, speaking to the girls on the extensions at Heather's house.

"Well, if she's queen, what would I be?" Heather wanted to know. "Can I be, like, the court jester or something?"

"Heather has a boyfriend, Rod," Jeanine reminded him, "so you better come up with a place for Jeremy. He has to come along."

"We can take him with us and just have him as your pet," Rod told Heather, "we'll get him for you. He'll be your little boy pet and we'll put him in chains so you can play with him outside."

"Let's put him on a hook," Heather squealed, "that way I can have him up in my bedroom."

"No, I want him chained outside," Jeanine said, giggling.

"You shut up," Rod snapped. "I decide what becomes of our pets."

"No. You shut up," Jeanine blurted, "you're a control freak."

"What I was planning on doing was just getting a ride with Rod until we got out of Florida and then I was leaving," Jeanine confided. "I wasn't going to hang around with him, I was just leaving on my own. I was going to ask Heather if she wanted to come or not, but if she wanted to stay with Rod, that was okay. I just wanted out. My parents were driving me nuts. I couldn't stand them."

Jeanine had always complained about her parents. She and Heather had been friends since seventh grade, and there wasn't a moment when Jeanine seemed content at home. Mr. and Mrs. LeClaire were both teachers in the Leesburg school system. They had high hopes for their daughter, but in Jeanine's eyes, they were pushing her too hard. Because Jeanine had become so moody, they had sent her to counseling. The LeClaires tried to understand her, but Jeanine felt she was being watched and analyzed every second.

"My father has actually ordered me to be happy," Jeanine reflected, "but you can't control emotions."

Part of the reason she clung to Heather was that the Wendorfs were relatively lenient. Rick and Ruth were cool about things like MTV and late-night sleep-over parties.

Jeanine loved them enough to consider them her "second parents." Whenever Jeanine spent the night at Heather's, she regained her sense of freedom and felt happy again.

The Wendorfs were the kind of role models Jeanine needed. Rick and Ruth were cool about everything, an easygoing couple who really had it together. Rick worked a lot; Ruth kept a vegetable garden. The Wendorfs led separate lives, yet were very close to each other. They respected each other's privacy, Jeanine noticed.

More than anything, the two of them cared about their daughters. The girls were a bit spoiled—each had her own phone, CD player, and VCR—but the Wendorfs could afford it. Anyway, Jeanine didn't care about material things; she too had all the trappings of a middle-class teen. What mattered most was that the Wendorfs didn't spend all their time poking into their children's business. They trusted their girls, and Jeanine wished she had parents like that.

Out of the blue, in mid-November 1996, Heather received a call from Scott. He sounded so shaken up on the phone, she barely recognized his voice. Scott was calling to report that Rod had gone nuts, that Rod was on the *warpath*. Scott said Rod had kicked Matt Goodman's teeth in. Scott told Heather that Rod and Matt were fighting a psychic battle, using rival coven members to make serious death threats.

"Why would Rod do that?" Heather asked, her voice shaky. "Why would he hurt Matt? I thought they were blood brothers."

"Matt went to the police," Scott told her. "Rod excommunicated him so he went and made false statements to the cops. He tried to get Rod locked up."

"For what?" she asked, her tone growing anxious. "What were the false statements?"

"Matt said Rod killed a cop. He made a sworn statement that Rod either killed a cop or threatened a cop, I'm not for sure."

"Are you saying Rod's in jail?"

"No, not yet, but there's a lot of bad shit going on up here. Matt's blaming Rod for killing some animals."

Heather didn't like the sound of it. But over time, she had learned not to put much faith in Scott. Too often, Scott had called with outrageous accusations, just as a prank. Heather knew Scott liked to build his life around imaginary scenarios, that he thrived on false drama. Still, this time, his tone sounded quirky. Heather felt a pit in her stomach.

"Rod's lost it," Scott warned her, "he's gonna kill you and Jeanine. He's coming down there."

"Rod couldn't do that," Heather argued, her breath getting short, "Rod loves us. He just would never do that."

The second she hung up, she speed-dialed Jeanine to discuss the situation. Jeanine decided to reserve judgment until they spoke to Rod. She felt sure Scott was lying, that there was no real crisis.

Rod, of course, wasn't surprised when the girls called him later that night. In a calm voice, he explained that Scott was going to pay for his little joke, mocking Scott for playing the Masquerade too much. He apologized for Scott's phony phone call, suggesting that his buddy might have swallowed a few tabs of acid and become delusional. Heather thought that was likely. Scott's voice sounded funny, she said, and during their conversation, he was saying off-the-wall things.

"Like what?" Rod wanted to know.

"Scott now says he's a million years old," Heather said, laughing.

Rod just burst out, snorting through the phone.

"Scott gets high and says all kinds of crazy bullshit," Rod told them. "He once told me he got possessed by a demon and had sex with Jesus."

"He did what?" Jeanine asked. "With Jesus?"

"He had a séance," Rod said, "and he turned into a female demon and had sex."

"I didn't even know he was gay," Heather joked. "I thought he wanted to marry me, but he can just forget it."

"Yeah," Rod said, his voice matter-of-fact, "there's a lot that would surprise you about Scott, and if he decides he wants you, he'll get his way."

"Maybe he was reincarnated into that prostitute," Heather said, teasing, "you know, maybe he's turned into what's her face, the other Mary ..."

"Yeah, right. Scott probably channeled Mary Magdalene," Rod said, his tone sarcastic.

"Oh, haven't you heard?" Heather asked. "Scott says he's going to father the next baby Jesus."

Jeanine was howling on her end of the phone.

"No, I'm supposed to be the mother," Jeanine snickered, "only this time, it's not going to be immaculate conception."

"Yeah, and it's not going to be the savior," Rod told her, "because I'm gonna have you bring us the Antichrist. You're gonna have a baby with a little six six six branded on its butt."

Even though they knew it was sacrilegious, Heather and Jeanine just couldn't stop laughing. Rod had that kind of effect on them. He could turn a scary situation into the most ridiculous conversation in the world. Sometimes, he'd speak in tongues, using gibberish to make his point.

He was outlandish, like a whirlwind taking over, and he'd always blow them away.

Whenever they spent a lot of time on the phone with him, both girls could feel Rod's spirit through the airwaves. Rod would claim that if he fully opened up his mind, the evil inside him would be capable of deleting all human life. Though the girls had their doubts, the two of them never wanted to test Rod. They were careful not to say anything to cross him. Even when Rod's statements didn't add up, Heather and Jeanine agreed it would be useless to enrage him.

Rod would say he had enough power to ignite the last world war, and just in case he was the king of the world, they wanted to hang on to their connection.

chapter twenty-seven

"Hey, Rod, what's up?" Heather whispered. She knew something was wrong.

"I'm in New Orleans," he said. "I had to come down here to take care of some business. I had to kill someone."

"Isn't that supposed to be illegal? Are you tripping?"

"I disposed of the body. I ate it."

"Oh, right, you ate it. You ate the whole body?"

"When you're a vampire, you find that your appetite is quite increased."

"Well, what did you do with the bones? You surely couldn't eat those."

"I ground them into powder."

"Well, where are you now?"

"In the next birthplace," Rod said, "I'll show it to you sometime."

"But exactly where?"

"You'll see, my child. You still have a lot to learn before you're fully embraced. The Ancients have chosen your new name as Zoey. Jeanine will be called Celeste. Once all of us are completely out of the realm of mortals, you will refer to myself as Vesago, and to Scott as Nosferatu."

"But why don't you just tell me what part of New Orleans you're at?"

"I must go, child. I have to take a trip into the lower spirit world. I have this certain little demon down in hell that I have control over, and he's not doing his job guarding the gates."

"Every single time I talked to him, it was something crazy," Heather recalled. "He told me this whole story about the circle of elements, that was part of the vampire thing. Rod had informed me that there are prophets of the elements, that these prophets go back for all eternity. When the prophet dies, it goes into someone else. He told me I was a prophet."

The moment Heather believed one thing, it seemed, Rod would push her one step further. He always wanted her to join him on higher levels of the supernatural. And whatever Rod planned, even if all logic and reason told her it was crazy, Heather would act interested. If he suggested they had to kill someone, she wouldn't object.

When the phone would ring in the evening, Ruth would often pick up an extension and hear her daughter accepting a collect call. She would argue with Heather—the collect phone bill had become an issue at the Wendorfs—but Heather would get huffy with Ruth. Heather's phone bill was never over $50 a month, and her dad assigned her yard work to pay off the calls. Heather didn't feel she should get fussed at when she spent hours mowing the lawn as punishment.

Over picky things like that, Heather would get angry. She would tell Rod she couldn't stand her parents, and invariably, he would commiserate with her about her tormented existence. The two of them would make plans to run off into the darkness, Rod promising to save her and Jeanine. Later, the two girls just bubbled over at the thought of breaking free.

"You know what we can do, Jeanine?"

"What?"

"We'll leave, but before we leave, we'll fuck with our parents' heads. We'll trash our rooms and just freak them out."

"Yeah, let's wait till they're gone somewhere," Jeanine suggested, "and we'll get a bunch of fishbowls and put, like, goldfish everywhere. They'll come home and all they'll have is these tiny little fish. And we'll be gone."

"That's great. And you know what I want to do? I want to nail all my furniture up to the ceiling, just to mess with them," Heather said. "I want to nail my bed up there. I'm gonna take every single thing I own and just get big fat nails and freak my parents out."

Jeanine thought it was a splendid idea.

Ever since Jeanine's parents had found a stack of Rod's letters, the LeClaires were aware of the vampire coven. After reviewing Rod's twisted poetry and artwork—with all its focus on coffins, graves, and demons—they had forbidden her to speak to Rod. The LeClaires had taken most of Jeanine's artwork, notes, and letters and insisted she hand them over. They tore through her room relentlessly, forc-

ing Jeanine to toss anything that remotely suggested the
occult, witchcraft, or vampires. Thrown in the garbage
were posters, drawings, spell books, and even her monster
videos, which had nothing to do with magic.

Both Jeanine and Heather felt violated when, after her
discoveries, Suzanne LeClaire placed a call to Ruth Wendorf
to tattle. Suddenly, even at Heather's, the girls were being
scrutinized. Ruth didn't ask to go through her daughter's
whole room, but she did want to look in Heather's backpack.

Ruth was upset when she found a mangled Barbie doll
in there. It was hanging from a noose and all the body
parts were rearranged. Ruth asked her daughter to dispose
of it, but Heather refused. It was just a toy, and it wasn't fair
for her not to be able to keep it, she felt. The fifteen-year-
old was ready to stand up for herself. She wasn't going to
be pushed around just because she wasn't a cheerleader
and an all-American type like her older sister, Jennifer.

"I could come in and kidnap both of you," Rod offered
during one of their phone conversations. "I could come
grab you and then leave your parents tied up. I could make
it look like a kidnapping."

"No, because I would want to take my clothes,"
Heather protested, "I would want to take at least that part
of my life with me."

"You could take your clothes," Rod insisted, "you just
pack a bag and grab it."

"Well, that would look kinda dumb," Jeanine inter-
jected. "Wouldn't it?"

"Yeah," Heather said, "you don't get kidnapped and
take a bag with you."

But Rod didn't necessarily agree.

chapter twenty-eight

"Everyone thinks that I totally mutilated this Barbie doll, that I stuck it on my backpack on purpose," Heather lamented. "It started when my friend Matt decorated my locker. He went and surprised me and hung neat things in there, and in the center was this hanging Barbie. I hung it on my backpack, and then one of my buddies grabbed it, and it popped apart, so I just stuck it all back together and noosed it up, so it wouldn't come off."

Heather didn't think there was anything wrong with a hanging Barbie, with wearing all black, or with having purple hair. She considered herself different, but not necessarily punk or Goth. She didn't like being labeled. She had a bizarre group of friends, and that didn't make her a bad person. However, her mom didn't see things that way. Ruth Wendorf had taken a volunteer job at the front office at Eustis High, just so she could keep an eye on her girls.

For the most part, it was actually Jeni who had been acting up, cutting school so she could run around with an older boy, twenty-one-year-old Tony Stoothoff. Naturally, Ruth wasn't very happy about her seventeen-year-old spending late nights out with Tony, but she was unable to prevent it. Tony and Jeni worked at the Publix supermarket in Mount Dora, and they arranged their schedules so that they'd both get off at the same time, somewhere around eight o'clock, and then Jennifer would claim she worked two hours beyond that, grabbing a couple of hours with Tony without her parents knowing.

Jeni thought she had everyone fooled, but then one night in October, Tony wound up crashing her new red Saturn. He smacked the car into a tree and was arrested for a DUI on the spot. Stoothoff's accident cost the Wendorfs plenty, and Rick was furious with his daughter for breaking the one rule he gave her, not to allow anyone else to drive her car, but ultimately, Rick decided to give his daughter a second brand-new Saturn. Ruth didn't agree with the decision, but Rick was hoping that, with Tony behind bars, Jeni would come to her senses and let go of her loser boyfriend.

Rick was torn about buying the second car; a hard-working white-collar man, his money wasn't something he easily parted with. Still, he wanted his girl to have all the advantages that he never had. Jeni was an honor student who had been accepted to Florida State University; she had dreams of becoming a medical doctor. Rick wanted Jennifer to be a happy teenager. He believed that she would soon find herself a boy with a bright future, but unfortunately, Jeni went straight back to Tony the minute he was bailed out.

With Ruth working at the front office of the high school, trying to keep closer tabs on both daughters, Rick felt a little more at ease. Ruth Wendorf checked classroom schedules and tried her best to ensure that neither of her kids cut class, and for the most part, the girls enjoyed seeing their mom busy working. Other kids loved Ruth, as did the faculty. In the few months she worked there, Ruth had made quite a few friends. She thought she had found the key to keeping her daughters under control, but both Jeni and Heather managed to slip by her.

On Monday, November 25, the day Rod Ferrell appeared, Ruth Wendorf had no idea that Heather was skipping AP art class. She would never have dreamt that her straight-A student was outside in the nearby cemetery, performing a blood ritual with Rod in the middle of broad daylight.

Heather and Jeanine had received the call from Rod the night before, when their friend Shannon had dialed over to Jeanine's. Shannon said she had out-of-town guests, and then, all of a sudden, Rod got on the line. He was in Lake County, he said, he had driven down with Scott. Rod wanted the girls to get their stuff ready to leave town and gave them a week to get it together.

But Jeanine wasn't so anxious to go. Just before midnight that Sunday night, Rod met her out on Lake Seneca Road, a few yards from her house; he was making his last-ditch effort to convince Jeanine to join his "family." He never mentioned that Charity and Dana were waiting in Scott's Buick Skylark, parked a couple hundred yards away. Instead, he kissed and flirted with her and told Jeanine that she had a whole new existence awaiting her. Jeanine said she still needed time to think. She wanted to stall, but Rod wouldn't budge his schedule. Jeanine would have to make up her mind immediately, he told her. Heather had already made plans to meet with him in the Greenwood Cemetery the next afternoon. Heather was ready to be "crossed over," he said, she had agreed to take off for Louisiana as soon as he gave the order.

As Rod walked back through the woods, Jeanine shook her head in disbelief. It was as if he had appeared out of nowhere, and even after all their phone conversations, he seemed like a stranger to her. Jeanine hadn't laid eyes on him for almost a year, and Rod's looks had changed drastically. He had gone from being a strawberry blond, "normal"-looking kid, to being this dark figure lurking in the night. His hair was long and jet-black. His nails were painted, he reeked of smoke, and he seemed kind of scary. Jeanine thought maybe he really was a vampire, his skin was so ghastly white, and she was rather frightened.

But then she reminded herself that this was her ex-boyfriend, someone she had cared about with all her heart. Rod's boyish charm made his offers of immortality all the more appealing, and Jeanine teased with him about waiting until Mardi Gras before she turned immortal. Rod said he and his family would probably still be in New Orleans the following spring, if, in fact, she wanted to wait until Mardi Gras, but he hinted that he wouldn't be waiting for her to become his queen. If she wanted him, and Rod said she was possibly the love of his life, then she would have to make a choice: either her family or his.

chapter twenty-nine

All at once, things seemed to move in slow motion. Heather and Rod sat quietly, looking around the cemetery as if it were a beautiful playground, their shadows falling between the thick lines of Spanish moss. Rod gave Heather a kind of feeling that caused a twinkle in her eye. She was hugging him finally, after so many months of just talk, and his strong arms made her melt. Heather felt like she just blended into the backdrop and hardly noticed when Rod reached around and cut himself.

She drank his blood freely, then cut her arm in return. The bright red stream seemed to take her stress away; it helped her handle her pain. Rod's dark eyes shimmered as he took her arm to his lips. The embrace was almost complete.

Of course, Heather still had a few more hoops to jump through before she could consider herself a true vampire.

She would be required to learn incantations. She would be subject to unknown sacrifices. For her to become more in tune with the dark possibilities of immortality, she would have to stretch her mind past mortal limits. Being "undead" was something that could be willed, Rod explained. All mortals had the capacity to conquer time, they just didn't know it.

"Human beings don't have to die just because they reach a hundred," he told her, "mortals can live three hundred years if they want to. Do you understand that? Age is a figment of your imagination."

"I don't know what you mean," she answered, trying to grasp his point.

"Mortals have the technology to clone body parts. Do you understand cloning? Do you realize mortals have the ability to grow new hearts, new lungs, new everything? With today's technology, mortals can prolong their lives to age three hundred, at least."

"But life expectancy is still only around a hundred, isn't it?"

"So what? Two thousand years ago, it used to be age thirty," he argued, "don't you get it?"

"Not totally."

"It's all up to you, Heather. You determine how long your life expectancy is."

"But think how ugly I would be at three hundred," Heather snickered.

"No, that's just it," Rod sneered. "As a vampire, you rejuvenate yourself. You're not mortal, so you don't have to age. It's a secret vampires have known for centuries. Mortals are just now starting to figure it out. Scientists are using cloning and chemicals to reverse age, to become immortal. Mortals are trying to mimic vampires, which means it's time . . ."

"You mean, I'm never going to age?"

"No, you age, but you can rewind yourself. Once you learn to occupy the immortal gene in your body, you can reverse the aging process."

"So, I'll be fifteen forever?"

"If you would like, Zoey. At first, when I was Vesago, I chose to stay at eighteen. I let myself grow to that age before I went to sleep in France. But then I rewound myself to sixteen when I decided to return as Roderick."

"Well, I like being fifteen, so that's cool with me."

"Every seven years your body will rejuvenate, and you will have the option to go back to your current age."

"And how long will I really live?"

"Well, if redwoods live thousands of years, so can you. Look around at the oak trees here. That's your proof of the quantum connection."

As Heather looked at the ancient trees, her face grew puzzled.

"You will have no more fear of being sick," Rod promised. "As a vampire, you will have no more fear of loss. Any body part that is wounded, you can rejuvenate back to its original state. Any person who is killed, you can resurrect. You can bring people to an immortal state by the transfer of your blood."

"You mean, I can *raise* people from *the dead?*"

"You just have to believe it, Heather. Anything you want to have happen, will happen," he said, smiling. "You just have to want it hard enough."

The two of them concentrated on merging into the same spirit. They lay entranced in a brief moment of intimacy, forgetting about the rest of the universe, but then suddenly Heather remembered she had an important message for Rod. Jeanine had called early that morning to confess she didn't know if she really loved him anymore. Heather said Jeanine was uncomfortable with the idea of going on a road trip. Apparently, Jeanine didn't trust Rod.

Heather confided she heard a rumor that Rod had offered to kill Jeanine's parents. Rod freaked Heather out, casually stating that he had, indeed, made the offer, but Jeanine wanted him to stay clear of her household. Jeanine's parents were off limits, Rod said, which was fine with him.

"You are the prophet, Heather, not Jeanine. You are the one designated to attend Black Mass with me," he told her. "My coven in New Orleans is looking for a way to overthrow God, and they have determined that you are the missing link."

"How can they do that?"

"The world will end soon, Heather. Everything as you've once known it will cease to exist. When the undead take over the earth, you will preside along with me. On that day of judgment, you will be there, Zoey, to deliver mortals into the hands of evil."

"But what about Jeanine? I'm not going unless she comes with me. We promised each other that."

"Before I give you more answers, I have one question," Rod said flatly.

"Okay, shoot."

"Do you want your parents dead or alive?"

"I want them alive, Rod. Why would I be telling you I'm gonna get my stuff and sneak out if I wanted them dead?"

"Well, Zoey, you once mentioned that someone would have to kill them before they'd let you leave."

"No, no, no, no, no. You've got it all wrong, Rod. I was

just kidding, I mean, does anyone ever take you up on that? When you ask that question, does anyone ever say *yes*?"

"Come to think of it," he sighed, "no one ever has."

"You don't want my parents winding up *undead* and then being around us for eternity, do you?" She paused. "Because if you killed them, I could bring them back."

"Good point."

chapter Thirty

That Monday afternoon, Jennifer Wendorf didn't go to class. She thought she was safe hiding out at Tony's house, but just before three o'clock, her mother showed up. Jeni met her mom outside, moving Ruth toward the parking lot, anxious to explain things and get her out of there. More than ever, she didn't want Ruth to report back to her dad, but oddly, her mom seemed preoccupied. Ruth had spent the afternoon trying to locate Heather.

"I don't want you to skip any more school," her mom scolded, heading back toward her car. "You're going to mess up your grades and wind up not graduating."

"But I had this big fight with Tony and I had to see him."

"Are you sure you didn't see Heather around campus anywhere today?"

"I missed her at lunch. She wasn't anywhere that I

noticed. She's been acting really weird the past few days, Mom, she hardly even says hello to me anymore."

"Well, Heather needs to learn a little respect," Ruth complained, "she's getting too big for her britches. She's been getting up in my face lately. I don't know what's gotten into her, but things are going to have to change around the house. Both of you girls are running wild and your dad's not going to put up with it."

"Maybe I can talk to her when I get home from work tonight," Jeni offered, "maybe it's just a phase she's going through."

"I think when you get home from work, your dad and I will sit down with you and Heather and have a talk."

"Well, I get off at ten," Jeni lied, "I have to work late."

Out at the Greenwood Cemetery, Rod had convinced Heather that she was born evil, that no matter how much she strived to be a good Christian and go to heaven, there was no place for her there. He promised to take her to the edge of eternity, to a place beyond heaven, where Christians never went, and Heather thought she understood what he was talking about. She felt she was truly one of them, one of the undead. If it was her destiny to live as a vampire with Rod, she wasn't going to fight it.

"I didn't see it as anything wrong," she confided. "It was just like I was in human form, just a regular person, and Rod just came over and embraced me. It felt good, really.

"I embraced him back and then things started changing," she recalled. "I went with him into the black depth, we crawled under this little stairway, and then I started a flying dream. It was pitch-black and I could see I was flying low to the ground and I could feel wings flapping. I

was flying down this street in this suburban neighborhood and following this creature. It was Rod, and his
color was absolute black."

Later Monday night, just after dark, Rod called from
Shannon's again, this time insisting that Heather pack her
bags immediately. He and Scott had a flat tire, he explained,
they were in a stolen vehicle and had to run from the
police. They were under a lot of pressure, Rod said. His
voice spelled trouble.

If the cops stopped them for any reason, he told
Heather, if the cops ran a check on the license plate, it
would mean jail.

Rod told Heather the group would be hitting the road
that evening. He ordered her to call Jeanine and make the
final arrangements. Heather knew Rod and Scott had two
girls with them, she had met the girls briefly that day—they
waited in the car with Scott when Rod embraced her over in
the cemetery—but Heather wasn't so thrilled about being
cramped with five other people all the way to Louisiana. She
was trying to buy time, arguing that it wasn't fair for Rod to
force her to leave just before Thanksgiving.

But over the phone, Rod seemed almost frantic, he was
being pushy, which was unlike him, and Heather was confused about why he was in such a rush. She asked Rod to
meet her a few yards from her house, down at the end of
Greentree Lane, insisting that she had to talk about things
in person before she'd give him a decision.

It was already pitch-black out, a half hour later, when
Heather waltzed down Greentree in her cutoffs, fishnets,
and combat boots. All she could see was the glow of cigarettes, but as she got closer, she realized she was inter-
rupting some big conversation between Rod and Scott.
The two of them got very silent as she approached, and,

noticing two figures in the backseat of the Buick, Heather started to go wave hello at Charity and Dana, but the boys escorted her away from the car.

"So what's up?" she asked, poking Rod in the chest playfully.

"If you're going," he told her, "it's got to be right now."

"But I'm not ready. I don't want to leave in a big hurry. The car's not really stolen, is it?"

"Actually, it's my dad's car," Scott said nervously. "I usually drive it, but we've been gone for three days and they're probably looking for me."

"The cops are after us, Zoey," Rod told her. "Scott violated curfew and his crazy mother always calls the cops. I'm sure there's a warrant out for him by now."

"We've got to split," Scott told her, stomping out his cigarette, "because this is the first place the cops would look for us."

"But I need time to say good-bye to my parents," Heather insisted, her voice getting hyper. "If I'm never gonna see them again, I want to at least say good-bye."

"That's fine, you can do that, but don't take too long," Rod said. "Or, if you want," he told her, staring blankly out at the woods, "you can go in there and start to pack and we'll follow you and tie them up so we can get going faster."

"Why would you do that?" Heather asked, getting panicked. "I don't need you to tie them up. I can sneak out my window and they'll never know."

"Well, I was just offering to make it look like a kidnapping," Rod said, looking over at Scott for support.

"Rod just wants to make things more interesting," Scott muttered, his face bunching up in a weird grin. "He's only joking, Zoey. You need to ignore his little games."

"But I already told you, we don't need to do that," she blurted. "I just need a half hour to say good-bye and get my stuff together."

"Okay, fine, Zoey," Rod said, "it's not a problem, we can wait."

"And what about Jeanine?"

"We'll go get her right now," Scott suggested. "We'll head over there and that'll give you a half hour."

Heather agreed to meet the Buick Skylark out at the exact same spot, and she ran down Greentree Lane with her heart pounding. As she jumped the fence and scurried toward her house, she could hardly believe she was actually running away. Heather had asked Rod to take her to see Jeremy one last time, and Rod had offered to do that. It hardly seemed possible that she would never see her boyfriend again. She hoped she could talk Jeremy into going with them, but in her heart, she knew Jeremy would never say yes.

Undetected by her parents, Heather flew through the side door and back into her room, where she pulled together some of her favorite jeans, jewelry, and T-shirts. She grabbed her teddy bear and artist sketchbook, crammed as much as she could into two backpacks, and then dialed Jeanine. But Jeanine couldn't talk; she was in the middle of cake and ice cream. Heather had forgotten about Jeanine's birthday celebration with her family. Jeanine didn't have time to hear what Heather had to say. She was busy. She rushed Heather off the phone and told her to call back.

Heather hung up and tiptoed around to the kitchen. Before she went to sit with her dad in the family room, she snuck open Rick's wallet and pulled out fifty bucks. She stuck the money in her jeans and quietly went and sat by

Rick on his favorite couch, where, for some strange reason, he happened to be flipping through pages of his high school yearbook. Heather had never seen it before, and she looked with interest as her dad showed her his childhood friends from Winter Park. He pointed to a few ex-girlfriends, remarking about how "hot" one of them was back then, and Heather looked at the image of a young woman in a miniskirt and go-go boots and just laughed.

As she leafed through his high school pictures, Heather felt like she was viewing ancient history. Her dad's outfits were so funny, his hairstyles so outdated. She sat for ten minutes and listened while Rick reminisced about the good old days, then slipped away to go see her mom.

Ruth was in her bedroom watching a made-for-TV movie, some Lifetime family drama, and Heather lay down on her mom's pillow, right next to Ruth on the quilted bedspread, pretending to be her little baby girl again. The two of them just lay there watching the television show, hugging each other without saying a word, and after a short while, during a commercial break, Heather got up and went to make a phone call.

"I'm leaving with Rod," she told Jeremy, her voice quivering. "We're heading over there for a minute so I can see you before I go."

"Why are you doing this, Heather? It's stupid," Jeremy said, trying to coax her, "you're just gonna get caught and wind up in big trouble."

"I have to go, that's why, you just don't understand. Why don't you come with me? It'll be an adventure."

"Why do you have to go, Heather? Who says you have to? Can you tell me that?"

"It's Rod," Heather said in a whisper, "he might kill my parents if I don't go with him."

Ruth (left) and Rick Wendorf (right) with their family in happier days.
(Courtesy of Heather Wendorf)

Ruth Wendorf with Jeni and Heather.
(Courtesy of Heather Wendorf)

Growing up, Heather Wendorf was surrounded by love.
(Courtesy of Heather Wendorf)

Heather
Wendorf with
her parents'
Ford Explorer.

Heather in front of the Wendorf house on Greentree.

Remnants of the Vampyre Hotel at the Land Between the Lakes.

Inside the Vampyre Hotel.

The animal shelter in Calloway County where puppies were found slaughtered.

Rod Ferrell at the
Old Salem cemetery.
(Courtesy of Jaden Murphy)

Jaden Murphy.
(Courtesy of Jaden Murphy)

Jaden and
Rod duel.
(Courtesy of
Jaden Murphy)

Rod Ferrell.
(Courtesy of Jaden Murphy)

Female member of Rod's Coven.
(Courtesy of Jaden Murphy)

The Embrace.
(Courtesy of Jaden Murphy)

Rod Ferrell, before he claimed to be "undead."

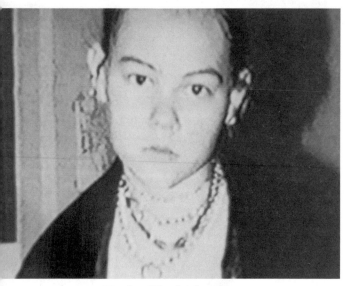

Heather Wendorf under arrest.

Jaden Murphy has his fifteen minutes of fame.

Charity Keesee after her arrest.

Scott Anderson in shackles.

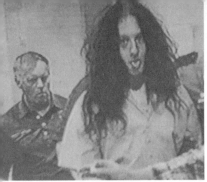

Rod Ferrell taunts the press.

Prosecutor Brad
King faces the
media throng.

Rod's mother, Sondra
"Star" Gibson,
self-styled vampire,
tells the press, "We
live forever."

"What?"

"He said he would. He keeps talking about killing them and I don't want them dead. If I don't leave, I'm afraid he might do something."

"That's crazy, Heather. Why don't you just catch your breath and listen to yourself for a minute? You're not making any sense."

Heather didn't have any more time to argue. She told Jeremy she'd stop by Orange Avenue to see him before she took off, and she glanced one last time around her bedroom. At least, she thought to herself, she had stuck a note in her back bathroom telling her family good-bye. At least they wouldn't think she was kidnapped, or something worse.

Heather had only written a few words. Her farewell letter didn't say anything much. But it was sufficient, she told herself, and she ran away from the house as fast as she could, without ever looking back.

Dear Mom, Dad, and Jeni,
I don't have much time but I must say that I love you all so very much.

I'm leaving for good, but I don't want you to worry about me, because I will be fine. I had to go with Jeanine because she needs someone to look after her.

Please don't try to find us.

Just know that I'll miss you and will always love you.

Heather

chapter thirty-one

Jeremy had gotten used to Heather talking about things like vampires and evil spirits. He didn't ever take her at her word, but that last phone call, the one he'd gotten around eight-thirty Monday night, sounded serious.

The timing was perfect, because for the longest time, Jeremy had been thinking about breaking up with Heather. Now, with her running away, his problem would be solved. Still, Jeremy stayed attracted to Heather; for months, he had managed to block out all the nonsense about rituals and blood, to look beyond that and appreciate Heather's beauty, her brains. Heather was tremendously smart, gifted in the arts, and she was cute. Jeremy had always wanted a girl like that.

Trying to appease her, he even allowed Heather to drink blood from him once. It made him cringe to watch her suck his arm. He had offered it, really, because he just wanted to see if she would go through with it.

To get her away from blood, Jeremy encouraged Heather to become involved with spiritual healing, with New Age energies and more positive things like crystals. He didn't want her to identify herself as a vampire and chose to disregard the part of Heather that was drawn to the underworld. He believed Heather was salvageable, especially since her friend Jeanine was a churchgoer who was busy trying to convert Heather. Heather claimed Jeanine was a vampire, but from what Jeremy could tell, Jeanine was attending church services regularly. Jeremy tried to derail Heather's twisted fantasies, but she would get defensive about her vampire coven, and he didn't want to attack her.

"She called it the family," Jeremy confided. "She showed me this photograph of her with Jeanine and Rod, the three of them were looking very dark and evil from the way they posed. I thought it was just a cool picture, I didn't think they were crazy."

When Jeremy first met Heather, back in September of that same year, and she started talking about this guy Rod, some dude who lived in Kentucky who drove around in a big hearse, Jeremy thought Heather was kidding. But then, Heather spoke incessantly about Rod, claiming that he had promised to return to Eustis to take her to faraway places. She said all kinds of insane things about Rod, but Jeremy never really reacted. Jeremy was a jock with a weekend job at the movie theater. He was a popular kid, a typical guy who didn't like to think about things too much. Heather was satisfying his needs, and that's what mattered.

Jeremy figured it was all a mind game anyway, something that Heather had come up with, trying to make him jealous. Since this guy Rod lived up north, hundreds of miles away, Jeremy never really cared to challenge her about it. From the details he heard, Jeremy considered Rod more of an annoyance than a threat. If anything, Rod sounded pathetic.

Still, Jeremy thought it was nuts that Heather would place so much stock in someone she described as an evil character. He wondered why such an intelligent girl would waste her brain cells on this type of lunatic. Rod sounded like he belonged on *Jerry Springer.*

"There was one time when she told me that Rod believed he was some reincarnated form of a demon," Jeremy recalled, "that he was this high power that she had to obey.

"She had to look up to Rod, but she never told me why," he mused, "I know she believed in ghosts and demons. She believed in everything, in angels, in second lives, in third lives . . ."

When they first dated, Jeremy and Heather talked about getting married. They thought they loved each other and fantasized about going off to a place such as Wisconsin and starting a family. Jeremy had a sister there, and he and Heather were convinced they could run off and get jobs and create a fairy-tale life.

But it turned out it was just puppy love, especially for Heather, who had no interest in settling down. Heather wanted to travel and see the world. She wanted to see places in Europe, she was obsessed with Paris, and somehow, she believed Rod was going to take her there. She told Jeremy that Rod had promised to whisk her off to France to live in a castle. Jeremy thought it was bizarre, the way Heather had come to think of Rod as her "daddy." Rod was the person Heather would follow to the ends of the universe, and Jeremy never understood it. The more he heard about Rod, the more he wondered why Heather would respect him. If Rod really believed he was centuries old, if he really fed off near-dead people and hung out in cemeteries, Rod was somebody Jeremy definitely didn't want to meet.

By mid-November, when Heather confided that she considered herself a reincarnated demon, even though Jeremy liked her parents and thought she came from good stock, he was ready for the relationship with Heather to end.

"Here I am thinking about my life, my future goals, school, work," he recalled, "and she's off in this world where it's good to play in, but she wouldn't come back to the real world. I was pretty speechless when she told me she was a demon.

"She said Rod put her under some hypnotic spell, like hypnosis, and she went into some other world and she was in demon form and she loved it. Heather thought she was something from hell that slaughters people, like some form of dragon creature."

On that Monday night, when Heather called with the request for him to run away, Jeremy thought it was just as good a time as any for him to finally end things, but then, after he hung up the phone, he was second-guessing himself. She had sounded so serious, so scared of Rod, and he felt he should protect her. Of course, Jeremy still cared about Heather, and he didn't approve of her running away. He had mixed emotions. He didn't want to be her boyfriend anymore, yet he was hoping she would change.

"I noticed little things about her," Jeremy admitted, "scars and nicks on her forearms. She would tell me that she did them all. I read in some magazine that depressed people did some weird stuff, self-inflicted cuts, and putting that together with Rod and her, and the reincarnation of demons, and then seeing her drinking blood, at that point I was grossed out beyond belief."

After thinking about the consequences and considering Rod's alleged threats, Jeremy realized he had to prevent Heather from running off with Rod. Even if he was going to dump her, it was his obligation to save her from disaster. Jeremy felt he owed that to the Wendorfs, a family whom he had taken on as his own, people with whom he had plans to spend Thanksgiving. Over the phone, Jeremy had tried to reason with Heather, he had tried to talk her into staying, but he hadn't made a dent. Jeremy wondered what could be running through that little mind of hers, especially after her bizarre description of Rod and his comments.

With much dread, Jeremy threw on his jacket and decided to wait for Heather in the parking lot in front of his apartment complex. The last thing he wanted was for his parents to overhear them, especially if Rod was going to be present. Jeremy was ready for a fight and intended to battle Rod, if necessary.

But when the Buick Skylark finally pulled up, it was just Heather with two other girls. The three of them looked sweet and innocent, all their belongings piled with them in the backseat. Jeremy wanted to know where Rod was, and Heather said he and Scott went to pick up Jeanine. She claimed she didn't want Rod around Jeremy, that she was concerned about what might happen, especially since they were both schooled in martial arts.

"He's crazy and he could hurt you real bad," Heather warned him. "He can kill you, you know."

"No, I don't think so," Jeremy said, "I'm pretty sure I can handle myself."

"Well, I guess you won't change your mind about coming with us?" Heather asked. "Just wondering."

"No," he told her, giving Heather a hug, waving hello at the two girls in the car. "I'm not going anywhere," he said firmly, "and neither are you."

"Oh, yes, I am. I'm going with Rod, I already promised."

"Heather, you don't have to follow this guy. I mean, why are you doing this?"

"I have to do whatever he says," she insisted, her eyes welling up. "I'm already crossed over and he said if I don't leave now, he's going to hurt my parents."

"No, he's not going to do anything like that," Jeremy promised, "nobody's going to let him do anything to your parents. You don't have to go anywhere. He's got you brainwashed."

Heather was about to cry, she was shaking and seemed scared about leaving. Jeremy grabbed her by the arms and held her, he said everything he could to change her mind, but he realized he couldn't help her. He wasn't getting through to her at all. Heather was programmed. She had her heart set on Rod.

"I wish you could go with me," she pleaded, a tear running down her face. "Why don't you come? It would be great to just run away and live together."

But just then, Charity stepped away from the driver's seat. She stood up against the car with her arms folded, anxiously awaiting Heather. Clearly, Charity and Dana were in a rush, and Heather had no more time to waste on good-byes.

"Come on, let's go," Charity yelled, "we have to get out of here."

chapter thirty-two

Rod and Scott had hidden in the woods behind Heather's, just long enough to watch the Buick pull off. At first, they were confused about which house was hers. They had gone to her next-door neighbors and peered in the windows, but were deterred by an alarm system.

Rod had a feeling they were at the wrong house. He had never heard Heather mention anything about an alarm, so he directed Scott over toward the ranch-style house a few hundred yards away. Rod had never laid eyes on the Wendorfs, he had no idea what to expect, so he examined the exits and entries, hoping to catch a glimpse of them. He and Scott were considering a break-in, but when Rod realized the garage door was unlocked, he decided they should just walk in like they owned the place.

"Are you sure you want to do this?" Rod asked, half under his breath.

"Yeah," Scott told him, "I'm ready."

"I'm gonna take out the dad, you'll take out the mom, right?"

"Okay," Scott said, holding up a wooden club, "I'll beat her in the head and just knock her out."

"Now, you're sure about this, 'cause I don't want to get in there without having backup. The old man could be hard to handle. He could have a gun."

"I'll back you, man." Scott motioned with his thumb up. "I'm cool."

"Then let's get it over with," Rod said, opening the door to the garage. "You know, I think we're gonna need something better than these clubs. Let's look around in here for something metal."

As the two young men entered the garage, their eyes focusing on a wall of tools, Rod decided not to pick up anything dangerous. He bypassed the machete, the chain saw, and the ax, and grabbed a crowbar instead. Rod wasn't really positive about killing these people, he told Scott. Maybe he could just beat them and grab the car keys and get out.

The boys could see the TV glare as they waltzed down the hallway toward the family room. It was cranked up pretty loud, and they were relieved to see Rick fast asleep on the couch. They were able to slip by him and cut the phone cords in the back bedrooms, then Rod asked Scott to check out the master bedroom. They could hear the shower running from that direction, but Scott didn't want to go back there by himself.

Obviously, Rod was going to have to take charge of the situation.

Scott was losing his nerve.

I hope you plain out don't move, Rod was thinking as he passed by Rick the second time, *'cause if you do, I will beat the fuck out of you.*

chapter thirty-three

From the moment he lifted his head, Richard Wendorf never had a chance. The blows from the crowbar started coming at him in even strokes. He never made it up off the family-room couch.

Rod Ferrell knocked Rick cold in the first few blows, but kept beating the forty-nine-year-old man, just to be sure he was dead. Rod was concerned that Rick might wake up—even after inflicting more than twenty blows to the head—so Rod took the crowbar and stabbed Rick through his chest. It was as if Rod was driving a stake into someone's heart.

It was a bloodbath, and Scott stood watching, absolutely frozen stiff.

When it was over, Rod picked the man up and flipped him over on the couch, trying to get Rick's keys out of his back pocket. No cash was in the wallet, so Rod grabbed

Rick's Discover card and left the corpse to search for Heather's mom.

On the white linoleum floor, in the brightness of the kitchen, he and Ruth confronted each other. She was standing there, squeaky-clean in her blue bathrobe, a cup of hot coffee in her hands, bewildered at the sight of these bloody strangers.

Then she saw the crowbar.

"What do you want?" she shrieked. "What are you doing here? Are you friends of Heather's?"

"Just shut up," Rod muttered, heading for her with the long piece of metal.

Ruth threw her steaming hot coffee at him, enraging him. He lunged at her and Ruth scratched his face with her nails.

The whole time, Scott stood by silently. He never moved a muscle, never said a word. He acted like he was watching a movie, like he wasn't really there.

Then as soon as Rod got his bearings, as soon as he recovered from the scalding burn on his arm, things began moving very quickly. With a karate kick he knocked Ruth to the ground, then started beating her with the bar. Rod struck her hard, hitting her in the head over a dozen times. He made sure he beat her to a bloody pulp.

Having satisfied his rage, he looked pleased with himself. As Rod gazed over at Scott for advice, he seemed to be on an adrenaline high. His face was empowered, his tone outrageous.

"What do you want to do with the bodies?" Rod asked, pumping Scott. "Come on, quit standing there."

"Well, we could throw the bodies in the pool."

"That's sick." Rod smirked. "Man, you are just one morbid motherfucker."

Rod told Scott to pilfer through the master bedroom for cash while he went back to check out Rick's other jackets, where he found a sturdy pocketknife. Then for kicks, while he was out in the family room, Rod decided to leave his mark on Mr. Wendorf. He flipped Rick back over and used a cigarette to burn a *V* in the man's chest.

Rod was used to the smell of fresh blood. He had no problem being surrounded by it. As he stood by Rick's body, getting his fill of the smell of burning flesh, Rod looked curiously delighted. He smirked and told Scott he felt like a god. Making these human sacrifices gave him a rush.

Meanwhile, the only thing Scott had come up with was a small jewelry box. Rod went through it and grabbed a set of pearls. The rest seemed like costume junk, and Rod had no time to stand there and pick through it. He looked over at the mom and motioned to Scott to come with him into the kitchen to review the damage.

"Doesn't her face look like a rubber mask?" Rod asked, smiling. "She doesn't look real."

"Yeah, I guess," Scott said meekly.

"That little bitch was so persistent. Did you see her lunge at me?"

"Yeah."

"She shouldn't have done that. She clawed me and it didn't exactly make me too happy."

"She wasn't very nice to you."

"That's why her brains are coming out of her head," Rod howled, "look at 'em oozing out of her skull."

"Well, they're dead. We don't have to worry about them gettin' back up."

"You egged her on, man. You weren't hitting her or nothin'. That's why I just had to go boom, boom. You just stood there, and now look at you. You're like a kid in an amusement park, just watching a freak show."

"Hey, let's blow this joint," Scott mumbled, "we need to get outta here."

Rod smiled and held up the Explorer keys. The two young men ripped off their blood-splattered shirts and Rod grabbed a garbage bag that he noticed out in the garage. He cleaned off the crowbar so he could take it with him and ordered Scott to drive the Wendorf car. Minutes later, the two young men were at a gas station washing up. The guys had no shirts on, having covered them with gas. They had left the evidence to burn in the Florida woods.

As the two of them removed every trace of blood, or at least as much as they could, Rod and Scott remained calm. They discussed their game plan for reuniting with the girls and agreed to tell Charity and Dana the news but not to tell Heather. They wanted to keep Heather in the dark as long as possible.

Back on Greentree, the Wendorfs' dogs had already discovered the bodies. Their white toy spaniel, Bichon, barked wildly beside Ruth, her curly hair turning bright red as she nuzzled herself against her mom.

Their large mixed Lab, Jake, had made his gruesome inspection of Rick and had bounced back out through the open garage door, barking furiously on the edge of the Wendorf property. But no one responded. One of the neighbors heard the barking, and just as he was about to check it out, suddenly the dog stopped. Apparently, Jake had returned to the scene to stay beside his master.

For over an hour, the house stood strangely silent.

Jennifer's arrival at 10:30 P.M. was the first hint of human life. When she noticed the Explorer was gone, she thought it odd, but Jeni figured her father had gone out somewhere to retrieve Heather. As she tiptoed through the house, noticing her dad asleep in front of the TV, she determined it was her mom who had run after Heather. She and her sister had been causing them both so much grief, Jeni knew it was all about to come to a head. She wondered if they were going to be forced to have that family chat when Ruth returned.

As Jeni moved toward her back bedroom, she made a point to keep her head down. She didn't really want to look at her dad and saw him through the corner of her eye, but she passed by quickly. Jeni didn't want to awaken Rick. Being twenty minutes late, she knew she'd be in for a reprimand.

When she picked up the phone in her room to dial Tony, Jeni found it was dead. She traced the wire, saw it had been cut, and figured maybe Heather had been up to something with her razor blades.

Without skipping a beat, Jeni pulled her cell phone out of her purse to call her boyfriend. In a whisper, she told him she had made it home okay. She was anxious to get off the line. She blew a kiss into the phone and said good-night. It was late and Jeni was starving. She wanted to grab something to eat before she went to sleep.

PART FOUR

TO
THE EAST

Ruth had come from the mountains of West Virginia. When she moved to the small city of Logan to marry Joe Queen, she was still such a farm girl, Ruth didn't even know what a pizza pie was. She knew about livestock, chickens, and hogs, but she was completely unprepared for the city, no less married life.

Born Naoma Ruth Adams, Ruth thought she had simple needs; the pretty blonde decided to be a homemaker, she didn't expect the moon. But, being young and superstitious, she felt she had jinxed things by being too anxious to settle down. She was well into her twenties when she realized she had made a mistake marrying Joe. By then, they had already moved to Florida and were raising their two adorable girls—Paula and Samantha.

Ruth loved being a mom but was caught in a rut. She

and Joe had fallen out of love by the time Paula and Sam were toddlers. The young couple just didn't get along, and when Paula turned sweet sixteen and decided to move out on her own, Ruth and Joe decided to separate. Ruth found herself a job at Crown Cork and Seal doing unglamorous factory work, but she was so down-to-earth, she never complained about it for a minute.

Working twelve-hour days, she managed to buy a car and keep a roof over her head, living in a little duplex apartment in the Orlando suburbs with her seven-year-old daughter, Sam. In those days, Ruth never dated much; she was a working mom and devoted homemaker, and that was enough.

It took almost eight years for Ruth to start thinking about a man seriously again. It happened unexpectedly one day, when she met Rick at her factory job. For him, it was love at first sight, and though Ruth didn't think Rick was anyone special, though she had no desire to even go out with him, her girlfriend at work, Bobby Spears, convinced her.

"You know, I met Rick and I think he's nice," Bobby mentioned, "don't you think so?"

"Well, he seems nice, he asked me out to dinner."

"Are you going?"

"I don't know. I'm thinking about it."

"Don't you think he's handsome? I sure do," Bobby persisted. "You should go out with him."

"Well, maybe."

Bobby did everything she could to talk her friend into dating Rick. He was a gentleman, Bobby told her, a guy who worked hard and didn't chase women. Bobby encouraged the match, and it was successful. It seemed like they had only been dating a matter of months when Bobby discovered her best friend was pregnant. Ruth had turned up at the Florida State Fair wearing a loose blouse, trying to hide it, and Bobby was just thrilled. However, Ruth wasn't so anxious to start a family again. She still had Sam and Paula to worry about, and actually, Rick had to talk her into moving in with him. Ruth wasn't ready, she contended, making Rick wait weeks for an answer.

Part of the problem was that Ruth was technically married to Joe—the two of them hadn't agreed to a divorce, and even though they lived separate lives, they were still emotionally attached. So it was with great trepidation that Ruth moved into Rick's house. Things were rocky at first, but after the birth of Jennifer, Ruth grew fond of her new life. She loved Rick, and though they never married, she was soon pregnant with Heather, living unofficially as Mrs. Rick Wendorf.

When Rick's company moved forty-five minutes north of Orlando and Rick got a promotion, Ruth was ecstatic. In her first years with Rick, Ruth kept her job, raising her second set of girls with the help of day care. She had her daughter Sam around to baby-sit, and she had her daughter Paula dropping by to help with Jeni and Heather, but still, being a working mom for the second time was tough. Ruth was tired of the grind. She wanted to spend the precious growing years at home with her little girls.

When Rick got his big promotion, involving a relocation to the "country," Ruth was told she no longer had to work. After twenty long years of being in the workforce, she finally had her break from hard labor. Rick loved her and wanted her to be happy. He was a great provider and would do anything for his wife and kids.

Rick and Ruth scouted the Lake County region for property and fell in love with the rural outskirts of Eustis, where they were able to buy five acres at a great price. For nearly a year, during the construction of their three-thousand-square-foot house, Rick and Ruth took the girls up to Eustis on weekends. Rick checked out the construction while Ruth planted the start of her vegetable garden, and the girls would play in the woods, imagining their brand-new bedrooms and swimming pool. These were some of their happiest days.

Not only did the Wendorfs raise their two girls with all the love and caring any parents could give, they provided Jennifer and Heather with all the amenities most American children take for granted. The girls had season passes to Disney World, camping trips in the mountains, music lessons, picnics, and craft prizes—Heather and Jennifer had just about everything a girl could want.

And Rick was a genius when it came to business and money. He invested his hard-earned dollars in companies like Disney and McDonald's, he knew how to pick them, and he was thrifty, he didn't throw money around. Not only had he saved enough for both girls' college funds, Rick had even bought stocks in his daughters' names, so the girls learned about dividend checks early on. Rick made sure they were schooled in the stock market, in the ways of making money. He wanted Jeni and Heather to be savvy businesspeople. He had great hopes for them.

An exemplary member of his family, Rick worked at the same company for twenty-three years. He had a middle-management job with a manufacturer of metal cans and plastic containers for orange juice. His mom and two brothers lived near his work, in a gorgeous little town called Winter Park, and Rick often spent time visiting. He was close with the rest of the Wendorf clan and shared a unique bond with his identical twin brother, Billy. Rick was beloved by the Wendorfs; they adored him. He was a caring son who felt responsible for his mom's well-being, and a loving brother who never missed a weekend golf date with his brothers and his dad.

Of all the Wendorfs, Rick was considered the all-around good guy. Of course he made his mistakes, he had been married once and divorced, but for the most part, he was a model human being. He and Ruth had a loving relationship, and he was determined to make things work. They had their share of the normal bickering, but there was no real fighting. At times they would step on each other's toes, in particular when it came to their daughters, when they frequently disagreed about how to handle things. Nonetheless, even when they had "mouthy teenagers" to deal with, Ruth and Rick seemed to love each other. For two adults being given a very hard time, Mr. and Mrs. Wendorf got along incredibly well.

According to Bobby Spears, the problems in the Wendorf household began around the time Jeni had been given her car, just after her sixteenth birthday. Because Jennifer habitually stayed out after curfew, because she consistently ran off without telling her parents where she was headed, Ruth was upset and Rick was growing frustrated. They tried grounding the girl, but she just wouldn't listen. She thought she didn't need her parents.

"After Jeni got the car, they would have to take it away from her every so often," Bobby recalled. "Then the next thing I'm hearing, there was this physical confrontation between Ruth and Jennifer."

Bobby was shocked when Ruth told her about the fist-fight, because in twenty-seven years of friendship, she had known Ruth to be the most levelheaded person in the world. Apparently, Ruth was hiding the fight from Rick, who would never have tolerated such behavior. It was in mid-1996 that Bobby met secretly with Ruth over at a little café in Mount Dora. Ruth had arrived there almost in tears. She was frightened for her child's safety, worried that something terrible might happen.

Bobby offered suggestions to help solve the problem with Jeni, but Ruth seemed beside herself. She was at a loss about what to do with her daughter and mentioned that Heather had been acting up as well, following in her sister's bad footsteps.

"Jeni's changed," Ruth complained, "she thinks she should be allowed to do anything and everything she wants to. Rick and I had to crack down on her."

"Well, if Rick's cracked down," Bobby said, "I know it's got to be serious, because those girls are the center of his life."

"She's getting really hard to handle, we had a big fight the other day."

"What kind of fight?"

"A brawl."

"Are you telling me you had a fight with Jeni that came to blows?"

"Well, yes, on Jennifer's part it did."

From what Ruth told Bobby, the fight had begun with Heather and Jennifer. Ruth heard screaming and had run into Jeni's room to find the two girls down on the floor beating on each other, and Ruth lost it. When she went to break the girls up, she tried to pull Jeni off Heather, and Jeni turned on her.

"Ruth was trying to hold Jeni and keep her from really hitting her," Bobby confided, "but the blows were striking her and Jennifer ended up rolling on the floor and I think Jeni got some bruises too, though I can't say that for sure."

Jeni eventually admitted that she had battled with her mom the one time—it was a fight over Tony—but she would not confirm that any serious physical damage came to her or her mom. If anything, Jeni felt stupid about the scuffle. Upon reflection, she called herself "ignorant."

"Tony encouraged me to be defiant. I was causing problems in the house and my mom was concerned," Jeni explained. "I was going through this rebellious stage and I was just with people who were a bad influence on me. I'd have yelling matches with my mother, and she said I was deceitful and manipulative, which was basically true. I thought I was older than I was, I didn't want to realize I was only seventeen."

chapter thirty-five

"Heather and I were actually best friends for a real long time," Jeni promised, "we had this little contract we signed, that whenever we grew up, we were going to live in the same house and live together forever."

But with Jeni going through the teenage transition, she didn't feel so family-oriented anymore. Her little sister would come to her for advice or ask for a ride in the car, and Jeni would have no time for her. Jeni didn't want to hang around people like her sister, her parents, or grandparents. She loved her family, but she had different priorities.

Jeni was cheerleading at ball games, she had things like homecoming to worry about, and she was busy buying her very first sequined gown, preparing for a life with Tony, who, much to her parents' chagrin, she planned to marry.

Mostly, Heather was the one who stayed at home. Since

she was still young, Heather wasn't allowed to stay out on school nights, so she'd spend her evenings watching TV with her parents, just hanging around helping her mom with different craft projects, helping her dad polish off homemade blueberry pies. The Wendorfs rarely had visitors, and when they did, it was often Rick's father, Jim, a retired lawyer who had spent years working for Billy Graham, who was trying hard to win his son's affection.

Jim had been trying to work his way back into Rick's life for some time, and Heather would listen quietly when Jim and Rick talked about the old days, about their years out in Wisconsin and how beautiful the land was back then, when it was still like the Wild West.

Rick and his brothers had been raised in Oshkosh and had moved around from Colorado to Texas, and then at some point, Jim Wendorf had uprooted the family and moved East. Not long after his relocation to Winter Park, however, Jim was estranged from his wife, and the Wendorf boys slowly began to resent him.

Jim was a born-again Christian with strong right-wing beliefs, and his sons respected him for that. However, it didn't give the man carte blanche to walk away from his marriage to their mom. It took years for Jim to mend fences with his three sons, and Rick became the most understanding and tolerant of the three, having his dad stay at his Eustis home for weeks at a pop. Jim finally remarried when he reached seventy, and he settled in a town called Umatilla, just a wide stretch in the road, about fifteen minutes from Eustis.

It was a great retirement place, Umatilla. It was quiet and inexpensive and religious. And by strange coincidence, Rod Ferrell's grandpa had retired there. Harrell Gibson had relocated from Kentucky in the latter part of

1995, when he had left Sondra and Rod to their own evils; he had given up on Sondra. Still, Harrell maintained his tiny place in Murray, he would continue to drift between the two states, and oddly, it was just around the time Rod was expelled from Calloway High, just before Rod disappeared with Scott in the red Buick Skylark, that Harrell had returned to Kentucky, feeling the need to hang around for the holidays, at least for Rod's sake.

In all the long-distance phone conversations between Rod and Heather, the fact that they had grandparents living practically next door to each other never came up. The two of them hardly discussed practical realities; Rod didn't think his family was really connected to him, only his supernatural family mattered. Harrell was an embarrassment to him, Rod would say, complaining about Harrell's Pentecostal ways. To Heather, Rod would make fun of his silly grandfather who tried to reform him and get him to go to church. Rod dismissed his grandpa as a man who lived in a Christian bubble. Talking about him was a waste of breath.

Rod thought Harrell was a dopey old man. Rod thought he could put anything over on him, but in the days before Rod left for Eustis, Harrell had a strange run-in with his grandson that he would later report to authorities.

Rod had asked Harrell for a ride over to his friend's place out in the middle of nowhere, and as Harrell drove his Jeep across a deserted bridge, he came upon Scott Anderson blocking the roadway. Scott was supposedly having car trouble, but apparently, Harrell had a sixth sense that the boys were up to no good, that he was being set up, and he refused to stop the car to help Rod's little friend.

Then all at once, Scott's car miraculously fixed itself. Scott had put the hood back down and had gotten the red

Buick back into gear in no time. With Scott following Harrell, and Rod insisting on driving the old man's vehicle, Harrell felt extremely threatened.

Harrell Gibson raced back into town thinking Scott was going to try to run him off the road, and the whole time, Rod fidgeted with something in his jacket. Rod seemed like he was about to pull a knife, Harrell recalled, so he stopped the car in front of the Murray Police Department and made his grandson get out.

Harrell told Sheriff Stan Scott that he suspected Rod and Scott were planning to "roll" him that night. The sheriff felt certain the boys were intent on leaving Harrell in the dirt so they could steal his vehicle, because, according to Harrell, the incident occurred on Saturday, November 23, just hours before the red Buick Skylark pulled out of Murray for good. Sheriff Scott told the old man he was lucky to have escaped with his life.

"I just don't know what was going on there," Harrell said blankly. "That Buick was barreling after me all the way down the road."

"Well, two things come to my mind, Mr. Gibson," the sheriff said. "I hate to say this, but I feel like your grandson was either going to seriously harm you, or he and his friend were going to knock you in the head and take your Jeep."

"You know, I think you're right."

chapter thirty-six

The night Jeni came in late from work, the night the TV was on in the family room and the Ford Explorer was mysteriously missing, she had seen her dad's feet in her peripheral vision. She thought about her phone cord being pulled out and figured her mom and Heather had been fighting over the phone bills again. She didn't really have time to process it, she was just hungry and tired. But as Jeni started to walk to the kitchen, she noticed the trail of blood.

She was shrieking, running to her mom, only to find her bludgeoned, her mom's body stopping her dead in the kitchen. *Dear God, this has to be a dream*, Jeni tried to tell herself, wishing it wasn't real, that she was imagining this out of a horror movie. She ran back into the family room and leaned over her father, shaking him, calling to him, but he was a gory, bloody mess.

"Dad, Dad, what happened?" Jeni yelled, her voice

frantic. Her tears were so great, she could hardly recognize herself. "Oh my God, Dad," she was saying. "Oh my God," but her voice was muffled by her sobs.

"It seemed so surreal to me," she confided. "My dad, you know, he was lying on the couch, and he was just covered . . .

"My mom, the first thing I saw was her broken glasses," she recalled, "and it seems like it happened in slow motion to me, like I saw her glasses, and that was just built up even more, and just when I saw her, I screamed."

Jeni ran from the corpses, her heart breaking, chest pounding, yet when she called Tony back to say her parents had been killed, her boyfriend thought she was joking. She was hyperventilating, but it sounded like laughter, and Tony figured she was pulling off a prank. Jeni had no time to argue. She rushed him off the phone to dial 911.

It was just after ten-thirty when she placed the call. Jennifer Wendorf reported an emergency at 24135 Greentree Lane, requesting two ambulances.

"Both your mother and your father, they're not breathing at all?" the female dispatcher asked.

"I don't know, I didn't check. They're my parents, I can't get that close."

The dispatcher wanted to know if anyone was with Jeni in the house, and that's when it suddenly dawned on her that her life could be in danger. Jeni was patched through to the local police department, who promised her that law enforcement was on the way, and she reported her sister, Heather, was missing. The police dispatcher requested that Jeni move away from the house, that she stay on the phone and move cautiously toward her driveway until help arrived.

But Jeni was too petrified. There was blood everywhere, on the floors, on the walls, and she was afraid to leave Heather's room. She had grabbed the portable phone and had run to the back of the house with it, planning to lock herself in the back bedroom in case anyone was lurking on the property. But Heather's door wouldn't lock. It was busted.

The dispatcher had Jeni stay on the line for ten minutes, asking for details about the house, wanting to know whether the front door was broken into, and things like that. The woman was trying to distract the poor girl, and for a minute, it was working, because suddenly, Jeni decided she should go see if maybe her parents were okay.

"I'm going to stay with you," the voice said. "I don't want you to feel like you're here by yourself."

"Yes," Jeni whispered, "can I go check to see if my parents are even alive?"

"Do you feel comfortable going up there to do that?"

"I don't know. I worry for them. I don't know how long it's going to be until the medics . . ." Jeni's voice became unintelligible.

Jennifer wanted the ambulances to get to her quickly, hoping against all hopes that *maybe* her parents had a chance to survive.

"I've seen these things on TV," she said, her voice quivering, "and I know things like that can happen, but I can't believe—oh, my gosh, do you know about how long? Do you know when they're going to get here?"

"You're doing fine, Jennifer, you're doing fine," the dispatcher said. "The sheriff's department is right in front of the ambulance, and they're just a few minutes away."

chapter Thirty-seven

When they were done washing up, Scott and Rod were in a race to meet up with the girls, and when they approached Greentree, they whizzed right by the Buick, which was tucked away on the roadside, just a few hundred yards from the Wendorf place.

Before they motioned the girls to follow the Ford Explorer, when Heather caught the first glimpse of the family vehicle, she thought it was her parents, and she ducked down so they wouldn't see her. She figured her parents found the good-bye note.

But when Heather peeked and saw it was *Rod and Scott* in the front seat, both of them bare-chested, her mind started racing. She asked Charity what was going on, she questioned Dana, but neither girl had any idea.

Heather didn't understand. No one had ever said anything about stealing a car.

Heather was confused about what was happening. She had no idea why the boys had stolen the Ford Explorer, and fearing the worst, she realized Rod must have gone into the house to get the car keys, that he might have tied her parents up or hurt them. With Charity following the Explorer so closely, Heather started to twitch. She was so nervous, she could feel her stomach doing flip-flops. She felt weak, like she was about to pass out, and she wondered if it had anything to do with her crossing over.

Heather needed to talk to Rod, and she told Charity to flash her brights. Heather wanted Charity to get the boys to turn back, and Charity tried flashing them, but it was no use. The Explorer was traveling at high speeds, and the next thing Heather knew, they were driving on highways she wasn't quite familiar with. Charity was blindly following Scott, and Heather was freaking out.

"Get him to stop, Charity," she yelled, "this isn't the right way. We have to go pick up Jeanine."

"I can't," Charity told her, "I can't get his attention."

"Well, honk the horn," Heather persisted.

"No, he'll get pissed," Charity said. "Let's just follow them."

But Heather pitched such a fit that, eventually, Charity managed to flag Rod down. Heather insisted that if Jeanine wasn't going along, she wasn't interested in leaving. She wanted Charity to communicate her wishes to Rod and demanded that Charity drive her back to the LeClaires.

Heather's heart pounded as she watched Rod and Scott have their roadside conference with Charity. Looking over at Dana in the front seat of the Buick, Heather felt dazed. She was furious that the boys had stolen her dad's car; she knew it could only mean trouble. If they got caught speeding, the Explorer tag would be traced, Heather presumed. But then, no sooner had the thought occurred to her, she saw Rod and Scott were busy switching license plates. They were transferring the Kentucky tag onto the Ford Explorer.

In her mind, Heather kept going over Rod's offers to hurt her parents. Out on Greentree, when she and the boys were huddled behind the Buick in a circle, Rod had offered to knock her parents out. He had offered to tie them up. When Heather told him not to, Rod just became nonchalant. The last time they had discussed it, Rod agreed to leave the Wendorfs alone.

The plan was, the boys were supposed to go get Jeanine, then after the girls had stopped off at Jeremy's, they were going to drive the Buick over to Jeanine's to meet up with everybody. But after the girls left Jeremy's, when they pulled the Buick up behind the LeClaire residence, Heather snuck around back only to find Jeanine sitting around, doing homework in her room. Jeanine wasn't packed, she wasn't anything. She was even aware that the group was leaving that night.

Of course, Heather didn't have time to ask Jeanine questions. She was nervous about Rod's strange behavior and just wanted support from her girlfriend.

Jeanine thought Rod's comments were a bit outrageous, but then, Rod always offered to do weird things, to kill people or drain part of them and then bury them alive. Rod had talked about draining the LeClaires, Jeanine reminded her, he had joked about "having them for dinner." Jeanine thought it was funny that Heather was so upset about Rod's stupid threats. She wanted Heather to put things in perspective, she reminded her about all their long-distance conversations, about how Rod was always claiming he killed people.

Jeanine convinced Heather that Rod was just a big talker. She calmed Heather down, and promised to get her belongings together. Jeanine just needed twenty minutes or so. She had decided to run away after all.

Now, as Heather thought about things, she wondered why Jeanine had been left behind in Eustis. As she sat in the backseat of the old Buick, watching Charity finish her talk with Rod on the side of the roadway, she could tell by the expression on Charity's face that Charity didn't have good news.

Heather had hoped that somehow Rod could have been convinced to turn around, at least to pick up Jeanine. But from the looks of things, Charity hadn't had much success convincing him. As she approached the Buick, Charity looked distracted. She was wild-eyed when she slipped behind the wheel of the car. She started up the Buick without saying a word, even though Heather hounded her.

"Just shut up," Charity finally howled, "don't ask any more questions. Rod has done something I can't explain."

"But, what is it?" Heather pleaded. "What did he do?"

"I can't, I just can't say."

"Look, I won't get mad. I just want to know."

"Rod's the sire. He's your daddy. You ask him when we make the next stop."

"But, where are we going?"

"Rod decides that."

"Look, I don't care what it was," Heather insisted, "I just want to know. Why won't you just tell me what happened?"

Heather was dumbfounded. Charity refused to answer. The girl just kept her eyes on the road and the gas pedal steady.

Heather finally slumped down in the backseat and was just trying to understand what went wrong, desperate to know what was going on. She racked her brain thinking about what the plan with Rod had been. All she remembered was that the boys were supposed to go get Jeanine, then after she and the girls had stopped at Jeremy's, they were supposed to drive by Jeanine's to meet up with everybody.

But then, Heather realized that when she and the girls had snuck up behind the LeClaire residence, she had walked to Jeanine's window only to find Jeanine doing homework. Jeanine hadn't even been contacted by Rod that evening.

Now, as Heather was being driven out of town in a crappy old red Buick, as the "shitbox" moved down the road, lagging behind the boys in the Wendorfs' Ford Explorer, Heather looked at Dana and Charity in the front seat and wondered how she had wound up heading off into the darkness with strangers. Heather certainly didn't feel like these girls were "family," as Rod called them. She felt nothing but scared.

Heather felt betrayed and kept thinking about the day's chain of events, trying to figure out why she had been forced to leave town without Jeanine.

Heather ran through the events again and again. She couldn't understand why her plan with Rod hadn't been followed. It was so simple, she thought. When she had left Rod and Scott earlier that evening, she had been given a half hour to pack. Heather had waved good-bye to them at the end of Greentree Lane, had seen the guys walk over by the woods on Greentree, and had wondered about where they were headed. But then, at the time, she was in such a rush.

As the guys walked off, Heather stopped Charity in the Buick, just curious about what the guys were up to, and before Charity pulled away, she told Heather the boys were "going to get some things" for the trip.

Heather never second-guessed it. Since Rod didn't drive, it was normal for him to walk through the woods. Rod usually traveled on foot; no one questioned that.

But now, as the car moved east, Heather kept tracing back to the occurrences earlier that night, when the red Buick had pulled up to Greentree to retrieve her. She realized she had never truly thought about where the boys were headed when they walked into the woods. She thought about Jeanine's surprise earlier and wondered why the boys had never made it over there. Heather had been so caught up in saying good-bye to her parents, she had been so concerned about being taken to see Jeremy for the last time, she hadn't thought about how the boys were planning to round up Jeanine.

"We turned off someplace and they switched plates," Heather recalled. "Charity told me to stay in the car, and I'm trying to hear what she and Rod are saying, but it's muffled. She gets back in the car and I'm wondering what the hell is going on, and then I realize we're **not** going to Jeanine's house."

As Heather was being driven along a dark highway heading east, toward highway signs that said Sanford, she realized something was really wrong. They were heading in the opposite direction, away from New Orleans, and she was getting panicked. Heather pointed to the road signs and told Charity it looked like they were on their way to Daytona Beach, but Charity didn't answer.

"Hey," Heather was shrieking, "we've got to go back to Jeanine's."

"We can't," Charity told her, "Rod said she's not going with us."

"Why not?" Heather asked, indignant. "This is not the plan, Charity. I'm not going without her. I didn't plan for this. Flash your lights at him, you've got to pull Rod over."

The Kentucky girl told Heather she had been instructed to keep driving until Rod decided it was safe. Heather wanted to know what Charity meant by that, but Charity remained tight-lipped. Heather tried to squeeze information out of Dana, but Dana just shrugged her shoulders and looked away. Dana lit another cigarette and slurped on her Mountain Dew, looking out at the neon signs as they got closer to the small town of Sanford.

Dana felt sorry for Heather—the girl looked like a caged animal back there—but Dana was under direct orders to keep her mouth shut.

Heather looked like a fawn caught in the headlights—she looked frightened, without knowing why.

They were still headed the wrong way when Charity flashed her lights again, getting Scott to pull over for the second time. She wanted them to say something to quiet Heather, but the boys had refused. When she came back to the Buick, Charity was hesitant.

Even though Rod had said he would deal with Heather later, Charity couldn't stand Heather's panic. The girl was wigging, insisting they turn back and take her to Jeanine's.

chapter thirty-eight

When Jeanine's mom, Suzanne, had discovered her missing from her room that night, she had gone out looking for Jeanine in the neighborhood. As Suzanne LeClaire stood at the end of her street, searching through the dark woods behind her, she had a psychic feeling that her child was back there.

Then, from out of nowhere, Suzanne watched her daughter step out from behind the shadows. Suzanne was shocked. She had no idea what on earth had led her to that exact location at the edge of Lake Seneca, but she didn't question her instinct. She was so relieved to see her child standing there, she didn't even show a hint of anger.

"Honey, it's not safe for you to be out here on the roadway by yourself," Suzanne said, remaining calm. "Why are you out here?"

"I don't know, I'm confused, Mom."

"Where were you going? To Heather's house?"

"I'm waiting for Heather. She needs me."

"Well, where is Heather?"

"I've got to wait for her to come back. Some people are driving her over here."

"Who? Who is she with?"

"Just some people."

"Well, who are they?" Suzanne demanded.

"She's running away, Mom."

"But why? Why would she do a thing like that?"

"She wasn't happy at home."

Earlier, Suzanne had a strange premonition that Jeanine was planning to bolt. She had felt anxious about her daughter that evening, particularly because Jeanine had gotten into a big argument with her dad. Apparently, Mr. LeClaire was refusing to take her down to the DMV to get her driver's license. He wanted his little girl to wait a while, and Jeanine was just livid about it.

"I had a kind of foreboding feeling," Suzanne recalled, "then all of a sudden it dawned on me that Rod was probably involved in this."

The minute Jeanine admitted her plans to run away with Rod and Heather, Suzanne grabbed her daughter and insisted they get back home to call the Wendorfs. She asked Jeanine to wait in their computer room while she dialed the Wendorf number, but the phone was busy. Suzanne kept dialing the residence, but their line was a constant busy signal, so she finally requested an operator to place a break-through emergency call. The operator came back to report the phone out of order. She couldn't break in on the line.

Suzanne told Jeanine to get busy on her homework

assignment—the girl had a report due on Edgar Allan Poe the next morning—and jumped in her car and drove the four miles over to the Wendorf place. It was about 10:45 P.M. when she pulled onto Greentree, and suddenly, Suzanne was confronted with a roadblock. There were ambulances, police vehicles, just all kinds of cars in the Wendorf driveway. For some reason, the property had been taped off, and at first, Suzanne had trouble getting anyone's attention.

The initial thing that crossed Suzanne's mind was that Jeni had come home drunk and had wrecked her car in the driveway. Suzanne became so worried about Jeni, she had forgotten all about Heather, and then finally, a detective came to the roadside to talk to her. He didn't really say much, he was trying to ask her to leave, but Suzanne insisted she speak to the Wendorfs.

When Suzanne divulged Heather's runaway plan, the detective became very interested in what she had to say. Right away, he asked Mrs. LeClaire to run and get Jeanine. The officer said it was imperative that he speak to Jeanine about Heather.

chapter Thirty-nine

By the time Suzanne returned with her daughter to Greentree Lane, the street was swarming with news teams. As they approached the driveway and heard the reporters talking about a double homicide, they couldn't believe their ears. While they watched broadcasters make their live on-site reports to local stations, Jeanine and her mom tried to comprehend the facts, but were briskly escorted into a patrol car for questioning. Outside, in the Wendorf driveway, the speculation about the murders had become great. Police had leaked some interesting details—the numbers 666 had been written in the dust on the garage door.

For Jeanine and her mom, the news of the Wendorf murders seemed impossible. They heard the names Ruth and Rick Wendorf ringing in their ears and wondered how Jeni and Heather were. They weren't being given very much hope, and when they learned that Heather was missing, Suzanne grew concerned that something terrible might have happened to her. Suzanne prodded her daughter for information, however, Jeanine was in shock. She wasn't talking.

But Lake County law enforcement forced Jeanine LeClaire to cooperate. Jeanine was hesitant to talk at first, but before she knew it, she was being asked to give deputies an official statement. When Jeanine was told they needed to check her for gunpowder, just as a formality, Jeanine felt funny about it. The girl had no objections, she wanted her name cleared, but she didn't understand why she was a suspect.

Unfortunately, one of the newspapers printed a story that Jeanine LeClaire had tested positive for gunpowder residue, and even though the information was false, the local report sparked off a string of media hounds at the LeClaire residence. Of course, when police leaked the information that Heather Wendorf and her friends considered themselves *vampires*, that Heather had run off with a vampire coven, CNN, *USA Today*, Barbara Walters, and even *Oprah* called the LeClaires for interviews.

Needless to say, the media only made matters worse for Jeanine. Between missing her friend Heather, feeling guilty about the Wendorfs, and being falsely accused of being mixed up in the crime scene, Jeanine landed in a Charter mental health center for a week. The LeClaires blamed it on the unwanted press.

Meanwhile, Lake County sheriff's detectives had taken days to complete their investigation of the Wendorf household, having sorted through clots of blood, mangled brain tissue, and shredded bone. The rage of the killers had led investigators down a path of insanity . . . there were no rational answers they could offer the Wendorf family.

The technicians and detectives had collected over a hundred latent fingerprints on the premises. The killers' marks were found everywhere—on the walls, the door handles, the bureau drawers. A forensics photographer had tracked the pattern of blood with a video camera and had discovered two sets of bloody footprints—one, a heavy combat-boot style, the other, the zigzag pattern of athletic shoes.

Nonetheless, in their diligent search of the five acres belonging to the Wendorfs, in their sweep across several Lake County roads surrounding Greentree Lane, law enforcement found no sign of a murder weapon.

The crime-scene technicians had taken their careful measurements, they had marked blood spots, had collected bone fragments, had searched through an endless amount of gore in the pretty little home, finding tiny specks of blood all the way back to Heather's bedroom, but they still had no clue as to why the middle-class couple had been victims of such savagery.

It would take two or three hours for Heather's friends to start mentioning the word *vampire*. At first, investigators thought it was a tease—the idea that these murders could have something to do with vampires was outrageous—but then, on Rick Wendorf, there had been noted this mysterious *V* that was carved into his chest.

When law enforcement had come pounding on his door at three o'clock in the morning, just hours after the murders, Jeremy Hueber told deputies that Heather had run off with Roderick Ferrell. Soon after, Jeanine LeClaire confirmed that Rod Ferrell was indeed with Heather, stating that she thought the group might be headed back to western Kentucky.

An all-points bulletin went out over the wires, and before daybreak, Florida law enforcement had sent a helicopter, along with a team of patrol cars, in search of the blue Ford Explorer.

chapter forty

While Heather sat catatonic in the backseat of the car, the two girls had been busy transferring their belongings over to the Ford Explorer. At Rod's insistence, Charity had pulled over. Rod wanted them to ditch the Buick just a few miles past Sanford. He was in a hurry.

He ordered Dana to leave half of her bags behind in the woods, and at first Dana balked, but Rod was irate. He had no time to waste watching her repack a bunch of crap. Dana was carrying so much stuff with her, the girl had at least seven bags, and Charity convinced her she didn't need all that. Charity helped Dana handle her job. They both moved as fast as they could, and though it was rather chilly outside, the girls managed to lather up a sweat. Clearly, the temperature was the least of their concerns. They were both following orders.

Only Heather found herself shivering as she lay in the

backseat of the Buick. Unlike Dana and Charity, Heather had no belongings to transfer, and she lay there frozen, rolled up into a ball, clinging to her backpacks and big teddy bear, pretending to be asleep.

When Dana finally settled herself in the back of the Explorer, Charity informed Heather it was time to get going. But Heather was groggy. She didn't want to budge. She was clearly unhappy about leaving the Buick, and she tried to tell Charity they would be much better off following Rod.

"My parents are going to kill me if they find their car," she protested. "I really don't think we should take it."

"The Buick's dying," Charity told her, "it's not gonna make it even halfway to New Orleans."

"But we'll get caught, and when my parents find out—"

"You don't need to worry about your parents," Charity quipped, cutting Heather off. "Your parents aren't gonna find out."

"What's that supposed to mean?" Heather asked, her face flushed.

"Well, to put it bluntly, Heather, I don't know how else to say this, but your parents are dead."

As the sounds formed, Heather studied Charity's mouth. For a split second, Heather was so concentrated, focusing on what Charity was saying, Charity's face became the whole world.

When Heather snapped back to reality, she just smirked. She warned Charity to stop kidding. Heather didn't think it was funny.

"I'm not playing with you," Charity said. "I'm sorry to be the one to have to tell you, but that's what Rod was saying the first time we stopped. Dana knows too."

"You're lying, I told him to stay away from my parents."

"Look, Heather, he and Scott went into your house. They say Rod killed your parents. But, I mean, maybe they're just bullshitting."

"They're full of it, Charity, you know how Rod talks. He just makes stuff up."

"Well, that's why I wasn't even gonna say anything."

Heather tried to let go of Charity's arm, but she couldn't. With a faint grasp, Charity was escorting her to the Explorer. Heather couldn't bring herself to cry, she could barely breathe, she was so flustered. Heather just wanted Charity to take the words back, to make everything okay again.

"Rod's full of it," Heather whispered, her eyes open wide. "If he said that, he's just trying to scare us."

"Well, you're probably right," Charity agreed, holding open the back door of the Explorer. "I'll find out."

chapter forty-one

"**I** was on some dark highway, I didn't know where we were at," Heather recalled. "I was sitting in the backseat between Dana and Charity. I had to sit up, and I was half in a daze staring daggers at Rod, and then I saw this huge crack in the windshield. I found out later that Rod got pissed and punched it."

For the first few hours, Heather decided not to say a word to Rod. The Explorer barreled down the interstate, now heading west, as they approached the Florida panhandle. They slept overnight in the car, somewhere off the highway near Tallahassee, and the first thing in the morning, Rod and the group went into a Wal-Mart to buy a few snacks—the girls wanted Little Debbie cakes and Doritos. He also picked up a large hunting knife and decided Dana should sign for all the stuff—pulling out Rick Wendorf's Discover card and handing it to her.

At a gas station in Tallahassee, Dana used the card again to fill up on fuel. Heather watched while Rod chatted with a man in uniform. Rod pulled out a cigarette and gave it to the security guard, and the two of them looked like they were enjoying themselves. Rod always claimed that the law was on his side, but watching him in action, Heather just couldn't believe it.

Heather had thoughts of fighting off the entire group and running away through the woods, but she felt that, even if she could manage the battle, she would never get very far. *If he really killed my parents,* she told herself, *he could just as quickly kill all of us.*

Heather was too frightened to say or do anything. She sat in the car like a zombie, feeling half-dead, just staring at the highways as they drove off toward Alabama. Everything was a blur to her, she melted into the road signs and the greenery. She wondered where she really was—everything on the interstate highway looked the same.

Then, all of a sudden, Scott thought they were having car trouble and he had to pull over. Everyone was getting upset, but then it turned out the Explorer was merely out of gas. Never one to panic, Rod discovered Rick's cell phone in the glove compartment, which he grabbed. He calmly requested the keys from Scott and suggested that the girls get some rest, they still looked tired.

Outside the vehicle, Rod ordered Scott to keep his eyes peeled. Rod didn't want to have to lock Scott and the girls in the car while he and Dana hoofed it a few miles to the nearest rest stop. Even though Rod had a five-mile walk ahead of him, he promised he wouldn't be gone long.

From the rest stop, Rod used the cell phone to dial his grandfather, and he was amused to hear that Harrell Gibson was so concerned. Harrell wanted to know if Rod was okay, explaining that the sheriff had called looking for him. During their brief talk, Rod admitted he was driving a stolen vehicle, and right away, Harrell insisted his grandson turn himself in.

Of course, Rod wasn't listening to any practical advice, and when Harrell wanted to know where Rod was calling from, Rod pretended the signal on the phone was breaking up. He shut the power off and teased with Dana about how stupid some folks in Kentucky could be.

Meanwhile, back in the Explorer, feeling a bit more brazen with Rod gone, Heather told Scott she thought she could use her powers to drain him. In a fit of anger, she snatched her dad's pocketknife off the front seat and pointed it at Scott, holding it up to Scott's head, threatening to cut off his hair. But Scott just sneered. The sight of ittybitty Heather wielding a pocketknife was so funny.

Instead of being annoyed, Scott pulled the knife away, just happy that Heather was finally speaking to him. Scott had a tremendous crush on her—he and Rod had even cast a love spell—and now Scott became animated about being immortal and traveling to the city of the undead.

Scott was beating around the bush, trying to ask Heather to be his dark mate, but out of nowhere, Heather started shaking. Scott repulsed her, he was a nerdy guy she would never give a second glance to, much less sleep with, but she felt she was going to be trapped. From the looks of things, she thought Rod had crossed her over, expressly for Scott. She had visions that Rod was going to force Scott on her.

Heather told Scott that she felt weak, that she felt like she was dying. Her body seemed to have a mind of its own, she said, and as she uttered the words, Heather started shaking so violently that, not knowing what to do, Scott jumped into the backseat to hold her down.

"This is part of the crossover," Scott promised, "you just need to be fed."

"Yeah," Charity agreed, "let me give you my arm."

Charity leaned over to the front seat and grabbed a new razor blade from Rod's trench coat. Charity quickly slit herself, and with Scott still holding Heather, Heather drank, claiming it did, indeed, make her feel a bit better.

"You're going to feel a physical death," Scott said, using a fatherly tone, trying to placate Heather. "You've been fully embraced, so you will be in pain for a while."

"But I feel light-headed," she complained, "like I can't feel my body."

"We all go through that," he reassured her, "we get the feeling that our life is flashing in front of us. It's part of the transformation."

As Heather was listening, she found herself beginning to get caught up in her own dreamworld. She felt like her body was leaving her, as if she could see the three of them sitting in the Explorer from up above. She believed she was astrally projecting herself and thought she could see everyone in her family, her aunts and uncles, her sisters, even her parents. Heather envisioned Rick and Ruth sitting happily around the TV, still alive and safe at home.

Then suddenly, a cop pulled up behind them, his lights flashing, and Charity insisted the three of them duck out of sight. Heather's mind was still floating, as was Scott's, but Charity looked scared to death.

Then, just at that moment, they heard Rod's voice. Rod and Dana had magically reappeared, the two of them arriving with a container of gas. The kids in the car listened as Rod did a great job of sweet-talking the patrol officer, keeping the cop toward the rear of the Explorer as he poured the fuel into the tank. And somehow, Rod was able to get the cop to leave without ever showing him a driver's license.

Rod laughed about how dumb police really were, bragging when he got back into the Explorer, taking over the wheel with Dana giggling at his side. He knew exactly how to play people, Rod told his flock, reminding them about his "family" in New Orleans who were anxious to see him return.

Rod was looking forward to the time when his new coven would meet everyone, explaining that he had much work to do. There were voodoo queens and witch doctors who had to be contacted; Rod needed them to consecrate his favorite cemetery before he could begin the formal training. He spoke of the various ghouls and lupines they'd encounter before reaching his kindred, acting like these creatures belonged to him.

Rod talked about New Orleans as if he'd lived there for centuries, creating the illusion that he had been in Louisiana back in the 1700s, and as he reminisced about the French Quarter, known to him as the Vieux Carré, he marveled over the beauty of the wrought-iron banister rails and sighed about the wooden shutters of his innocent youth. Of course, Heather had been told a whole different story, the one about Rod being five hundred years old, the one about his childhood in France. She wondered how Rod could shift backgrounds with so much authority. It seemed as if he did it so easily.

"Lupine territory covers everything east of the inner harbor on the north bank of the Mississippi," Rod told them, "but from the inner harbor west to Williams Boulevard is vampire territory. Lupines control most of the area outside the city, so if you're smart, you won't venture beyond Bayou St. John."

"Where's that at?" Dana wanted to know.

"You'll see," Rod promised, "after a while, you'll learn the grounds."

"How many kindred do you know there?" Dana asked.

"The kindred population will vary. During Mardi Gras, it can grow to over a hundred."

Now that he was driving, Rod was feeling tremendously in control, and he decided it was time to have a little fun scaring Heather. In front of the group, he asked Charity to reconfirm the bad news about the Wendorfs, but Charity just grinned, acting like Rod was kidding. Rod looked over at Dana, wondering whether Dana could be Heather's "protector" against evil spirits, but suddenly, Dana wasn't laughing anymore.

Rod's words were swinging between fantasy and reality. He had the mind of a child, and he was difficult to read, especially for Heather, who wanted to believe Rod was just playing another evil trick. No one in the car was making much sense; they all seemed scared to come forward with the details about the Wendorfs, yet they acted like they were playing a fantasy game.

It was confusing, and by the time the Explorer crossed the state line into Louisiana, Heather thought she was going through another "dying" phase. She told Charity she felt weak. She confessed she thought she needed more blood. Dana cut herself to let Heather feed, and after about five minutes, Heather's body stopped shaking.

But then, out of nowhere, Rod decided to pull a strand of pearls from his pocket and dangle them in the rearview mirror.

Heather's eyes bulged.

"What are you doing with those?" she shrieked. "Why do you have them?"

"You recognize them?" Rod teased. "Whose are they?"

"Cut it out, Rod," Charity said. "Why don't you just give them to her?"

But Rod wasn't going to make things so simple. Rod draped the pearls over the back of the driver's seat, and just as Heather reached out, he snatched them away.

"Give them to me," Heather yelped, "they're mine."

"Why? Do you want a souvenir? You want a reminder of your past life?"

"Yes, I want them," Heather insisted, "I want to put them on my squishy bear."

Rod thought it was a cute idea. He was delighted to watch Heather stretch the pearls around the stuffed animal's neck. The strand made it look like the teddy was choking.

"It was so pounded into my head that I was a coven member," Heather reflected. "I felt like we were a family, like Rod was the maker and I was the one he made. I don't know, it was like a hierarchy or something. It was always pounded into me, we weren't separate people. We were an entity.

"I didn't want to be around him," she confided. "I basically wanted all of this to be a dream, but I knew I wasn't going to wake up and it would be all better. I had to process all of this. I had to get it through my head that this all happened."

chapter forty-two

"Scott was already head over heels," Heather confided. "He thought, boom, we're supposed to be together, like that, because in past lives me and Scott were together. In your past lives, you supposedly lived the same existence with the same people. The whole point of life is to go on a quest to find those same people again. You gather up again and reunite."

Before she ever met Rod, Heather believed in reincarnation. She had grown up with the idea. So it was easy for her to make the leap, to think that she and Rod had lived together as vampires; that is, until she was actually faced with Scott.

Over the phone and in letters, Scott seemed like a great guy. He was good at role-playing, and he was wonderful to fantasize about, especially the way Rod described him. Rod was great at building people up, so much so, he had almost convinced Heather to have phone sex with Scott. Before they met, Rod had custom-designed Scott for Heather. The figure he created was some kind of cross between an action hero and immortal warrior, and Heather couldn't wait to meet the guy.

But in person, Scott Anderson was just a dorky sixteen-year-old boy, with a mousy mustache, frizzy black hair, and thick glasses. He was nothing Heather had dreamed of, he had none of Rod's looks, and certainly none of his charisma. Rod strutted through life like a peacock; Scott was no match for him. Heather wondered why Rod ever chose Scott as an immortal, but then, she couldn't question such things. Destiny didn't change its course because of thick eyeglasses.

Even so, Heather found herself laughing at Scott, particularly when the two of them were alone together. Throughout their road trip, Scott seemed to be her personal bodyguard. Heather could hardly shake him for a minute. At every rest stop, he followed her around like a puppy, trying to drop hints about immortality.

When Scott alluded to wrapping his body in dark capes, when he spoke about becoming the darkness of the night himself, Heather's mind didn't follow. She found him stupid, like one of those little kids playing dress-up that Rod always made fun of.

To try to prove himself, Scott had shown her *The Complete Book of Witchcraft*, from which he claimed he could conjure Heather a new life. He promised to initiate Heather when they reached their permanent home, and she pretended to be interested, just to keep peace.

Here and there, Scott referred to the Wendorfs as if they were alive. He spoke in such a way to make it seem they had only suffered a symbolic death, and Heather tried to

drag more information out of him, but whenever she tried
to get specific, Scott would become evasive. She listened
carefully as Scott described slaughtering "totem animals,"
wondering what, if anything, that would have to do with
the symbolic death of her parents. She just wouldn't allow
herself to put the pieces of the puzzle together.

"You and I are Rod's offspring," Scott told her, "we are
awaiting our new birth, one that will bring us to the home
of the dead."

"What animals were sacrificed? You guys didn't hurt my
dog, did you?" Heather asked, getting worried. "Because
Jake is the greatest dog in the whole wide world."

"Symbolic death is just one of the various stages of
initiation, but in order to become eternal, there must be
blood sacrifices."

"You didn't answer my question."

"It is not up to me to tell you, Zoey. You must cleanse
yourself of all your earthly attachments, of all your human
thoughts. Only then will you see the answers."

Heather tried to look into her mind's eye, she tried to
see through Scott's double-talk. Sitting silent in the car for
so many hours, she allowed herself to meditate. Heather
envisioned herself completely naked, standing at an altar,
bathed in light, and tried desperately to raise her higher
power, but it was useless. She was too worried about what
was going to happen to her, afraid that she was living out
her wildest nightmare.

Heather needed to talk to Rod, but at every rest stop,
he seemed too preoccupied with Charity to notice anyone
else. Apparently, Charity was carrying Rod's baby, Heather
discovered, so Rod was all wrapped up in pampering her.

If Rod did something so serious, Heather kept telling herself, he
wouldn't be acting so happy.

Rod seemed to be enjoying himself too much to have pulled off any kind of monstrous deed. But still, at each resting place, Heather tried to grab Rod's attention. She needed to hear it from him straight.

When they reached the suburbs of New Orleans, Rod finally pulled himself off Charity to deal with Heather. He didn't want to talk long. Rod told Heather he just wanted to take her aside for a minute.

"This is a stupid joke," Heather said, walking hand in hand with Rod toward a deserted corner of the parking lot, "I think we should go back to Eustis."

"You know, you're the only one that's not showing you're scared," he said, "and that's good because I need people to be strong. We can't turn around."

"Why?"

"All the rest of them are scared, Zoey, but I can tell you're not."

"Why should I be?"

"Your parents have been killed"——he paused, blowing a trail of cigarette smoke into the cold winter air—"but you're totally cool."

"Yeah."

"I had to hit your mother after she threw a bunch of hot coffee all over me," Rod said softly. "She took about five minutes to die."

Heather stood gazing at the sky, holding her weight up against a dead tree.

"Your dad, you don't have to worry about, he died in his sleep."

"Did you stab them, or strangle them? What did you do to them?"

"I used a crowbar, that crowbar in the car. You saw it."

"Oh, yeah," she whispered, "I did see it. I thought my

dad had left it, 'cause he's always leaving tools in the car."

"Scott was supposed to get your mom, but he literally turned himself around and froze. So I had to finish off what he was supposed to do."

"Why did Mom throw coffee at you?"

"'Cause I said her husband was lying dead on the couch."

"And she threw hot coffee?"

"Yeah, and she started scratching me, she tried to kick me. That's when all the shit happened."

But Heather didn't want to hear about it. She had inched herself away from the dead tree and was suggesting she and Rod rejoin the group. She wanted to get a move on.

"If we're going to live in New Orleans," she asked, "what are we going to do for money?"

"Are you worried we're all running out?" Rod asked, smiling. "Trust me, little one, you needn't be so concerned."

Rod alluded to some plans he made for them to "visit" a few homes outside the city limits. These were places that belonged to the Ancients, he promised, where they could dwell freely among their kind.

chapter forty-three

Heather sat playing with fire, flicking her cigarette lighter on and off and putting her fingers through the flames. She was seated at the center of the circle, the whole group had formed around her, and they huddled in the cold Louisiana night, Rod having built a small campfire to keep them from freezing. The next morning would be Thanksgiving, the fourth day they had been on the run, and they were all tired and dirty, a rather unsightly crew.

When the boys went off into the woods to have a look around, Heather asked Charity about the animals. The only thing Charity knew was that Rod and one of his buddies had supposedly filled a Super Soaker squirt gun with butane to torture kitties. She hadn't seen it, but Charity heard about squirting butane under cats, then throwing a match to watch them blow up. Charity told Heather she had come across a Super Soaker at Rod's place and was warned not to touch it.

"Did it smell like gas?" Heather asked.

"I never went near it," Charity told her.

"Well, would you have reason to be afraid of Rod?"

"No."

"You think he could kill?"

"Well, a friend of mine, Peter, said Rod would kill, but I never thought that was true."

The only experience Charity ever had with Rod's violence was the time he got mad at her friend Peter over an unwanted sexual encounter she had with him. Charity reported it to Rod, telling him that Peter had forced her into a compromising position, and Rod just went nuts. According to Charity, Rod tracked Peter down, "beat the living daylights out of him," and left him for dead. Charity later saw that Peter was a mess—the kid had bruised ribs, cuts on his face, and a black eye—but she figured the fight was a result of a night of heavy drinking. She dismissed it.

Now, as she sat around thinking about things with Dana and Heather, Charity realized that she had been kidnapped by Rod. She confided that she hadn't come along to Florida of her own free will, that Rod had threatened to hit her over the head with a baseball bat and take her if she didn't go willingly.

"What do you think of Scott?" Heather was curious. "Does he know anything about witchcraft? He was trying to tell me about astral projection."

"Scott wouldn't know the difference between astral projection and movie projection," Charity said, laughing. "He tried to teach me and Dana about using glowing ropes to take you where you want to go, but . . ."

"The only thing Scott knows is martial arts," Dana chimed in, "and vampire stuff."

"Is he a satanist?" Heather wanted to know.

"He told me he was atheist," Dana confided.

It was unusual for Dana to talk much. The shy, silent type, she had barely said a word the entire trip. Mostly, Dana operated as a lackey for Rod. She was practically his servant, carrying out commands. A large-framed nineteen-year-old, twice the size of Charity, Heather felt threatened by her. Heather wasn't sure why she fed from Dana; she didn't trust the big girl at all.

Right before the group camped out, Dana and Charity had accompanied Rod into a vacant house. Scott and Heather had stood guard at the front door while the other three broke in—ostensibly looking for food. All five of them had checked the property for alarm systems, and all of them watched, holding their breath, as Rod used the crowbar.

As soon as the door was pried open, Dana and Charity hit the kitchen, coming out moments later with a grocery sack. Rod, meanwhile, had gone upstairs to loot the place. He was looking for cash, but had come away with nothing other than change, just a few piggy banks. Along the way, he had managed to grab a bow and arrow and a shotgun.

With Scott driving ninety miles an hour, trying to get away from the suburban New Orleans neighborhood, Heather and Charity were scared to death, certain that Scott would crash into a tree. But Dana sat in the front, watching the streets so they could get out of the area safely. Once they were back on the interstate, Dana rationed out the foodstuff. It wasn't much—all they'd gotten was a package of Oscar Mayer hot dogs, some bread, mustard, and a couple jugs of juice.

* * *

"Rod went in and filled a bag of stuff, and it was creepy," Heather confessed. "It was so surreal, my life at this point. I felt so detached from the whole world, because it was crazy. I had no home. I had no past. I just felt like I was nobody at that moment. I felt like I was the one observing the world, but I wasn't a part of it."

chapter forty-four

Nosferatu is an archaic term, derived from the Greek *nosphoros*, "plague carrier." The word had passed into popular usage in Romania and came to mean "undead," but the word dropped from use in the twentieth century, although Rod used it. It became the name Rod assigned to his vampiric child, Scott.

Not that Rod wanted to perpetuate myths about vampires or legends such as Vlad the Impaler. Rod said characters like that were fake. He disliked the Hollywood image of Dracula, who stupidly wore a tuxedo and cape to attract prey. Rod hated that phony Hungarian accent. He said there had never been a vampire population in Transylvania, asserting the whole tale was based on gossip. Vlad, according to Rod, was not a fifteenth-century Romanian ruler; Vlad was a fourteenth-century prince from the kingdom of Walachia who made fleeting appearances in the Carpathian Mountains.

Rod found it funny, the way people talked about him. They gossiped about his being a vampire just because he had pale skin and extended canine teeth. To his followers, he scoffed at the idea that vampires grew fangs or slept in coffins. A true vampire, Rod would say, was someone who slept, not during the day, but rather, "during the daylight of consciousness."

To be "enclosed" in unconsciousness, that was Rod's idea of being entombed; that was his perpetual "coffin." To be a vampire was a psychic endeavor. He would tell Scott it had nothing to do with animated corpses. Being a vampire wasn't a matter of staying away from crucifixes and holy water. Things like that, along with notions about garlic and fangs, were all just "vampire folktale." It was mind-boggling to Rod that certain people wanted to perpetuate such false images.

He impressed upon Scott that to become undead was to become a poltergeist-like phenomenon—capricious and mischievous, like himself. In a narcissistic rage, Rod would rant about the olden days, reminding Scott how much better their existence had been back in the 1400s, when they had free rein to satisfy their compulsive urges to feed. To kill strangers, to give them the gift of death, that was how they would fulfill themselves. Their evenings were spent draining the physically and mentally weak.

In those barbaric times, Rod would reminisce, when he and Scott were part of the aristocracy, they had been able to seek the destruction of human flesh without detection. To suck the "lifeblood" of paupers and servants, Rod claimed, was a pursuit he truly missed. Of course Rod claimed he still traveled back to the old days, taking psychic journeys to visit France before the Inquisition, but unfortunately, his trips to the past didn't allow him to physically manifest. To appear human, he had to return to the present.

Rod would remind Nosferatu that they had an immense task to accomplish by the year 2000, that there was no time for satisfying petty physical pleasures. Vividly aware of the monsters he governed, Rod took a disturbing comfort in that. He was belligerent, filled with hatred for mankind. Rod planned to unleash death to all mortals who came before him.

He was disappointed in his followers, especially in Scott. Even their feat of human sacrifices hadn't transformed Scott into Nosferatu. Rod's little fledgling had been terrified by the stench of the bleeding corpses. Rod had hoped Scott could rid himself of mortal habits and fears. He had struggled to empower Scott, but the boy remained timidly human. In his mind, Rod concentrated on delivering Scott to an astral plane, he strained to bring Scott along with him. But all Scott could conjure were the small details—a crushed-velvet cape, a red tunic—it was only a fantasy for him.

Now, in a New Orleans alleyway, Scott "performed" for the coven. He envisioned himself living as a member of the nobility in France and tried to describe how his life was when he was first in New Orleans, in the days after the Revolution. But Scott's grade-school education prevented him from pulling it off. The boy didn't know the first thing about American history, no less European philosophies. Scott had intended to keep up with Rod's literature, with some of Rod's references, but when it came down to it, Scott's description of his great French castle, his rendition of his life in France, wasn't believable. Scott just couldn't spin a tale the way Rod could. He didn't have the gift.

Scott claimed he had "a million memories" as a dark prince, but when he was asked to elaborate, the young man would refuse. Scott did not remember, for example, what part of France he had lived in. It was obvious that he had zero knowledge of his French heritage, of the language or customs Rod occasionally described. Poor Scott didn't have any real sense of the past—that was painfully clear to Heather. He was nothing but a country bumpkin, but Heather decided to keep her thoughts to herself.

Anxious to acquire Rod's sophistication, hoping to utilize his supernatural skills, Scott had no problem calling himself Nosferatu, no difficulty swallowing throatfuls of blood. He would do anything to gain Rod's favor, to be accepted by the others as a true eternal, and to that end, Scott agreed to perform a ritual in the St. Louis Cemetery. Rod left Scott in charge of the rest, walking off as soon as they parked the Wendorf vehicle, because Rod had a few stops to make in the Vieux Carré. Rod snickered as he moved off into the shadows. From a distance, it looked as though he was laughing out loud, yet they couldn't hear him, the buzz of the city was so great.

It was pitch-black out, almost midnight, and things seemed ominous. Heather could feel a presence as Rod said he had "certain preparations" to make. It was as if something murderous was about to happen.

Stalling for time, Scott decided to lead the coven in a ritual of walking. They covered the outside boundaries of the cemetery in a circle, beginning from the north and to the east, then to the south and to the west. Their tracks followed each other, making the outline of a great star, and when they reached the main gate of the cemetery, Rod was already there, his arms stretched out, his black trench coat giving him the shape of a dark angel. He was beckoning a wandering demon, calling softly to the ghost of the gates.

Rod pointed to the air above, his bony fingers conjuring a spirit-messenger as he named "the passing." He forbid the others to watch, so they waited patiently while Rod slit himself, smearing his blood in the shape of an upside-down cross at the stone gate. Then, taking on the name Vesago, Rod recited a "thanksgiving" to the gods of the undead. He leaped over the gate with the agility of a prowler, pulled his knife as though it was a sword, and swiftly marked a circle in the name of Nanna. The dark angel stood quite solemn in the center of the sphere, giving Scott the signal to enter, as he began reading from the Necronomicon. Rod was invoking Nanna, a spirit of the underworld, and coming from Rod, it was powerful.

"In the name of the covenant sworn between thee and the race of men," he read, reciting the chant, "Lord Nanna, the lord of all sin, hear me. In the name of the god of the Crown of Night, hear me and remember."

It didn't take long for Rod to finish. During the chant, he had acknowledged all sin in the world, holding himself up to the gods as a symbol for all evils. When the others were allowed passage, as they began their journey through the cemetery, Rod spoke to the "Horned One." He demanded that Charity slice herself to offer fresh blood to the gods, but Charity felt too weak. Dana offered her blood instead, claiming she needed "to release it," and in the moment, Rod was appeased.

Venturing into the valley of death, into such an interesting old cemetery, where the coffins were aboveground and the spirits were readily accessible, Heather became spooked. When Rod referred to her as his "hellish queen" for whom he was conjuring dog-faced demons and "messengers of the gods of prey," she wished to hasten their departure. Rod was telling Satan he wanted to wrestle with the Old Gods, to "stare Death Herself in the eye," but for Heather the novelty of vampires was wearing thin. She felt Rod was psychotic, talking in circles to the blank Louisiana sky.

As Rod conjured demons, her inner voice wavered. One minute, she'd be laughing at Rod's audacity, the next, she'd be petrified by his insanity. Rod seemed to have no problem flying in the face of God. If he really could conjure demons, Heather thought, she didn't want to be a part of it.

Heather already had enough monsters plaguing her—she was shaking all over again—she certainly didn't need Rod to call on Satan.

chapter forty-five

It was striking Heather gradually, in waves, like a chill running over her entire body, that her parents were truly lifeless. She thought of their spirits, wondering if they might be with her, perhaps waltzing around the tombstones, but in her mind, she kept telling herself that the murders weren't real.

In the darkness, Heather felt like she was floating above the cemetery, as if her body had no weight. She had taken in a stream of Rod's blood; it flowed down her throat to her veins. She had tried to make her heart pound with it, to feel alive from the warmth that coursed through her, and somehow, Rod's blood had engrossed her.

Perhaps it was because Rod was so familiar. Heather wasn't sure why, but there was a disturbing comfort in being around him, in shunning mortal life. Of course, a sickness rose in her when she tried to envision *what he had actually done.* But then, Rod would use all his charms to keep her distracted. He had a way of keeping Heather entranced.

"Tell me your thoughts," Rod wanted to know.

"I'm not sure I'm thinking anything," Heather said, shrugging her shoulders.

"You lie. You're thinking of your God. I can read you," he said in disgust.

"Well, if I was, what's wrong with that? What if we get caught? Who's going to help us?"

"Your God is an incompetent spirit who has won prestige through serendipity," Rod hissed. "He doesn't happen to be the powerful ruler that everyone thinks he is."

"Oh, really? Well, who is more powerful than God?"

"Lucifer, and all his prophets. Remember, as the prophet of fire, you are the messenger, Zoey. Why must you deny this? You have been chosen to drink up the evil from mortal souls."

"But, what if I don't want to?"

"You have taken a *vow*, Zoey. You have become my child. You have been with me always, as my eternal child. You have been with me since doomsday, sixty-five million years ago, and today you will discover the ecstasy of the underworld. You are destined to repeat it. You have unfinished business."

Heather wasn't sure she was a prophet, really, but Rod had mentioned it so many times, she was starting to believe it. She felt like some high spirit when he coaxed her, like she could conjure energy from dead things and bring more energy into her own soul. Heather was so easily convinced by him that somehow she felt her life flash in front of her, like she had already traveled beyond her mortal lifetime right there in the St. Louis Cemetery. The recent killings made her feel that she belonged to Rod all the more. Heather had begun to feel the terrain of his mind. He was grimmer than she had ever imagined he would be.

It took no time for the coven to suddenly find themselves down by the Mississippi River. Heather hadn't noticed the car ride, she hadn't paid attention to the downtown streets. All she could feel was the moon touching her skin, which felt as strong as the sun. Then, out of nowhere, Rod was ordering her to discard all her personal belongings—her photos, scrapbooks, and other signs of human childhood—but Heather didn't argue. For her, girlish keepsakes were no longer relevant.

Heather had tears in her eyes when she was asked to let go of the pictures of her parents, but of course Rod showed no mercy. He had taken her away from the group for the moment, he had mesmerized her with his eyes, the moonlight beaming off them like diamonds. And for an instant, Heather had forgotten all about her parents. When she was alone with him, she felt an adulterated passion, she felt caught in the rapture, overpowered by something preternatural.

Then suddenly, Heather saw Rod pull a blunt object from his trench coat. Certain Rod was about to strike a blow, she braced herself, but Rod tossed the metal bar into the river. He had waved it like a magic wand, and Heather watched as his contorted face returned back to porcelain when it was all over. Rod seemed to gain a great satisfaction knowing the crowbar had evaporated into the dark river.

But all at once, Rod's face contorted again. He gripped Heather by the arm, and snatched her so quickly it appeared he was about to throw her off the bridge, to drop her screaming into the ice-cold Mississippi. But instead, he held her there, brushing her body against the guardrail. He stood mocking her, teasing his little girl.

"Are you rid of earthly ties?" he asked in a whisper. "Will you give thanks to the gods of the undead?"

"Yes, I give thanks," she mumbled.

"They can't hear you," he howled, bending Heather over the rail.

"I give thanks to them, Rod," she said, her voice becoming shrill. "Please let me go."

And such was the manner of disposing of her past, Heather dumping all her personal possessions, most of her childhood memorabilia, into the river. When they returned to the group, Charity and Dana were asked to do the same. Dana was the only girl who managed to hide certain keepsakes: a few prom pictures, a stack of love letters, her résumé, some bank statements and bills . . .

By the time they left the banks of the Mississippi, Rod had become drunk with power. He was busy swallowing a bottle of red wine as he directed Scott to drive through the inner city. Without realizing it, the five of them found themselves walking around in a bad section of downtown. Rod was dragging them through a nasty ghetto. It was just after midnight, Thanksgiving morning.

Heather felt she no longer knew who she was. She didn't care about what was actually going on around her. She watched Charity brush Rod's hair, she watched Scott and Dana exchange blood, she watched herself walking down ghetto streets, and none of it mattered. She was unaware of time and place, immune to life's meaning. Rod seemed so cheery about the murders, as did Scott, so much so, they seemed to be role-playing. It was *all a game*, Heather kept telling herself. But in her mind's eye, she knew the truth. Her life had become utter chaos.

As the group continued to walk deeper into the ghetto,

Charity was voicing her displeasure. She didn't appreciate Rod's little follow-the-leader game, she was scared and insisted she be taken back to the car. After a while, Charity started pitching an absolute fit, she was screaming at Rod, and she attracted the attention of a patrol car, a night cruiser with two policemen, which had stopped on the corner to *observe* the stray teens.

Rod directed the group to keep their mouths shut. He was brazen with the cops, having made the first moves over to the cruiser. He complained that he and his friends were lost. He asked the police for directions back to the river, and the cops offered to give Rod and his group a ride. As Rod declined, he flashed open his coat and bragged that he always carried a knife. He was able to protect himself against roaming crack heads, he assured them.

His friends watched in disbelief while Rod spoke. He carried himself with such ease, Rod had the cops eating right out of his hand. By the time he was done, Rod had shifted their conversation to talk about Thanksgiving Day festivities, wondering if there were any parades, any roads being blocked off in downtown New Orleans. Rod engaged the police in pleasantries.

Then suddenly, Rod became anxious to get his friends back to the French Quarter. He told the cops he was visiting with cousins for the holiday and claimed that he really had to get the group back.

And the police never asked another question. As Rod bid the officers good-night, as the cruiser slowly pulled away, Heather and the others stood dumbfounded.

Of course, that had been her best opportunity to run.

Of course, a part of her really wanted to.

Heather really did want to bolt.

But she felt she couldn't.

PART SIX

THE
REVELATION

chapter forty-six

Only a few members of the Lake County sheriff's office were present when Dr. Laura Hair performed the autopsies. A member of the Fifth Circuit Medical Examiner's Office, Dr. Hair had been called in by the sheriff's office the afternoon of November 26, 1996. She had proceeded to 24135 Greentree Lane and had waited for police to clear out so she could take the appropriate measurements and get a basic idea about the extent of the wounds. Mr. Wendorf's face had been bashed in so badly, he was unidentifiable, officers warned her. They had tried to prepare the medical examiner. She had been told that the male victim's face looked like "hamburger meat." But no words could truly have prepared her for the level of gore she was about to encounter.

When Dr. Hair had gone through the house, making her initial observations, she had hoped things would have gone more smoothly. She had hoped, for instance, to take Mrs. Wendorf's blue housecoat off easily. She had hoped to turn it over to police without blood getting everywhere, but the housecoat didn't have buttons, it had a zipper. It had to be cut off the woman's body before the victims could be transported to the Medical Examiner's Office.

Of course, it was never an easy matter, Dr. Hair's job, and the Wendorf homicide investigation proved to be one of the most gruesome in Lake County history. The investigators had located fifty-six separate bloodstains, had found a tooth knocked out of Mr. Wendorf's mouth, had noted bone fragments in the dining room, and had taken samples from blood and skin for DNA testing. Now, it was up to her to determine the cause of death, to deal with the corpses in an orderly manner.

At exactly 11:00 A.M. the next morning, Dr. Laura Hair resumed her work.

The findings: Mr. Wendorf suffered twenty-two chop wounds, mostly skull fractures and brain lacerations, causing his death. The male victim had also been wounded in his right chest area, having been lacerated with a blunt object, as well as marked with a symbol that resembled a V.

Mrs. Wendorf had some bruising that indicated a struggle; samples of skin were taken from under her fingernails. The female victim had suffered a cut on her lower right arm, a laceration around one knuckle, and another cut on her left hand, on her ring finger. Aside from the defensive wounds, Mrs. Wendorf had been struck twenty-one times, sixteen of those being sharp wounds to the head. Like Mr. Wendorf, she had been hit with some blunt object, possibly a crowbar.

A large depression had been made in her skull where

the brain stem had been lacerated all the way through. Mrs. Wendorf's skull had been beaten so hard, a three-inch hole remained where the brain had been cut through. She had practically been decapitated.

By the evening of November 27, arrest warrants had gone out on the five suspects: Roderick Justin Ferrell; Charity Lynn Kessee, aka Sarah Remington; Howard Scott Anderson; Dana Lynn Cooper; and Heather Ann Wendorf.

Lake County officials noted that the suspects were "armed and dangerous" and were in the vicinity of Baton Rouge, where one of the suspects had made a phone call from a pay phone at the Centro-plex. The Baton Rouge Police Department had been directed to look for a 1994 blue Ford Explorer bearing a switched Kentucky plate, and the display of a company logo, Crown Cork and Seal.

chapter forty-seven

On Wednesday night, Charity called Jodi Remington at her home in Piedmont, about twenty miles outside Rapid City. Charity had called to ask for money, and Jodi, who worked for the local sheriff's department, informed her child that the Wendorf murders were being covered on national news. Jodi told Charity she already knew what happened—she had seen the story on CNN. It would be for the best, she had insisted, if Charity could get the group to a well-lit area.

Charity had promised she would try. She had mentioned seeing a Howard Johnson's Motor Lodge, and her mom assured her that she would wire money to the location.

While Jodi Remington held her breath in South Dakota, Baton Rouge police were being called in for the sting. Meanwhile, the minute they got the information that Charity Kessee had made a phone call to her mom in South

Dakota, two Lake County investigators had changed their course in Atlanta . . . they were hightailing it to Louisiana.

Officer Ashton Thomas Dewey heard the call on the air-waves. Somewhere around 9:30 P.M. November 28, 1996, Sergeant Ben Odom requested backup units. Roderick Ferrell had surrendered without a fight. The sergeant had five teens in custody at the Howard Johnson's and needed assistance in transporting the juveniles to police offices on Mayflower in downtown Baton Rouge.

"It ended up, I had Rod Ferrell in my unit," Dewey recalled, "and en route to the office, Rod began to initiate conversation. He told me he was glad that I was transporting him because of my age. He was happy to be caught because he had been on the run for several days."

"I'll tell you everything you want to know," Rod boasted, his manner brazen, his attitude rather arrogant. "I just want to see my girlfriend."

"Hold up before you start to say anything else," the officer warned. "I don't know what all this is in reference to. You've been advised of your rights. Let me go over those rights again with you. I don't want you to make any statements now."

"Well, I know my rights, but I'll tell you anything you want. I just want to see Charity. I need to see my girl-friend, 'cause she's carrying my child."

"Well, let's wait until we get into the office, because I really don't know what the situation is. I don't know what you're being charged with. You should be quiet right now, because I really can't answer your questions."

"Well, dude, I think you're cool. I'm glad you got me. I'll give you the whole nine yards and make you famous, dude."

"Well, I don't know what kind of case you're talking about," the officer said calmly, "and I can't make any promises to you. The sergeant may or may not let you see your girlfriend."

Once Ashton Thomas Dewey secured Roderick Ferrell in the interview room, having taken all his personal items, right down to his shoestrings, he became acquainted with the case by viewing a CNN video clip. By then, Sergeant Odom had shown up, along with the other four suspects, and Dewey was reporting that he had patted Rod down, that the boy didn't have any weapons on him, that Ferrell was requesting to have contact with his girlfriend in exchange for a full confession.

chapter forty-eight

Rod insisted that he didn't care about life, especially his own. He was sick of living, of being accused, explaining that he left Murray because "all the cops were bugging me for something I didn't do." Rod said that all he wanted was to take Charity on a road trip. He wanted to have a getaway with her because she was supposedly pregnant.

"Just tell me if I'm going too fast," Rod asked casually, holding the cops' undivided attention. Three of them were in the room, hanging on his every last word.

"Go ahead," Odom said, trying not to interrupt, being very good at listening.

Rod listed the names of the people with him in the Explorer, confirmed that these were the same suspects held in custody, and went into his tale about their road trip from Murray to Eustis, detailing their stop at Heather's house. Rod said it was somewhere around 7:00 P.M. on

Monday when the two boys walked away from Scott's Buick. They had instructed Heather to go pack, then to hook up with the girls so she could see her boyfriend.

"Me and Scott stayed behind," Rod confided, "and after we made sure they were gone, we walked down the road to Heather's house."

"Okay."

"We walked up the driveway, looked around the house to check the perimeters. They left all the doors unlocked, so we went to the garage, looked for special items. We found special items."

"What kind of items?" Odom asked. "Weapons?"

"Yeah. That's all I was concerned about. Weapons, food, and cash."

Rod gave the officers a detailed depiction of what went on at the Wendorf house, stating that he and Scott had seen Rick sleeping on the couch, had heard Ruth showering in the master bath, had helped themselves to something to drink in the kitchen, and had gone to the back bedrooms to pull the phone cords.

"Scott was following behind me like a little lost puppy," Rod brooded, "so, before the mother got out of the shower, I went to her dad and smacked the fuck out of him until he finally quit breathing. So, yes"—he paused— "I'm admitting to murder."

"Okay."

"It took him about twenty fucking minutes to stop. I swear, I thought he was immortal."

"What did you hit him with?" one of the cops asked.

"A crowbar. I was going to use a machete or chain saw, but that was just too messy. Too nasty."

Rod had waived his rights to have an attorney; he had told the Baton Rouge police that he didn't care to have any adult there with him. He had been anxious to sing. He explained that Scott was "basically an accessory" who was good at talking about murder, but who hadn't been able to participate. Rod made it clear that none of the girls were with them when they killed and robbed the Wendorfs and claimed he hadn't discussed the murders with anyone "until ten minutes before we did it."

Rod said he couldn't recall what had become of the crowbar.

"Did you know Heather's parents prior to this?" Odom asked.

"I'd never seen them before until I killed them that night, so I wasn't even sure," Rod explained. "Hell, I went to the wrong house first. Didn't kill anybody though, 'cause I looked in and saw there were little kids and that's my rule, I don't kill anyone that's little. Now adults, that's perfectly fine. Sixteen and up."

After the murders, Rod claimed there were only two things that bothered him: first, the idea that he would not be able to see Charity again; second, the belief that when he was five years old, his grandfather had brought him into a cult, a group called Black Mass, that had performed a human sacrifice and had forced him into a sex act.

"Did you feel any remorse about what you did?" Odom asked, clearly disturbed by the attitude of this boy.

"I'm used to sacrifices. I'm used to seeing people's brains fly out the back of their head," Rod said, impressed with himself. "I've been hanging around gangs and cults forever, and killing is a way of life." The young man grinned at the sergeant. "Animals do it. And that's the way humans are. We're just the worst predators of all, really."

chapter forty-nine

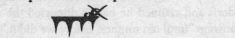

Two days before the fugitives were captured, when Lake County deputies were out interviewing potential witnesses and following leads, the authorities had come across some peculiar information. It had started with Jeni Wendorf, who suspected her sister's involvement with Rod Ferrell. At the time, the cops didn't press the issue. When Jeni mentioned that Rod was a vampire, that Heather was a vampire, they just shrugged.

But then, on November 26, a little girl came forward to incriminate Heather. Mandy Jones, Heather's classmate, told Lake County investigators that Heather was planning her parents' deaths.

"When was the last time that you heard anything about her wanting her parents dead?" an investigator asked.

"A couple weeks ago."

"How many times do you think she brought that subject up?"

"Um . . . probably once."

The second girl to blab to cops was fourteen-year-old Brandy Gonczy. Brandy had recently been with Jeremy Hueber, and she wanted to report that Jeremy had received a phone call from Heather, that Heather had bragged to Jeremy that she "got a couple men from out of state to kill her parents."

Jeremy Hueber denied ever receiving such a call. But the ball had begun rolling. Within days, a string of young people would waltz into the sheriff's office to report bad things about Heather, among them, Amber Blood, a girl who later failed a polygraph and admitted she had never even met Heather.

On November 27, a kid named David McIntosh gave a statement about being friends with Rod. David knew Rod from Eustis, he was introduced to him at a party. "From Rod's reactions and the speech he gave," David reported, "it seemed that he enjoyed pain. He enjoyed inflicting it, receiving it. He's just a very sick individual."

David portrayed Rod as an evil character with long sharp nails and weird hair who was interested in the occult. When Rod had returned to Eustis, earlier that week, he called David to brag that he had become a "full vampire."

"He was real dramatic," David recalled. "He asked if I had started drinking blood, if I partaketh of the nectar."

David McIntosh told authorities he had no desire to see Rod or his frightful little clan. When Rod had placed the call on November 24, David was mortified by Rod's comments. Rod had mentioned something about Heather running away from her parents, but David wasn't really paying attention.

Of course, by then the cops had developed their own sense of things. Almost from the start, they had heard enough to condemn her. Authorities were certain that Heather was a part of a cult, that she was operating out of a cult mentality, happy to join in the murder of her parents. The cops were out for Heather's blood, and soon the press began running stories. By the time the teens were jailed in Louisiana, public sentiment raged against Heather. She became the twisted little girl who wanted her mommy and daddy dead, who carried around "souvenirs" to satisfy her sadistic little mind.

It all started when Jeni had recalled this conversation she and Heather had a few months before the murders:

"Have you ever plotted Mom and Dad's death?" Heather asked.

"No," Jeni told her, "of course not."

"Well, if you ever wanted to, I know a perfect hit man."

"Who?"

"Rod Ferrell, he says he kills people all the time."

. . . But Heather says they never had this conversation.

chapter fifty

"People in their little worlds, imagining what they would do in that situation, they don't understand," Heather tried to explain. "Anything you would do in the real world, it's not the same as the world I was in. Now that I'm in the real world, I can see that I could have jumped to that cop," she reflected. "But I don't know that it would have helped, because I was still a part of that unreal situation."

By the time the Lake County officials arrived in Baton Rouge, it was already Friday, November 29. The five teens had been kept in dismal surroundings, without the benefit of showers or beds. They were chained to chairs in the gloomy Baton Rouge Police Department, given pizza and McDonald's burgers along the way, and were being judged by law officials as being kids without souls.

It seemed Charity was still in love with Rod, even though she knew he was a cold-blooded murderer, but more amazing, Heather appeared to be friendly with Rod. In those fateful hours at the police department, the teens' playful attitudes sparked outrage among officials, and this feeling transmitted to Sergeant Wayne Longo and Detective Al Gussler, the two officials assigned to the case from Lake County. They had been on a wild-goose chase for days, in search of the "vampires." By the time they arrived in Louisiana, Longo and Gussler were thoroughly exhausted. Clearly sickened by the "cult" teens, they could hardly contain their venom. They taped a series of interviews with each of the kids, and by the time they interviewed Heather, they seemed to have their minds already made up—they seemed convinced that Heather had solicited Rod to murder the Wendorfs—and were anxious to get her to prove them right.

Being seasoned law enforcement officers, they didn't start their interrogation with Heather. They decided to get as much ammunition from everybody else first, especially from Rod and Charity, and then try to trip Heather. Since Rod had already confessed to Louisiana officials, they began their chat with Charity Kessee, who, like all the other teens involved, had agreed to give an official statement without the presence of a lawyer or a parent.

At first, Charity wasn't sure she was really in trouble. She hadn't done anything, she insisted, and she wanted to be taken to see Rod.

Charity described nineteen-year-old Dana Cooper as her best friend, said she really didn't know Scott Anderson that well, and explained she had just met Heather Wendorf. She said they had wound up in Louisiana because Rod was supposed to meet with a voodoo priest, and she mentioned their run-in with a patrol car near the French Quarter, adding that Rod had flashed his knife.

Charity did a good job describing the highlights of their road trip. She talked about dropping the boys over by Heather's house, meeting up with Heather, and then taking her over to Jeremy's; she talked about being on the highways and running out of gas; she even described the burglary. Gussler and Longo didn't really seem to care about the reasons why, but they had to ask about drinking blood, and Charity explained she would cut herself "to make the anger go away."

The officials wanted to hear details about the murders. They kept bringing Charity back to Greentree Lane, asking her about dropping the boys off on Monday night, and Charity was insisting that she didn't know where the boys were headed when she left them on Greentree. But it was apparent the officers didn't believe her. She told the officials she was under the impression Rod and Scott were going to walk through the woods and head over to Jeanine's.

"What were your first thoughts?" Gussler asked. "What went through your mind when you saw the blood on these guys? When you saw the tire tool in Rod's hand?"

"I didn't see the tire tool," Charity said in a whisper. "He wouldn't get out of the Explorer, so I don't know if he had blood on him or not."

"Well, he couldn't have changed while y'all were driving down the road," Gussler said, "right?"

"He wasn't in the same car as us, he didn't have blood on him. I didn't see anything."

"Okay. Did everybody take a whack at Heather's parents when they were in the house?" Gussler wanted to know.

"We weren't with them, I don't know."

But Gussler clearly didn't believe the girl. The detective

was already armed with facts from Shannon Yohe about the group having been there the night before the homicides. He knew all about Rod and Scott bragging to Shannon in front of Charity and Dana, Gussler told her. He knew Rod had held up a knife, that Scott had described how he was going to "get his licks in."

As Charity spoke, the detective appeared to be revolted by her demeanor. The way the girl could sit there, acting so coy yet looking so dark and evil, it seemed obvious that she was covering for her cult-leader boyfriend.

Gussler had read the reports about the animal sacrifices at the Humane Society in Kentucky. When he questioned Charity about it, she defended Rod, insisting Rod was being blamed for something he didn't do. Of course Gussler became cynical. He advised the little girl to stop protecting Rod. Even though she swore she had told him everything she knew, Gussler was furious. He threatened to walk out of the interview room if Charity didn't stop tap dancing. He insinuated that things would be much worse for Charity when she got into a Florida court of law. She needed to cooperate with him, he implied, if she wanted to stand a chance.

"I'm trying to help you," Gussler explained, "I ain't trying to scare you. I'm just saying don't sink yourself."

"I'm not," Charity promised, "I've told you everything. I mean, Rod had been talking about killing people, he always talks about killing people, but he's never done it."

"Well, guess what?" Gussler asked, getting sarcastic.

"What?"

"He's a stupid idiot, that's what your boyfriend is," the detective raged. "I'm gonna tell you exactly. He's been charged with first-degree murder. Scott has been charged with first-degree murder. Heather has been charged with first-degree murder. You have been charged with accessory to first-degree murder. Dana has been charged with accessory to first-degree murder."

"How come Heather and Dana and I did? We weren't there. We were at Jeremy's house."

Gussler just shook his head. Charity kept asking why she was being charged, and the detective finally told her the way it was: she was with Rod in the car. No matter how Charity tried to explain her way out of things, there was no changing this fact. What's more, at Rod's insistence, Charity had initially lied to police about her identity—using her half-sister's name, Sarah Remington—which made her appear all the more suspect.

Gussler told Charity that he already had knowledge that Rod planned to kill the Wendorfs for over a year, but Charity said she never heard anything about it. The girl claimed she hadn't known the name Wendorf until the Buick landed in Eustis. When Gussler said he already had countless people in Eustis coming forward with details about Rod's plans to kill, Charity insisted Rod had only mentioned the Wendorfs once—when they arrived in central Florida—but then he dropped the subject.

"Rod was talking about killing an animal or something," Charity finally admitted, "he was talking about killing, and he said that Scott froze."

"Froze from what?" Sergeant Longo asked.

"I don't know," she said, her voice faint, "because when we had dropped them off, they said they were going to kill something and then . . ."

"When they left your vehicle?"

"Yeah."

"They said that?"

"Yeah, I figured, maybe he would kill a rabbit or something, out in the woods. He was walking to Jeanine's. I mean, there isn't too much in between."

At 5:38 P.M. on November 29, Sergeant Wayne Longo and Detective Al Gussler of the Lake County sheriff's department began the second interview with Rod, thanking the boy for his cooperation. Rod wanted to sum up the main details real quick, he said. He hoped they would keep their promise and let him see Charity when they were finished. In his second interview, Rod only had one question: he wondered if a sixteen-year-old could get the death penalty.

Rod began by talking about Heather and Jeanine, about how the three of them had corresponded for over a year, about their plans to run away together. He reminisced about his last days in Kentucky, bragging that several warrants were out for his arrest, something to do with making explosives. . . . Rod also talked at length about being engaged to Charity, saying she was "the only thing" he cared about.

According to Rod, he and his friends had left Murray on Friday night, November 22, around 11:00 P.M. He told authorities they had driven for two days to get to Eustis, stopping along the side of the roadway to catch up on sleep. He reiterated the sequence of events, including the stops at Shannon's and Jeanine's, and then talked about crossing Heather over in the cemetery, having picked her up on Monday afternoon, just outside Eustis High School.

"Did you discuss anything with her about her parents at that time?" Longo asked.

"We didn't think about the parent thing until ten minutes before we did it," Rod said, "that was kind of spontaneous. It wasn't premeditated."

"You didn't mention anything to her and ask her about if she wanted her parents killed?"

"Within the year, I jokingly said it once, but I never thought I would do it."

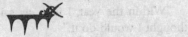

chapter fifty-one

"I'm sorry," Rod told law enforcement, his eyes welling up, "this is just like a big fucking joke. My life seems like a dream, so . . .

"My childhood was taken away at five. I don't know whether I'm asleep or dreaming or whatever. For all I know, I could wake up in five minutes."

"Rod," Sergeant Odom said bluntly, "I can assure you it's not a dream."

Investigators were leaving no stone unturned. They had already obtained warrants to search Sondra Gibson's apartment in Murray and had turned up a letter from Jeanine LeClaire, smeared with blood, which contained a hand-drawn map of the Wendorf residence. The details were chilling—from the pool to the glass doors to the exact location of the couches in the family room.

Attached to the map was a wish list of sorts: Canada, Ireland, Egypt, Rome, Greece, France. Though the letter to Rod wasn't dated, Jeanine had written "leave before school starts," which gave investigators the idea that these kids had been planning the murders since the summer, that Heather had enlisted Jeanine's help, had gotten her friend to draw the map.

Law enforcement didn't seem to pay much attention to the letter attached to the map. Jeanine's letter asked Rod to contact her at Heather's. Apparently, Rod had plans to visit Eustis with his mom, and Jeanine wanted him to drop his local phone number off at Heather's. She drew the map so Rod could leave his number in Heather's window.

When Rod called in June of 1996, telling Jeanine he was on his way to Eustis, as fate would have it, Jeanine and Heather were going to be out of town that week. They were leaving for North Carolina to visit the LeClaire's summer cabin. In her absence, Jeanine left the note for Rod, including the directions to Heather's window, placing a package for Rod in the attic window at the LeClaire residence on Lake Seneca. When Jeanine returned from North Carolina, the package was gone. Rod later called to thank her for the package of trinkets, never mentioning a word about the note or the map, and Jeanine never thought another thing about it. She never even mentioned it to Heather.

Jeanine had drawn the diagram of the Wendorfs' because she liked to doodle.

"Are you aware that Mr. Ferrell has told us everything?" Gussler asked Dana Cooper, continuing his interrogation in the Baton Rouge Police Department.

Dana shook her head yes.

Clearly frightened, Dana was the only legal adult of the bunch. The nineteen-year-old would be handled differently once she was extradited to Florida. She knew she would be subject to adult laws. Dana would soon discover that she was facing a sentence of life in prison.

Dana told the Lake County detectives she had only known Rod three or four months. He was a weird kid who people called "freak" and "vampire" because he liked to stay out at night. Right away, Gussler reviewed the information they already knew about Rod's conversation at Shannon Yohe's, about Rod's plans to kill. Gussler wanted to be "up-front" with Dana. He didn't want her to lie to him and get herself into any more hot water.

For whatever reason, Dana was overly talkative with the law, shaking her head affirmatively to Gussler's initial questions. Yes, she knew why they were there in the Baton Rouge police station. Yes, she knew about the Wendorfs being murdered. Yes, she waived her right to have an attorney with her.

"Now, Roderick Justin Ferrell was telling Shannon and everybody else that was present, there was something else he was gonna do, right?" Gussler asked.

"He was going to kill Heather's parents," Dana said blankly.

"Why would he kill her parents?"

"Now that, I don't know."

"Had you heard him talking about killing her parents in the past?"

"Nothing was ever mentioned about it."

"Okay, have you ever seen him with a letter, or possibly a sketch, of the inside of Heather's parents' home?"

Dana shook her head in the negative.

"No? Okay. When he was discussing killing the parents, I understand there was a discussion about different ways of doing it, and then Scott Anderson, what was Scott's comments at this time?"

"I really don't remember," she said, speaking slowly, as if she was in a dream. "All I remember is that Rod got out of Scott's car and he had a crowbar and he said he was gonna use that to kill Zoey's parents, Heather's parents."

"Okay, try to help me clear things up here. You say Rod got a crowbar out of the car and said, 'This is what I'm gonna kill them with.' Is that correct?"

Dana shook her head side to side.

"All I know is that whenever we got everything transferred to the blue Ford Explorer, we looked down and underneath the back of the front passenger seat was a crowbar with dried blood on it."

"Okay, but correct me if I'm wrong, I mean, you just made a statement that Rod got the crowbar out of Scott's car and said 'I'm gonna kill them with this,' right?"

"Yes, because we had a blowout on Scott's car and we had to change the tire."

"Okay, and that's when that statement was made?"

"Yes."

"Who all was present when that statement was made?" Longo asked. "Who was in the car then?"

"Oh, let's see. I believe it was just me and Charity. Because Scott was driving, and when we had the blowout, the cops came by and they assisted us. And when they were taking the spare tire out of the back, there was the crowbar."

"You saw the crowbar?"

"It was in the back of the car."

"What comments was made when he said, 'This is the tool I'm gonna use to kill Heather's parents'? What else did Rod say?" Gussler wanted to know.

"Well, at first, I thought he was joking around. I thought the original plan was just to sneak her out of the house and get gone. The original plan was to go to Florida, pick up Heather, and go back to Spokane to Charity's grandparents and stay there."

"Okay, we've got a little bit ahead of ourself here. The area where Shannon lives is called Pine Lakes. And when Rod made the announcement that night, I believe he made the announcement that he was gonna, number one, steal the car. And number two, kill the parents. Is that correct?"

"That's correct."

"Okay. And you heard that with your own ears?"

"Yes, sir."

"Okay. Did you hear Scott make any statements like he was gonna participate in this?"

"He just asked Rod if he could go."

"Okay, so you left Shannon's area. Was any phone calls made from Shannon's by Rod?"

"He called Heather and told her to get her stuff ready."

"Okay. So then you left and you went back to Heather Wendorf's residence?"

Dana nodded her head yes.

"Okay. Can you tell me what happened when you arrived there?"

"We parked a ways from the residence and we waited for Zoey to come out. Once Heather got out, me and Charity got her into the backseat and put her stuff in the back of the car, and Rod told us to take her to see her boyfriend, Jeremy, and to go see a girl named Jeanine. So that's what we done. And they said something about, right as we left, that they were going to kill her parents with the crowbar and get their vehicle."

"Okay. When you say they were gonna kill the parents, you're referring to . . .?"

"Rod and Scott."

chapter fifty-two

When they sat her down for questioning, there was no compassion for Heather. From the way the cops treated her, it was evident they were disgusted. They stared at her like she was a freak, part of some cult. They seemed to believe she was *grateful* that her parents were dead. The Wendorfs were worth more to her dead than alive.

The little girl was polite and somewhat shy. She was a frightened fifteen-year-old, just trying to be friendly with the law. She was trying to be cooperative with Al Gussler and Wayne Longo, and they were cordial, as cordial as anyone can be who intends to crucify. They wanted Heather to be comfortable speaking with them, she said she went by the name Zoey sometimes, and she invited them to call her either name, and that was fine. Between Nosferatu, Jaden, Shy, and Damion, they were becoming veterans with nicknames.

Zoey began by talking about her hobbies; she mentioned drawing, her favorite pastime. She said it was her artwork that had attracted Rod, the two of them had become friends back when he attended Eustis High School. She said she and Rod got along pretty well.

Rod seemed normal, Heather told the investigators, Rod had a few strange friends she talked to occasionally—she mentioned the name Damion (Matt Goodman) and said Rod sometimes exaggerated about himself, that he occasionally hyped himself up as being supernatural, but she didn't object to that. Heather told Lake County officials she believed Rod was a vampire. She said she liked to believe in supernatural things.

"How did you get along with your parents?" Gussler asked.

"When?"

"Well, let's take one at a time. Your dad?"

"Oh, well, we got along real good."

"So you liked Daddy?"

"Yeah."

"Did you love Daddy?"

Heather was speechless. The reference to her father in the past tense sent chills running through her.

"Was he hard or strict on you?"

Heather had no answer. Not the type to shed tears, she refused to show emotion.

"All right," Gussler plodded right along, "what about Mom?"

"Mom." Heather paused, catching her breath. "She's the one that usually sets the rules."

"So it was just you and your sister at home?"

Heather heard the detective, but she just couldn't answer. The thought of home made her sick, especially when she knew poor Jeni was out there, completely lost. Heather couldn't bring herself to talk about her sister.

"Okay, why don't you take a couple of deep breaths," the detective suggested, calling for a paper towel for Heather. She wasn't weeping, but she was welling up, on the verge of crying.

"Did you feel that maybe Mom was a little too strict?"

"Well, sometimes I felt she didn't understand, but that's just typical teenage youth."

"I'm sure I felt the same way when I was a kid. I almost don't remember, it's been too long. Did you ever tell your mom, or did you ever have a conversation with your sister that, a few times it had crossed your mind to plot their deaths?"

"No."

"Did you ever ask your sister if she had ever thought about plotting—"

"No."

"—their deaths?"

"No."

"No. Okay, just asking. We've got plenty of towels there," Gussler said, handing the girl something so she could wipe her face.

Detective Gussler said he wasn't trying to blow smoke or anything, but he wanted Heather to know that they had already talked to her boyfriend, Jeremy. They had already talked to half the world in Eustis, he said. He was trying to be honest with her, as he hoped she would be with him.

Gussler was irritatingly cute when he first brought up the vampire stuff—asking her what she drank—was it Coke? Was it Pepsi? Was it blood? And Heather gave matter-of-fact answers about the bloodletting. She didn't catch on that the detective was trying to make fun of her.

At his request, the girl showed Gussler the scars on her arms. Some were from bloodletting. Others were from times when she just felt mad.

Of course Heather talked about Monday, the day when she "crossed over" with Rod. Everybody in custody had crossed over, she explained, everybody she hung around with had crossed over, except Jeremy. Jeremy wasn't the type to cross over, she said. Jeremy hadn't come along on their road trip because he wanted to finish school. Her boyfriend was the dependable type, unlike Rod.

"What rank in the organization does Rod hold?"

"Organization?"

"Or group?"

"Group of what?" Heather wondered. "All of us or just Rod?"

"I guess, I mean, how many of them is there? Other than the five of you?"

"Oh, you mean all over."

"Oh, they're *all over*, huh?"

"Yeah."

"What do you call yourselves?"

"Vampires."

"*Vampires*"—the detective winced—"'cause you like blood?"

"Yeah."

"Any blood?"

"Yeah."

"You like to see blood?"

Heather had no response for that.

"I mean it's okay," Gussler told her, scratching his head, "we're just trying to understand. This is new to us."

"I like it no more than I like to look at a flower."

Heather tried to explain her ties to Rod, and how they

differed from her ties to say, Jeremy. She said she had run away because she was keeping her promise, even if it meant she had to leave her boyfriend behind.

Detective Gussler claimed he was "fascinated" by Rod, and wondered what could have happened to all his powers. Gussler was curious, because if Rod was a real vampire, then he should never have gotten caught. The detective was baffled about what Rod possibly had to offer, about why someone like Heather would choose to follow him. Gussler mentioned these concerns, just "thinking out loud," and Heather just let the man talk. She surely wasn't going to praise Rod, even though that's what it seemed Gussler wanted her to do.

"He's laid a big line on you, but he's a scared little boy," the investigator finally told her. "He's sitting in there with big tears in his eyes, and he's told everything that happened and tried to blame it on everybody that he could."

"What do you mean, blamed it on everybody?"

"Everyone he could. Why go down by yourself when you can take everybody?"

Heather was read her rights. She wasn't quite sure what she was arrested for, and instead of being told, she was made to guess. Heather wondered if it was because Rod was an outlaw, because she was guilty of traveling with him, but from Gussler's tone, it seemed more serious. Of course, to Heather, what Gussler was implying didn't make sense. She never wanted her parents dead, she told him, insisting that she had no part in their deaths.

"Do you still want to follow him?" the detective asked.

"On the road to where?"

"Wherever you planned on following him."

"I didn't know where he was gonna go."

"Does crossing over mean that you have to become somebody that has to kill people? I'm just asking your opinion, okay? I'm not asking what Rod has told you."

It was a shame what happened as a result of the interview with Heather. Most of what the girl said was twisted around and later used against her by Rod's defense team. The investigators mocked Heather's story, they did all they could to catch her in a lie, but to Heather's credit, her story never changed. She had nothing to hide, and she signed a search warrant to allow them into the Ford Explorer.

Heather was asked repeatedly about her alleged conversation with Jennifer, but said she knew nothing about plotting her parents' deaths.

Perhaps because she didn't appear to be all that upset about the murders, perhaps because she didn't seem angry with Rod—whatever the case, someone in the know had a field day leaking bits of information about Heather Wendorf to the media. Public sentiment was spewing hatred toward her. People wanted Heather to pay.

"Who would have sent a sketch of the inside of your house to Rod?" Gussler wanted to know, his voice booming at her.

"Sketch? I never did."

Heather didn't know what Gussler was talking about. She had never drawn a sketch, she hadn't been planning on stealing anything from her parents. She had never sanctioned the theft of the Explorer. She would never do anything like that, she said, but Rod had told the investigators otherwise. Heather was in on it, Rod said. Heather had sent him into her house to steal the Explorer keys.

The detective asked Heather what was running through

her mind when she and the other two girls had dropped Rod and Scott off in front of her house, right at her driveway, but Heather didn't know what he meant. In her eyes, she hadn't let Rod near her house: She had deliberately met him a few houses down, she had deliberately kept from giving him her exact address.

"Dropped who off?" she asked. "We weren't near my front yard."

Gussler reminded her that the Buick was parked a few houses down, maybe a hundred yards away from her home. She and the group had been seen—somewhere around seven o'clock that Monday night. A neighbor had spotted them.

"Just hear me out," Gussler said, theorizing. "They say you gave Rod the sketch of the inside of your parents' home. He knew that none of the doors would be locked. He knew that if he went through that bathroom door, he'd come down the hallway and Daddy would never know it. Now, would they all be lying?"

"If I did, then I do not remember. 'Cause, when would I give him the sketch? You know?"

"Now there's a question that can only be answered with a question. If you send somebody a sketch of your parents' house because they planned these dastardly deeds, you would certainly remember."

"But I didn't write him."

"You didn't write to him?"

"I never, never wrote Rod."

"Okay. So it's a complete *lie?*"

"I did not write him."

"You never sent those sketches?"

"I never sent those."

"Well, I'm not saying you did, but who might have

sent him a sketch of the inside of your house that would have known it to a tee?"

Heather didn't want to blame her best friend, but she figured Jeanine had to have sent it. There was really no one else. So finally, Heather mentioned her friend's name, she said she wasn't sure, but maybe Jeanine had drawn the map.

Heather wasn't doing a very good job of trying to convince him, and from his tone, Gussler had already decided that Heather was responsible. According to Rod's statement, the girl had only been upset about the murders "for an hour and a half." It was clear that in Gussler's view, Heather Wendorf had the heart of a cold-blooded killer. No matter how much Heather told Gussler otherwise, no matter how much she said she was still upset and sad, Gussler just didn't see it.

He obviously thought Heather was the worst kind of monster, a punk kid—complete with dyed-purple hair and a dog collar—who wanted her parents dead so she could collect their money. The detective couldn't wait to throw the book at her.

"You stopped fifteen times at different locations," Gussler scoffed. "Anytime you could have chosen, even before leaving Lake County. Why did you choose to stay?"

"I thought you all were going to blame me that I did it."

"We're trying to understand why you didn't stay and defend your mom and dad, who are no longer here to do it themselves, but you chose to go with the man who killed your parents. We're trying to find out *why*. You don't seem to think there's anything wrong with that, other than the hour and a half being upset."

"You don't know how upset I am inside."

"But you sat out there making funny faces at Mr. Rod sitting across the room, making his funny faces."

"Just bringing a little levity to the ground."

"Pardon?"

"Bringing a little levity to the ground. If I didn't, I probably would have gone crazy in there."

"Sergeant, I've got nothing else. As far as I'm concerned, I've heard a whole bunch of lies and I don't want to hear no more. Lady, when we see you again, you know where it's going to be?"

"Where?"

"It's going to be in Lake County, Florida, at our place, okay?"

As soon as Gussler stormed out, Wayne Longo took over, quizzing Heather about her parents again, asking her why she considered it a joke.

"How can you stand to be in the same room with him and laugh and smile at each other? Do you know what Rod did to your parents?"

Heather nodded in the affirmative.

"Tell me."

"He killed them."

"No. Tell me what he did to your parents."

"I don't know."

"Yes, you do, because he told you."

"He beat them with a crowbar, I don't know."

"If you had it to do all over again, what would you do?"

"I wish I had never seen Rod in my life," Heather whispered, her little body shaking. "I wish I had never met him."

chapter fifty-three

Howard Scott Anderson didn't realize that the Lake County officials were covering their bases. Before the sixteen-year-old was read his rights, the cops believed they had enough information to send the kid to the electric chair.

Poor Scott thought of himself as an innocent bystander. He decided his confession could help him. Rod was his childhood friend, Scott told the Lake County officials, Scott had known him since second grade. He had accompanied Rod to "see some friends" in Eustis, and then, "some things happened" on Monday night.

"Okay, what happened, Scott?" Gussler asked, expecting the boy to stammer.

"We went to Heather's house."

"Okay."

"We saw her, and then the three girls left, and me and

Rod entered their house, and then I froze up and he beat them to death."

"Okay, and you observed that?"

Scott nodded his head, admitting it, but was insisting that the murders were spontaneous. Scott promised that he and Rod had no plan to kill the Wendorfs, but was told they already knew the whole story—it had been confirmed by the four other people. The Lake County officials thought Scott was trying to insult their intelligence. They didn't appreciate it.

"Do you want to help yourself?" Longo raged. "Do you want to start over again and get the story straight? 'Cause we're gonna give you one last chance. All right? 'Cause remember, we've already got the story. We are giving you your opportunity. You want to be stupid and sit there dumbfounded, we will get up and leave and let the chips fall where they fall."

"Scott, it doesn't make one damn bit of difference to me, because the next time we see ya, son, you know where you are gonna be?"

Scott looked at him without changing his expression.

"Back in Florida," Gussler said, "guaranteed."

"They have read you your charges, I assume."

"No."

"You have been charged with first-degree murder. Two counts."

"Two counts," Gussler repeated, looking straight at Scott, who sat staring blankly into space, "do you know what that means?"

Scott didn't answer.

"You don't have any idea what that means? What two counts first-degree murder is?"

"Yes, I'm aware," Scott said finally, becoming slightly annoyed.

"It's not a game," Gussler ranted, "it's not a board game. It's not a bullshit game to sit and lie and play silly little games with. It's a very serious situation. Two human lives are gone for some stupid reason. Can you understand that?"

"Yes."

"Now let's start over," Gussler said, toning down a notch. "Our investigators have talked to probably forty people if they've talked to one. You guys had a bad habit. You went around telling everybody what you were going to do. And everybody may have seemed like your friend, man, but they don't tolerate killing. Everybody was more than happy," the detective gloated. "Our phones were ringing. They're still out there investigating while we're sitting here, and they're getting statement after statement."

Al Gussler told Scott that he could either tell "the truth, the whole truth, and nothing but the truth," like his big leader, Rod, had already done—Scott could try to help himself and be smart—or else, they would find out all the facts another way.

Not that Lake County officials could make Scott any promises. But if Scott would come forward, if he would tell them why they killed the Wendorfs—it just couldn't be because they didn't want to get caught stealing a car—if Scott could just explain the reason, it might be to his benefit when he stood up in front of a judge.

"How much was it discussed about Rod and yourself taking these people's lives?" Gussler wanted to know.

"I never knew about it until he called over from Shannon's house."

"You heard him call from Shannon's house and what was the conversation?" the detective asked, getting huffy.

"Well, I don't fucking really recall all of it."

"Well, do the best you can, that's all I'm asking."

"We were going to get Heather and leave."

"Okay."

"I didn't know we were gonna end up killing her parents, not until we got to the road in which she lived on."

"You know, once we get out that door, the next time you see us, we are on the witness stand. And we can leave here with two things in mind: We can think, this guy tried to help us, he tried to explain to us, tried to get us to understand why this happened. Or we can be thinking, all he did was sit up here and bullshit us, and go for the jugular."

"What do you want to do? Do you want to try to help us?"

Howard Scott Anderson did try to help. He tried to clear things up as best he could, but then the officials started turning everything around on him, making it seem like he and Rod had plotted these murders for over a year, like they had made plans to steal the Ford Explorer when they were back in Murray. Scott admitted that he and Rod had talked about taking a trip down to Florida for quite some time, that they had discussed it for about nine months, but insisted that nothing about robbery or murder was ever brought up.

The Lake County officials kept taking Scott back to the Monday. They wanted to talk about the afternoon at the graveyard, when Heather had been crossed over. Scott said he hadn't been present for that. He couldn't tell them anything about it: He really had no dirt to offer on Heather. Scott had only just met the girl, and to his knowledge, she was completely in the dark about what went down at the Wendorfs'. She didn't know about anything until after it was all over.

As for Rod, Scott finally admitted that Rod had been mildly angry, that during their long drive down from Kentucky, Rod had complained that he was "tired of sitting." According to Scott, Rod said he "wanted to kill someone" and talked about killing Heather's parents or Jeanine's, that was Rod's comment. At the time, Scott didn't think much of it. It was just Rod's way of passing the time on the road.

"Do you think if Jeanine were to have come with you all, you would have went ahead and killed her parents?"

"Yes."

"You would have helped," Longo asked, making certain.

"Like I told you, I froze when he done Heather's parents."

"What did you go up to the Wendorfs for?"

"I thought I would be able to do something, but . . ."

"Do something? *Like what?*"

"Like help him. Help him kill them, but then when I saw him make the first blow, I knew I couldn't."

"So your intentions were to go up there and assist him in that?" Longo asked, amazed.

"Yes."

"And how were you going to assist?"

"He was going to go after the father, and I was going to go after the mother."

Scott admitted that he and Rod had predetermined their roles about twenty minutes before they went into the house, that Dana and Charity knew about it, about what their intent was. He told the law that Dana and

Charity didn't seem to like the idea, but then again, neither of the girls had tried to talk them out of it.

"They knew they couldn't stop us," Scott blurted, telling authorities that he and Rod had initially planned to beat the Wendorfs with wooden sticks, but then Rod found the crowbar in the garage, which would make things "quicker."

"Scott, did you ever take the time, son," Gussler wondered, "to ask yourself before you ever entered that house, if, well . . . We're just tying to understand, because we've been in this business more years than you've been on this earth."

Scott looked at Gussler without a hint of remorse. He had no answer.

"I just don't understand you," Gussler went on. "After he murdered these two folks, and he was rummaging through the bedroom, did you participate in that a little bit?"

"Yes," Scott admitted, telling the detective they had both rummaged through the drawers for cash and had come up with four dollars.

"All right. Did you get to participate a little bit on either one of the victims? Maybe with your pocketknife, a couple of stabs here and there?"

"No."

"And what was your destination when you were heading down here?"

"New Orleans."

"And, on the ride, say, you and Rod might be off and away for a while, did any of the girls try to leave?"

"No."

"Did they appear they were having a good time?"

"Heather wasn't having a good time at the beginning. She was angry at Rod for killing her parents."

"But, of course, she stayed with you all," Gussler said, mystified. "There's people that just killed my parents, I wouldn't be with them but maybe one minute."

"She seemed remorsed for the past few days."

"Can you explain to us what it is to cross over?"

"Changing from human to the undead. Basically a vampire."

"Has Rod ever talked about killing people before?"

"Yes."

"Who?"

"He said he used to be an assassin."

"Who did he say he killed?"

"He never gave me any names."

"So you are saying that you were in the house. And Rod was in the house, and which one of the girls came into the house?"

"None."

"You have any other questions, Sarge?"

"What are those initials on your arm that you carved in there?" Longo was curious.

"I didn't carve them. Heather did."

"What are the initials?"

"Fett."

"What does Fett mean?"

"It's her boyfriend's name, Jeremy something."

"Heather carved her boyfriend's initials in your arm with a razor?"

"Yeah," Scott said, nodding his head, trying to look cool.

chapter fifty-four

Scott Anderson had agreed to take Lake County officials on a tour of New Orleans; they wanted to recover the crowbar, if possible. Dressed in shackles, Scott brought the crime unit to the banks of the Mississippi, but the currents had removed any hope of finding the murder weapon. The frogmen came up from the freezing-cold river empty-handed.

Searching the grounds, they discovered a carving on a tree stump. It was a heart, with the words "Zoey and Fett" cut into the center. The tree bark became part of the official evidence list, along with hundreds of other minuscule items, and it would eventually become the subject of gossip. People would insist that the carving said "Heather loves Rod."

The way the rumor mill was pumping, by the time the Wendorfs' funeral was held, folks were certain that Rod was Heather's boyfriend, that she had gotten him to kill her parents so they could run off and live happily ever after. At the funeral of Richard and Ruth Wendorf, a lot of myths were already in place. Most people just made up stories. They ignored the facts, including the fact that Rick and Ruth had never married. People didn't care about minor details like that. But Naoma Ruth wasn't a Wendorf; she was the wife of Joe Queen.

Ruth's two daughters by him, Paula and Samantha Queen, were understandably upset by the way they were ignored during the funeral arrangements and services. It was their mother who had been killed, yet Paula and Sam were left no seats in the front row during the funeral service and were offered no heartfelt condolences from the Wendorfs. It was the Wendorf show, this funeral and burial, the Wendorfs controlled every facet—including who would and would not talk to the press.

The services were held in December, at the Baldwin-Fairchild Funeral Home in Winter Park. More than two hundred people filled the chapel for the closed-casket ceremony; it was standing room only, with people lining up in the back of the tiny place. The funeral was an emotional ordeal for everyone, but particularly for Jennifer, who, unlike her sister, was filled with visible grief and torment. Jeni was a bleeding heart, and in addition to being in shock, she was scared for her sister. Along with the other teens, Heather had just been extradited and locked away in the Florida Department of Juvenile Justice in Ocala. No one from the family had seen her—Jennifer had been forbidden.

"If Heather had anything to do with this, not a penny of Rick's money will go to defend her," Billy Wendorf told Paula when they had a moment alone.

"I can't believe Heather was involved," Paula argued, "let's wait until we get her side of the story."

But Billy had no time for that. He believed the press, he believed the police, and he wanted Heather prosecuted. In his eyes, his twin brother had been murdered because Heather wanted her freedom. Nothing could veer him away from that, not even the preacher, who tried to put aside the "speculations" about Heather, asking the congregation to pray for the Wendorfs' youngest child.

"God loves Heather," the Reverend Peter Nordstrom said during the funeral service, "and nothing is ever going to change that."

But it had changed for the Wendorfs. Jeni was a part of Billy and Gloria Wendorfs' family now, she was subject to their rules and beliefs, and even though she didn't agree with them, Jeni had to honor the Wendorfs' wishes and stay clear of Heather. Billy and Gloria were the only family she had. A senior in high school, Jeni Wendorf was miserable in their home. She had been shifted out of Eustis High to a school in Winter Park, which had three times the student population, and Jeni had to forfeit her popularity and her cheerleading, which made her feel even more ill at ease.

The death of her parents had cost the girl everything— her home, her sense of belonging, her friends, her favorite teachers, even her pets. Jeni wanted to see Heather, she didn't want to think that Heather was some kind of cult killer, but the seventeen-year-old was forced to make a choice. Billy didn't want her to have any contact with Heather, and Jeni couldn't jeopardize her living circumstances.

"They wouldn't let Heather call me," Jeni confided. "They felt it was in my best interests and they picked a lawyer for me. Uncle Billy was the legal representative of the estate, and he said that if Heather was legally convicted of murder, by Florida statute she had no right to the estate. He tried to get me to sign papers to sue my sister, but I didn't want to take anything from her."

For most people, it was just after the funeral that one thing became clear: Billy and Bobby Wendorf were going to do whatever they needed to make sure the death of their brother was avenged. They were telling the media that Heather needed to serve jail time, they were calling her a murderer. When their dad, Jim Wendorf, told the press he didn't blame Heather, his sons got angry.

"Billy and Bobby told Jim that if he didn't stop," Paula recalled, "they said if he didn't stop talking to reporters and defending Heather, they would disown him. They would never speak to him, nor have anything to do with him again."

"I won't have Rick's monies going to defend his murderer," Bobby told Paula and Samantha when the three of them were back at the house, having a little cigarette break after the burial.

Heather's older sisters, who had flown in from Texas, who had spent hours and hours making connecting flights during the Thanksgiving weekend, who had walked into the Greentree residence and witnessed the blood all over the walls, could hardly believe their ears.

"At the time, we had no clue about what happened down there," Samantha said. "But, I know there's nothing in the world I wouldn't do for my sisters, and, even if Heather was involved, Mom and Rick would say it was a mistake if I didn't stick by her."

chapter fifty-five

As the investigation continued, as technical services developed diagrams of the Wendorf interior, detailing each square inch of the crime scene and sending specimens to crime labs for analysis, Rod Ferrell's DNA was found to match evidence at the Wendorf house, including the skin taken from under Ruth's fingernails.

Al Gussler and his team of investigators continued to interview folks, both in Florida and Kentucky, and were busy collecting names and stories. They had an intense interest in Amber Blood, a fifteen-year-old girl who had volunteered information about Heather by calling the Crime Stoppers Hot Line.

In her sworn police statement, Amber told Lake County detective Ken Adams that she had gone to Eustis High with Heather and Rod, that she'd known Heather for about two and a half years, that she knew Heather was in a vampire cult.

"Her and Rod mentioned once about the cult, and they talked about blood and torture," Amber told the detective, her voice earnest.

"Okay," Adams said, "and you also mentioned that she thought she had been a demon in her past life. Did she tell you that?"

"Yeah. Heather told everybody that."

"You mentioned the clan or the group that she belonged to. Were there many of them in that group?"

"All I knew was that she was in it. I'm pretty sure Rod was in it too. I met him at her house a few times."

"Okay, describe Rod. Since you only know him by his first name, describe Rod to us."

"He's tall, quite tall. He's got long, long hair. It's like a darkish brownish brown, black color. He's not skinny, but he's not fat, you know, and he dresses in black. He looks very scary, and he's got, like, an oval face."

"Okay. And you stated that you've seen him out at Heather's house a couple of times. Whereabouts at Heather's house?"

"In the front yard, closer to the fence."

"Okay, was he by himself or . . .?"

"No, it was him and Heather."

"Okay. And why did you stop by?"

"I wanted to see if maybe Heather and them wanted to come to a party."

"Okay. And you say this is when you heard them talking about killing something? When was this?"

"October of this year."

"Okay. And have you ever heard them talking about killing things before?"

"Just, like, animals, cats, not really dogs, but like cats and birds and little things like that."

"Okay. And this was Rod and Heather?"

"Yeah, and some of the people they hung around."

"You remember who the other people were?"

"No, I can't."

"Okay. And you say the next time you talked to Heather was November of this year? How do you remember?"

"Because I moved to my mom's in Orlando the end of November. The Saturday I talked to Heather was before I moved, when I was still with my dad."

"Okay. And what happened while you were at your dad's?"

"Heather called, and I remember the part where she just said, 'I'm finally gonna do it. I'm gonna kill 'em. We're gonna do it. Rod and Dana are gonna do the most. I'm gonna help a little bit, the rest of 'em are gonna watch.' And then she said that her parents hated her, that they always loved her sister better, that her sister was the more popular one between everybody."

"Okay. Was that her feeling as long as you had known her?"

"She always thought her parents loved her sister better."

"And she had stated, prior to this, dislike of her parents?"

"She was always saying she couldn't stand her parents. She hated 'em."

"So tell me what words Heather used to make you feel she was talking about killing her parents?"

"In cold blood we're going to murder them."

"Okay. Did she say anything else in regards to that?"

"She said they were gonna take her dad's Jeep or Bronco, it was like a Jeep thing, and they were gonna switch the license plate on it from somebody else's car. She never said who else's car. She said they were gonna leave the state, change their names and stuff, and they were never coming back."

Amber Blood's police statement was recorded on December 10, 1996. Days later, when the statement was published as part of the Florida public record, it would cause a media frenzy.

And it would be months, not until March of 1997, before Miss Blood would repudiate her statement. In the meantime, Miss Blood received a lot of attention, being called by both newspapers and local TV stations. Her little game didn't end, really, even after she had been asked to take a polygraph and had failed.

Not until her sworn statement before special prosecutor Brad King, did the fifteen-year-old girl finally admit that her police statement was a bold-faced lie. Miss Blood had gone to school with Heather, but the two of them were never friends. Heather had never called her.

During her deposition with King, Amber Blood admitted that she herself was into wicca, which she referred to as "satanic witchcraft," but said she didn't know if Heather was into it or not. She didn't know if Heather was a vampire, and she had never laid eyes on Rod.

As far as the Wendorf case was concerned, Miss Blood had gleaned her knowledge strictly from local and national news reports.

chapter fifty-six

The business of special prosecutor Brad King, also known as Darth Vader in certain circles, was to secure death. He was, without doubt, one of Florida's toughest prosecutors. Even though, in King's eyes, asking for a death sentence was a no-win situation, it was a necessary evil that he was responsible for.

Of course Rod's defense team, led by public defender Candace Hawthorne, was doing all it could to nullify the evidence, to keep the tape of Ferrell's confession out of the courtroom. Rod's case became the subject of a series of vampire jokes and gags, with plastic fangs and replica coffins, but the task of saving Rod's life was certainly no laughing matter. In his confession, Rod had already hung himself. All his attorney could hope for was that the jury would take into account all the mitigating factors and sentence him to life without parole.

Meanwhile, not only were all the national news shows calling, not only were the talk shows and newsmagazine shows hounding the public defender's office in Lake County, even HBO was bugging them for "just a few minutes" with Rod. HBO had already begun filming a documentary, as had producers in England. It was unbelievable the controversy a few "vampires" had created. Calls were coming in from as far away as Japan.

Numerous TV folks were asking for film rights, at least a half dozen people planned to write books. The attorneys representing the five teens were bombarded with daily requests. Reporters were visiting from as far away as *Australia*, but the defense attorneys and prosecutors involved all said the same thing: no interviews with any vampire until after the trials.

Apparently, Rod didn't realize he was supposed to keep his mouth shut, because shortly after he had been indicted by a grand jury, Rod decided he would try to beat the first-degree murder charge by placing a collect call over to the *Orlando Sentinel*. Rod phoned the reporter because he needed to "set the record straight."

"I know who did it," Rod said, calling collect from the Lake County jail in Tavares, just a few miles from Eustis. "It was a rival vampire clan," Rod insisted, describing his "sire," eighteen-year-old Jaden Steven Murphy, as a practitioner of witchcraft, as an evil entity.

During his two fifteen-minute conversations with the news reporter, Rod got angry at the grand jury, implying that the panel of civilians had completely ignored the facts. Rod said he was "framed" by this rival, who he claimed was "totally immoral."

Rod described himself as "very gentle-natured" and

accused his rival of killing animals, of "mutilating two dogs and beating forty others."

"I knew Rod better than anybody," Jaden told a Kentucky news reporter, responding to Rod's wild accusations. "I've been stereotyped as a satanist mainly because of closed-minded people," admitting that he had taken the name Jaden off a Star Trek episode.

"Rod and I would talk about how we would avenge the death of someone. But then it became a battle in Rod's mind as to who had more power."

Jaden told the press that Rod started to get "weird," that Rod was "mixing fantasy with reality." Jaden insisted Rod had been ostracized from the vampire role-playing group long before the murders ever took place. Jaden wanted the press to know that his vampiric lifestyle didn't sanction killing of any kind.

Nonetheless, reporters from around the globe trekked up the hills, hiked all the way to the top of the Land Between the Lakes, just to get a glimpse of the "Vampyre Hotel." The abandoned stone building, Rod's hangout, was just a skeleton of a place all covered with graffiti. It was really nothing to make a big deal about, this creepy kid hideaway.

And even though it was nestled in hills and was inaccessible, fifteen miles away from downtown Murray, residents of Calloway County demanded that the place be torn down.

Because so many outsiders were flocking there, because Murray was starting to get a reputation for being vampire central, enough fuss was made that a local ordinance was passed and the Vampyre Hotel was actually demolished. Afterward, the people of Murray thought everything would quiet down, but of course, it didn't.

The newspapers continued to spread rumors about Satan worship and blood rituals—about "strange occurrences" in Calloway County. Even with the killers behind bars, local townsfolk had begun to think that Murray, home to the National Boy Scout Museum, was suddenly a breeding ground for the occult.

People in Calloway County had become so paranoid that dozens of calls poured into the sheriff's office reporting sightings of vampires and other weird phenomena. In fact, one sixteen-year-old was charged with "hindering prosecution," a class-D felony, because, on the day before the teens were trapped in Baton Rouge, when there was still a national manhunt under way, the young western-Kentucky boy made false statements to Murray police.

Claiming that he sighted Rod Ferrell driving the blue Explorer in Calloway County, the "informant" invited authorities to visit with him at his home. Murray police drove miles outside town to hear the sixteen-year-old assert that Rod Ferrell was threatening to kill him and his family, that Rod had astrally projected himself back to Murray.

Also in the spotlight was the game Vampire: The Masquerade, which most people had never heard of, though they understood it was some variation of Dungeons & Dragons. Newspapers blasted the game, wondering how a role-playing book could have escalated into such brutality. However, by that time, most people had already made up their minds about the five teens. These kids were nothing but Satan worshipers who cut themselves and sucked blood. They were sick little puppies who were happy murderers.

It was rumored that, among the many items police confiscated from the Wendorf Explorer, there were "bloody sheets" and a "witch's spell book," but the truth was, only minuscule particles of blood were traced in the car. And the "spell" book, Rod's Necronomicon, was a mass-market paper-back, widely regarded as a work of fiction. The editor's note says it had been written by a "mad Arab" in the eighth century A.D. and gives acknowledgment to the demon Per-durabo—touches that make the book seem authentic—but it is clearly not a sorcerer's handbook.

Of course, no one writing news accounts bothered to focus on all the typical childhood items found in the Wendorf Explorer—little things like Lion King and Aladdin videos, like horseshoes and lucky-charm bracelets. Ignored largely by the press were teen belongings includ-ing country-music tapes, love poetry, art books, Cover Girl makeup, and pressed flowers.

No one cared about the TV remote-control clicker that was discovered in Dana Cooper's belongings. No one bothered to consider that these kids honestly thought they were just running away, that perhaps four of them, at least, were planning to start over, just looking for an adventure in the big city. Such items as baby pictures, Christmas cards, and glamour shots—all found in the Explorer—didn't mesh with the "vampire clan" stories that were being peddled by the media.

If it didn't involve blood or horror, it didn't get cover-age. It seemed, when it came to the subject of the Wendorf murders, people only cared about three things: blood, guts, and revenge.

On Christmas Eve, 1996, while other kids were safe at home dreaming of Nintendo games, the five "vampire" teens were being mocked by their fellow inmates in Florida. Their saga had become the subject of a trashy headline story in the

National Examiner, and their pictures were splashed across grocery newsstands in every burg of the country.

According to the article, the bludgeonings of Richard Wendorf, age forty-nine, and Ruth Queen, age fifty-four, were said to have stemmed from the "game-playing youths' beliefs" in Vampire: The Masquerade, from their need to "suck the blood of corpses in order that they actually become vampires."

In the *Examiner* piece, a "vampire expert" was quoted as saying that the teens involved were part of a "major movement" among American youths who were trying to "earn high marks from Dracula." The article noted that White Wolf, the creator and distributor of Vampire: The Masquerade, had already sold half a million copies of the game.

"YOUR KID COULD BE NEXT!" the headline screamed, recounting the gory details of the murders that "rocked a Florida community." The story reported that five teens "graduated from sitting around the table throwing dice to masquerading as vampires and DRINKING BLOOD."

Frightful pictures of the "vampire cult" members—with the exception of Heather—were prominently displayed next to comments about bloodletting becoming a "horrendous trend that could trigger an epidemic of violence across America."

chapter fifty-seven

Dear Jeni,

Sorry I didn't get to call you on Sat. They wouldn't let me get Tony's number out of my personals because they locked it up. Last week, all the girls here acted up, and in here, the good also get punished with the bad. But isn't it like that all over? Of course.

Right now I'm pretty nervous about the jury thing on Tuesday. If they decide in my favor, I could be released on Wednesday. If that were to happen, it's most likely that I'd be out before you get this. When you read this, my future will be known.

I really don't have much to complain about here, it's what you can expect from a place like this. Some of the girls like me. At least I have a kindred spirit that understands what others can't.

I don't know if I'm supposed to say this, but when my lawyer came to see me, I had the opportunity to read the transcript of your interview. <u>All of it.</u> I know that you don't think that my first letter from Louisiana was sincere, even though I poured my heart out onto paper, as I am now.

I remember my first letter was from Jeanine, even though I prayed it would be from you or at least someone else from my family. When I was in Louisiana, I called Bobby, or so I thought. How many Robert Wendorfs can there be in the central Florida phone book? Anyway, the operator said she was yelled and cursed at. It was embarrassing and disappointing.

As you can imagine, my days have been boring and monotonous, but I hear that you're enjoying yourself. Beaches, road trips, and party upon party, the things I can only read about in books.

I also get to read transcripts from people I've never heard of before, saying they were my best friend. Another person trying to get a piece of the pie. Why are people telling lies about me? I've never hurt them. All I want to know is <u>why</u>. Do you know how it feels to have the whole world against you?

You said that what happened that night, you'll never be able to forgive. It sounds almost as if you've convicted me. How do you know that I did anything to be forgiven? You just assume? Don't write to me and make statements that you should be making to the four others.

You also say there's many questions you have that will never get answered. It hurts me to hear you doubt my <u>word</u>. I know you love me like I love you, but do you love because you feel obligated? I entreat and ask you to read I Corinthians 13: 4–10. That is my definition. And yes, as I have been here I decided to expand my mind by reading the Bible. I duly recommend it. It changed me so that I will never look at life the same again.

All I ever asked for in life was for people to understand me. That's all. Perhaps that was too big of a request.

Believe me when I say I've straightened up my life. I pray that you'll do the same. I want you to be as happy as I am right now. I'm happy enough to say that, even though I pray for good news on Tuesday, I know I won't be devastated if I don't get it. I know that God will be with me, and if doing time is His will, I will accept it.

Remember, if you need any other info, Jeanine will keep in contact. She has from the beginning. Farewell.

Love, Heather

chapter fifty-eight

James Hope, a court-appointed attorney, made his initial contact with Heather in late December, two days after the grand jury had convened. A few weeks later, after the lawyer had read the transcripts of the police interviews, after he had seen Heather's four codefendants talking to police on videotape, he made an unusual decision.

Hope suggested that Heather offer her own testimony to the grand jury. This rare tactic left Heather open to cross-examination, but she agreed to go forward. Heather had read the transcripts of people like Brandy Gonczy, Amber Blood, and Mandy Jones. She knew these kids had accused her—even her sister accused her—but Heather insisted that she was not guilty.

Prior to her decision, James Hope had spent hours with her, had given Heather an understanding of the charges that were filed against her: murder in the second degree and principal to robbery. He explained why, when the grand jury had met on December 16, they had found probable cause to indict the four others.

Roderick Ferrell, Howard Scott Anderson, Dana Lynn Cooper, and Charity Kessee were each having trial dates set in Lake County. They each had played a part, the police statements indicated, and now Rod and Scott were facing the death sentence. Dana and Charity were looking at the possibility of spending life in prison. Each would stand before Judge Jerry T. Lockett, a hanging judge who had a reputation for being the toughest of them all.

Though a jury would recommend a sentence, in the state of Florida the final decision would be up to the judge. Even though Dana was the only person over eighteen, all four teens were being tried as adults, so legally, Lockett held all the cards. Heather's defense attorney tried to emphasize that. He told her that Judge Lockett had no problem letting people fry, and, should she be charged as an adult, she would be in serious trouble.

However, in the case of Heather Wendorf, the grand jury still hadn't come to a decision. The eighteen-member panel had yet to decide if probable cause existed, and rather than rush things back in December, they had decided to reconvene toward the end of January.

"I don't know if it was simply a matter that it was late in the day," Hope speculated, "or maybe the grand jury had done enough work in December. But I think Amber Blood did not come across well.

"Miss Blood was, in fact, impeached while she was in there," Hope confided, "and it was my impression that she gave the grand jury some reason for pause."

Throughout November and December, while all the other attorneys were rushing to gain information from their clients, while they were scrambling with their vampire teens, with the media hype, with their personal images and reputations, James Hope was sitting back.

"I had no knowledge that my client would not be indicted along with everyone else," Hope admitted. "But I was waiting for all the dust to settle."

James Hope had confidence in Heather. When he finally met with Brad King at the prosecutor's office in January, when he laid out his client's position, Mr. King already had the benefit of the discovery. In addition, King had conducted an extensive number of interviews himself.

Behind closed doors, one could have heard a pin drop, the special prosecutor listened to Hope so intently. Notorious for being tough on offenders, King was not one to let anything slip by. If anyone on earth could have prosecuted Heather for murder, Brad King was designed for the job.

But after a lengthy discussion, the prosecutor concluded that what Heather Wendorf was saying was consistent with all that he knew. Based on the investigation, based on the review of all the items that King had, with two notable exceptions—a statement by Amber Blood, and a statement by Sondra Gibson—everything corroborated Heather's story.

By the time Hope had his meeting with King, Amber Blood had already recanted her statement. Rod's mom, Sondra Gibson, meanwhile, who claimed to have "overheard" Heather "ask Rod to kill," was still scheduled to take a polygraph. Other than Sondra's statement, Brad King had nothing to refute Heather's position.

Then on January 27, the day before the grand jury reconvened, Sondra Gibson changed her testimony; she had failed her polygraph. At that point, Brad King placed a call to James Hope, asking if he would still be willing to put Heather on the stand. Hope said yes. He didn't want his client to drop the ball.

"If they don't believe you, they can indict you for first-degree murder," Hope reminded her, "or, they can indict you for lesser things."

Heather understood that once she took the stand, her attorney wouldn't be able to say a word. Hope would have to sit there "like a bump on a log." A board-certified criminal attorney for over ten years, Hope had never placed a client in front of a grand jury. Of course Hope could raise objections, by way of privileges that Heather might have, but only if the questioning went contrary to the grand jury's main purpose. As it happened, however, Hope didn't invoke any of Heather's privileges.

"I made sure that Heather knew as much about the case as I knew," Hope recalled. "Her being one of the prime characters, I had her explain to me, in her words, all that she knew. That was the extent of the preparation. I didn't give her a mock cross-examination. I didn't stress any questions I thought she might be asked."

chapter fifty-nine

In the Circuit Court of the Fifth Judicial Circuit, in and for Lake County, the following no true bill was presented and filed:

> We the Grand Jury of Lake County, having been presented the obligation to determine if Heather Wendorf should be charged with any crimes involving the deaths of her parents, do hereby report as follows.
>
> At the time of our original consideration of this issue on December 16, 1996, there was testimony presented from a civilian witness (whom we will not name) that Heather Wendorf had discussed with that witness the fact that Heather Wendorf and Roderick Ferrell had planned, not only Heather Wendorf's departure from home, but also stealing the Wendorfs' Ford Explorer and killing the Wendorfs.

In the course of our previous proceedings, we determined that the testimony of this witness was inconsistent with the statements of <u>each and every one</u> of those persons indicted by this Grand Jury on December 16, 1996. In their statements to law enforcement, the four codefendants, as well as Heather Wendorf, consistently stated that Heather Wendorf had no prior knowledge that the murders, robbery, or burglary would take place.

Because of the concerns about this witness, and at the State Attorney's suggestion, we adjourned our session in order to allow time for this witness's story to be more fully evaluated and to allow for any other evidence to be brought forth. The other evidence principally concerned alleged statements of Heather Wendorf, overheard by Roderick Ferrell's mother. During our adjournment, both of these witnesses' stories were reevaluated by the Sheriff's Department and the State Attorney's Office.

At our session today, the civilian witness recanted the testimony that Heather had talked to them concerning planning the robbery, burglary, and murders. This recantation originally occurred at the time of the witness's polygraph examination. It was subsequently confirmed before us. Ferrell's mother, in her polygraph examination, stated that she had no recollection of the statement earlier attributed to Heather Wendorf. This being so, we deem her to be unreliable as a witness.

In making our determination, we act in accordance with the instructions we were given at the outset of our service, the advice of our State Attorney, and the facts presented to us. We recognize that we, as the Grand Jury, are the "guardians of all that is comprehended in the police power of the State of Florida."

We have as much an obligation to protect the innocent as to pursue those who may have violated the law. In this regard, we must find that there is <u>NO LONGER PROBABLE CAUSE</u> to believe that Heather Wendorf was a knowing participant in the terrible acts that occurred at her home.

While she certainly acted inappropriately in planning to leave home, and arguably so, in remaining with the others after learning what had been done, we recognize that these acts are not crimes. We also wish to unequivocally state that these actions were wrong.

Heather Wendorf, her sister, and the families of both Richard Wendorf and Naoma Ruth Queen will live the rest of their lives with the consequences of Heather's choices of associates and activities. Nothing that anyone can say or do will change the loss they have suffered. We wish them God's mercy and grace in the recovery that must follow.

So Heather went free. It took only a few hours for James Hope to collect her belongings and sign the necessary paperwork to get her out of the detention center in Ocala. On January 28, 1997, a court-appointed guardian, Lou Tally, would become legally responsible for Heather.

For a few weeks, the girl went to stay with her maternal grandmother, Gertrude Adams, who lived not far from Eustis, in Orange City. But then, according to Heather, her granny tried to shoot at her. When the old lady shot a few bullets in the air above Heather's head, poor Heather went

catatonic. She was sent by ambulance to a psychiatric ward
for evaluation, and after a couple of days, when Heather
was given a clean bill of mental health, with the help of her
guardian, she was placed at the home of a prominent attorney in Lake County, where she lived in high style with his
wife and many children. Heather was hoping to be
accepted by her former classmates and neighbors.

But people in Lake County hated her. The law enforcement folks involved in the case were still fuming. They
fueled the media, which, in turn, fueled the public disdain for Heather. In particular, the local sheriff, George
Knupp, was determined to see Heather behind bars.

Even though Heather had testified before the grand
jury for over two hours, even though her codefendants
had not implicated her in any way, Sheriff Knupp was
sure, once he brought further evidence, that he could get
Heather convicted of a murder charge. The sheriff became
so hell-bent on having a second grand jury appointed
that, two years after the murders, because of Knupp's
written petition, which was printed on the front page of
local newspapers, Brad King decided a second grand jury
should review the case against Heather.

Meanwhile, after she had been released to live out her
childhood in Lake County, Heather Wendorf had become
a twentieth-century version of Hester Prynne, wearing
her parents' murders on her chest, like a scarlet letter. The
girl could not walk any street without being whispered
about or jeered at. Some people went so far as to walk
right up and tell Heather she was *hated*.

Heather dropped out of high school and tried to drop
out of sight, but it was impossible. With each detail of the
upcoming trials and continuing investigation, the "cult
case" continued to make headlines.

chapter sixty

In the few weeks of transition, when Heather first stayed with her granny in Orange City, her family tried to save her. Granny was so religious, a lot of people thought she was a fanatic. Granny took Heather to a high-tech church in Orlando, a place where everyone had their Bibles and sang contemporary Christian music, where people followed along with the preacher from two huge screens.

It was the World Outreach Center of Benny Hinn, a Middle Eastern evangelist who, from his pulpit in Orlando, cast demons out of humans. Granny was hooked on Benny Hinn's TV program, *This Is Your Day*, and she imposed it on Heather regularly. Heather would laugh to herself as she watched the holy man sort through thousands of letters, as he reached his hands toward the TV screen, healing people through the airwaves.

According to Granny, if it wasn't Christian, it was the

devil, but after four weeks of attending church, Heather still didn't "get" it. Benny Hinn was laying on hands, he was having folks leap out of their wheelchairs, but none of it seemed real. Heather refused to go to church with Granny, and that seemed to be when the old lady decided that her granddaughter was, in fact, a devil worshiper. For a short while, Granny tried to wage a spiritual war. Granny wanted God to perform a miracle for Heather. Granny and Aunt Lily called it "crazy praise" when people would shout and scream about their love of God. They thought Heather needed to take notes; they wanted her to understand.

But of course, all that ended when, as Heather later testified, Granny fired her pistol. Aunt Lily blamed the incident on Heather's white witchcraft. Heather and her tarot cards were removed from Granny's house, and that was that. When Heather was admitted to the psychiatric hospital for evaluation, nobody in her family even went to visit. Granny and Aunt Lily told Lou Tally they were fed up with Heather. They told Heather's guardian that, in their eyes, nothing could help her.

Heather just couldn't win. No one believed she was innocent; most people felt she belonged in the Lake County Jail with the four others. Many believed that Heather had solicited and plotted the murders. At the very least, people agreed that, because Heather had taken that ride in the Explorer, she was an accessory after the fact. The public resented Heather's freedom, she became a hot topic of conversation, and folks were very opinionated about her. And then, when the press revealed that the Wendorf estate was worth a million dollars, that Heather would be receiving her full half of that, public outrage grew out of control. People hissed and cursed at her in the streets.

Heather had gone into hiding. Having found a boy-friend to cling to in Orange City, she attended a high school program in that area, requiring her guardian to drive her hours and hours each week. Back in Lake County, not only was Heather subject to abuse, *Jeanine LeClaire* was being mocked and taunted in her high school. Jeanine continued to associate with Heather, but paid a price for that. She eventually would feel pressured enough to move away from Eustis before finishing high school.

The few kids who had practiced witchcraft with Heather, the few who had dabbled in vampirism, were now hiding behind their McDonald's uniforms and Wal-greens smocks. These teens had their weekend jobs, they were finishing high school and preparing for college, and they wanted nothing to do with Heather's bad reputation. To the police, to the media, most of them denied that they ever tasted blood. The few people who had been in Heather's circle now made it seem like she was making things up about them, like she was a complete outcast, drinking blood and casting spells by herself.

Even Jeremy Hueber refused Heather's calls. He still cared about his former girlfriend, but then, his life was already hellish enough. Shows like *Unsolved Mysteries* were calling, an entire media brigade had camped out at his mom's house, so Jeremy had to keep his distance.

Unsolved Mysteries had intended to shed light on the crime, but in the Wendorf "cult murder" case, the TV coverage seemed to revictimize Heather. In February 1997, when *Unsolved Mysteries* aired their segment on the Murray "vampire teens," Gertrude Adams started to doubt Heather's word. According to Heather, shortly after her grandmother viewed the program and listened to Murray police advising parents to "be on the lookout" for warning signs of vampirism, Granny decided Heather was still in love with this vampire stuff, that Heather was a child of Satan, just like Rod.

In the months to follow, other programs would air: Jenny Jones hosted Jaden Steven Murphy, who went to Chicago to brag about being a vampire—and to bad-mouth Heather. Maury did a show called "I'm Scared My Teen Is Evil," which included a short interview with Rod, and a studio appearance by his mother, Sondra, who was only too happy to fly to New York to tell America her son was a "good person."

Meanwhile, Hard Copy sent reporters to Eustis High, in search of vampires on campus, but their staff came up short. Among the many misconceptions being broadcast by the national media was the notion that the teens had murdered the Wendorfs so they could drink their victims' blood.

chapter sixty-one

To fellow inmates at the Lake County Jail, Rod was promoting a new story: he said it was his best friend, Scott, who had come up with "an idea" the night they had gone to retrieve Heather from Greentree Lane. According to Rod, Scott had directed Dana and Charity to drive Heather off in the Buick Skylark. Rod said Scott "borrowed" his combat boots and used them to climb inside the Wendorf home.

In his second call to a reporter, Ferrell told the *Orlando Sentinel* that on the night in question, he had fallen asleep in the woods on Greentree Lane and was awakened by Anderson, who showed up driving the blue Ford Explorer. Rod reported that it was Scott who had taken the vehicle. It was Rod's understanding that Scott had left Heather's parents "unharmed."

"I don't think Scott is capable of killing anyone more than

I am," Rod told the paper. He was sorry he couldn't really remember anything more regarding Monday, November 25, but of course, he was the victim of "multiple personalities" and experienced "blackouts" quite often. It was one of Rod's ten personalities, apparently, that possessed him to stick his tongue out at news reporters when he arrived at the Lake County Jail in early December.

For the paparazzi, Rod had licked the glass window in the booking area. He was caught on camera blowing a kiss to reporters and howling the words "God bless America." Those were the days when Rod was still cocky. Those were the days before his trial and sentencing, before Rod had his hair cut off and had counsel advising him to clean up his act.

Rod was quite a different creature when he had first arrived in Lake County, in the days following his confession. For one thing, he was no longer concerned about his punishment. He was already bragging that he could escape from jail; escape was no problem for him. It was just a question of when. In his mind, he was still a vampire, still capable of supernatural acts.

In fact, Rod told Officer Desiree Nut, who was working the corrections desk over at the county jail, that he could "take out" the night guards anytime he wanted. Rod tried to tell Nut all about the case, he tried to proclaim his innocence. He told the corrections officer that he wouldn't stay behind bars for long.

"I don't know why Heather got off," Rod was insisting. "She had it done. She wanted her parents dead."

"I don't want to hear about it," Officer Nut warned him, "you really shouldn't be talking about it before your trial."

"But Heather was in on it. Charity and Dana just went along for the ride."

* * *

Scott Anderson made no attempt to correct the negative publicity. He suffered in silence, for the most part. The sixteen-year-old was sorry about what happened. He broke down and told an inmate that he tried to stop the murders, but couldn't.

chapter sixty-two

In preparation for his trial, Roderick's team of attorneys were considering a mental health defense, specifically "insanity by hallucination." To prove that, the public defender's office retained three mental health experts to visit defendant Ferrell, all of whom would testify on Rod's behalf.

Among other things, Rod was diagnosed as suffering with a "schizotypal personality disorder." Somewhat similar to a schizophrenic, Rod's personality seemed fragmented. Other psychological stressors had to do with frequent geographical moves, cult activity, alleged childhood abuse, impaired peer relations, and his chaotic family system.

It would be a year before Rod Ferrell's psychological report was faxed over to Brad King's office. Dr. Wade Meyers sent it just weeks before Rod's trial date. Roderick Ferrell's trial, everyone understood, would proceed as scheduled, with no change of venue, no additional time granted by Judge Lockett. The judge wanted to "get on with it."

The doctor's report described Ferrell's many suicide attempts as something Rod did because he was "feeling like he was immortal and sort of proving that to himself." Evidently, Rod was quite an unhappy person; he seemed to suffer from different kinds of hallucinations and persecution complexes. Rod claimed he started "hearing voices" when he was age three. He exhibited "odd perceptual experiences." Rod described hearing things, seeing things, even tasting and feeling things, that weren't based in reality. He told the psychiatrist, for example, that he could pick people up with one hand. The young man had a lot of strange ideas. He was intensely involved with his vampire fantasy, claiming he could smell people's blood.

When the MD looked at Rod's drawings and writings, he determined that Ferrell was "on the fringe of not being in touch with reality." Dr. Meyers considered Rod to be "borderline." One of the first things Rod admitted was that he had abused every kind of substance—from heroin to acid to dope to alcohol. Rod was even into glue sniffing. Certainly, his drug use exacerbated his fantasy state. Rod told the psychiatrist he had dropped acid a few hours before he walked into the Wendorfs.

In their initial interview, Meyers would note, Rod exhibited antisocial behavior; he was anxious and withdrawn. Beyond that, Rod had "thought" problems, attention problems, and social problems that would manifest themselves in aggressive and delinquent behavior. Rod tended to be unusually self-deprecating, excessively complaining, to be, at times, extremely vulnerable, and to exhibit feelings of defenselessness.

Regarding the murders, which they only touched

upon lightly, Ferrell told Dr. Meyers he "didn't do it," but of course, the psychiatrist had already seen the police confession. Months later, Meyers would be forced to testify that he "questioned the veracity" of Rod's word. According to the expert, Rod Ferrell's version of what happened on the night of November 25, 1996, showed he had a "very active imagination."

In conjunction with the clinical analysis, Meyers had Ferrell take two computer-scored psychological tests. These were standard tests, the Millon and the DICA, given to many defendants to determine the possibility of an insanity plea. However, in Ferrell's case, the tests failed to provide a valid personality profile. Dr. Meyers later told prosecutors that this didn't necessarily mean Rod was being dishonest, it just meant that he had "so many problems, it was too much for the test to tease out."

The doctor's report concluded that one major mitigating circumstance needed to be considered in determining Ferrell's culpability: according to Meyers, Rod did not have the ability to appreciate the criminality of his conduct.

Of course, the prosecutor boldly disagreed with the doctor on this point. In Brad King's eyes, Rod fully appreciated his actions. Rod had limits. Rod knew exactly what he was doing, his own confession had proved that. King would later remind the jury that Mr. Ferrell told Baton Rouge police he only killed people "sixteen and up."

"People with schizotypal personality are very sensitive to stress," Dr. Meyers told Brad King, responding to him during a heated deposition, "and when they are under stress, their personality can disintegrate. They're going to have less control over their judgment, less control over their behavior, less control over their emotions."

"So, your opinion is that at the moment in time that he

took the crowbar and went into the house and beat the Wendorfs to death"—the prosecutor paused—"your opinion is that he didn't have the mental ability to conclude that he should not do that?"

"I wouldn't put it that way. I'm saying that the crime would most likely not have happened had he not had all these stresses going on in his life, in addition to having a schizotypal personality disorder and depression."

"Okay."

"It seems to me," the doctor asserted, trying to make himself clear, "that you're asking me if he was, in my opinion, legally insane at the time of the crime. I'm not saying that."

"So, you're saying that he could appreciate what he was doing was wrong?" King wondered.

"Well, I think his appreciation of what he was doing was disturbed."

"Okay. Would it be fair to say that this disorder, this schizotypal personality, that didn't cause Rod to go in there and kill somebody, did it? Did his mental illness affect his ability to say, 'No, I'm not going to do that'?"

"I don't think it affected him so much that he would be legally insane."

"Okay. Do you believe in the death penalty?"

"Some studies show it doesn't have a deterrent effect," the psychiatrist said, "but other people say it does. Were I to know that the death penalty was a good deterrent, that it was going to save people's lives, then I would say, yes, I'm for it."

"Would that opinion change depending on how old the person facing the penalty is?" King wanted to know.

"Oh, yeah, sure. I absolutely would disagree with the execution of a minor because they're just not mature.

They're still developing, they're not adults, and I think it's wrong."

Meyers went on to describe the basic problems Rod had: schizotypal personality disorder, drug abuse, and a learning disability. He asserted that things started to go wrong for Rod early on in his life—beginning with a case of encephalitis Rod had as a toddler. Dr. Meyers concluded that if somebody had noticed Rod's developmental problems early on, if someone had counseled him about his strange perceptions and delusional thinking, Rod might not have gotten caught up in fantasy.

"Do you derive any sense that the vampire role-playing book played any part of what was going on with Mr. Ferrell?" King asked.

"I think it offered power and solutions to somebody who felt pretty powerless. Rod was somebody who didn't have a whole lot of answers to life. He certainly didn't have a very good identity. He didn't feel good about himself. He didn't feel he could achieve very much in life. I think that gave him an alternative method to have some power, a way to feel good about himself."

"Did the book talk about animal sacrifices as a way of getting power?"

"I don't recall that it did."

chapter sixty-three

"**R**od was feeling very paranoid and was concerned the police were coming after him," Dr. Harry Krop later explained. The psychologist, describing Rod's state of mind before the murders, told lawyers that Rod thought he was going to be accused of kidnapping.

Speaking in Rod's defense, Dr. Krop later testified that Ferrell's "personality conflicts" stemmed from the alleged sexual abuse Rod experienced as a young child. In talking about his sexual history, Ferrell claimed he had been presented to a "Black Mass cult" at age six, that his grandfather had introduced him as the "chosen guardian." Rod alleged he was then sodomized by several adult males.

"They were fertilizing the demon spirit within me," Rod told Dr. Krop. "I felt helpless."

According to Rod, both his mother, Sondra, and his aunt, Lyzetta Crews, were aware of what happened, but did nothing about it. His aunt Lyzetta would later claim that it was not only Rod who suffered with this particular "problem." In her testimony, Lyzetta Crews hesitantly told the court she had been a victim of Harrell Gibson herself.

With her dad, Harrell, staring at her from his front-row seat in the Lake County courtroom, Miss Crews said her dad tried to kiss her, that she felt so harassed in her own home, she was forced to move out when she was fourteen. In a separate interview with Dr. Krop, Lyzetta claimed that she had been "fondled and touched inappropriately" by her father.

Harry Krop also interviewed Sondra Gibson. A full psychological profile was done on the mother, and Sondra later testified that when Rod came back from a fishing trip one day—he had gone out with his grandfather—the boy was "very upset." Rod was throwing up and didn't exactly spell out what happened, but Sondra finally got him to "indicate" that he had been subjected to "oral and anal sex by four or five men in the woods."

Sondra told Dr. Krop that after his fishing trip with Harrell, Rod started drawing sexual pictures and also started drawing pictures of devils and demons. Sondra said she "screamed at her father." She claimed she tried to confront Harrell, but her dad told her to stop making up stories. Harrell threatened to throw Sondra out on the streets if she didn't quit lying. He accused Sondra of being a loose woman. He later said Sondra exhibited inappropriate behavior by "displaying herself" for Rod, lounging around their backyard in a bikini. Harrell repeatedly denied any and all allegations regarding sexual abuse and satanism.

"You heard them say Rod considered his grandparents die-hard Christians," Harrell told reporters, denying that he or his friends ever engaged in cult activity. "Would a Christian do this?" Gibson asked, his tone filled with sarcasm.

To the media, Harrell dismissed Rod as being a kid who lived in a "teenage dreamworld." The old man was quite anxious to "set the record straight" with the press. He wanted everyone to know that his daughter was crazy, that his grandson was no killer, that he was not the person on trial, that it was Heather Wendorf who needed to explain things. Harrell's main goal was to remind everyone that Heather had created the entire Wendorf mess.

"The sexual abuse victimization did have an impact on the whole formation of Rod's personality," Dr. Krop testified. "Rod viewed himself as a nymphomaniac. He saw himself as a superstud, and sex became a much more important part of his interactions with other people than it should be for a sixteen-year-old."

For Krop, Rod had described his consensual sex life, which he said began at age eleven with a "sixteen-year-old whore who wanted my virginity." Rod referred to himself as a "very promiscuous young man" who had always been an "excellent sexual partner."

According to Dr. Krop, Ferrell had been emotionally deprived as a child. Ferrell was in need of attention, especially from a male adult figure, but unfortunately, his time spent with his biological dad, Rick Ferrell, was limited to sporadic moments.

Rick Ferrell would later testify that he saw Rod no more than a handful of occasions "up until the time Rod was age eight." Rod's father recalled that they both liked to play the game Dungeons & Dragons, which was one of their primary pastimes, and lamented that Sondra Gibson kept him from enjoying visitations with his son.

"His father's interest in Dungeons and Dragons is really what gave Rod this image," Dr. Krop would later testify. "Over time, Rod really saw himself to be a leader and got a lot of reinforcement as the chief vampire."

Regarding Rod's allegations of sexual abuse, Dr. Wade Meyers would be the second mental health professional to offer testimony. The expert, who had previously dealt with therapy clients raised in satanic cults, would testify that "some of the things" Rod mentioned "seemed to add up."

According to Meyers's notes, Rod was acting as the high priest, the sacrificer, in a pretty tight cult called the Darkness of the Black Mass.

Dr. Meyers would later testify that Rod mentioned the fishing trip with his grandfather. The expert said the description of Rod's behavior that day would match that of a child who had been sexually assaulted.

chapter sixty-four

"I never viewed her as a mom," Rod confided, reminiscing about Sondra from behind bars. "I viewed her as my best friend. We hung out together, watched movies, drank Cokes, ate pizzas. It felt like hanging out with your best friend rather than your mom. Visitation, it's still like that. It's like having a visit with my best friend. I was never into the mommy-and-daddy bullshit anyway."

The experts testified that Rod had a mother who was psychologically younger than he was. They said that, as a child, Rod had nobody to raise him. After interviewing thirty-five-year-old Sondra for over three hours, Dr. Meyers concluded she had the mentality of a twelve-year-old.

As for Rod, who was good at throwing language around, who was good at sounding mature and intelligent and making himself *appear* to be bright, in reality, he had

trouble with a logical train of thought. Rod was like someone you'd shake hands with at a big cocktail party, who
might talk to you on the surface but would not say anything real. Rod could not carry on an in-depth conversation.

He described his life as being "sometimes full and sometimes empty, depending on what happens," which sounded
possible, but his reasoning behind the statement lacked any
substance, any compassion. All Rod's talk was contradictory.
He described himself as "emotionless," insisting he was
"full of emotion, yet empty." He considered people to be
nothing more than "objects" and, at the same time, said he
was in love with Charity.

"Truth and lie are all the same within me," he claimed,
using a voice that strained to sound cryptic. "It's hard to
figure out if I'm having a good life or not."

Everyone who dealt with Rod agreed that he wasn't
operating within the realm of the "consensual reality"
most people share. Most people agree on, say, 90 percent
of the world, then everyone has their own 10 percent
skew on reality. But Rod was much more into his own
reality than what was going on with the rest of the world.
He was unable to process his environment adequately. He
was more susceptible to illusionary things.

Playing fantasy games and then extending it into real
life, living in a "coven" or "clan," all that made sense to
Rod because he had a tenuous grip on reality to begin
with. The role-playing game merely greased his fingertips.
Here was a kid who was not in school, who was not
working, who had no structure to his life whatsoever. By
the later part of 1996, Rod was just wandering around
Murray day and night, feeling odd, feeling alienated. The

one time he tried to visit the Calloway County high school, he had been arrested for trespassing.

But his vampire family met his needs. It gave him a father, it gave him rules, it gave him freedom to pursue his fantasies, and Rod liked to live inside his head. He didn't pay sufficient attention to his surroundings. He was too busy with what was going on inside. Rod tended to intellectualize things, but then would overevaluate the big picture and forget about all the details. He was constantly looking at the world globally, trying to view it from beyond.

The psychological experts each noted that Rod perceived himself and his environment only *vaguely*. Because he was caught up in a grandiose vision, ordinary people didn't meet his needs. Rod was satisfied living in a fantasy because he couldn't deal directly with people. He was suspicious, mistrustful, oversensitive to criticism. He would infer the attitudes of others, and even though he was usually wrong, he could only see things his way. Rod thought people were jealous of him. He viewed himself as being persecuted and was paranoid to the point of being delusional.

"A nuclear war may not be such a bad idea," he once wrote, indicating it would be a good end to everyone's suffering, especially his.

Above all, Rod liked to claim that he was "influenced" by others, whether they were people, spirits, ghosts, or unknown entities. Even then, however, he would remain narcissistic, very self-absorbed about it. Rod thought of himself as the big man on campus, as someone who had control over the souls and spirits that inhabited him, as someone who could become the oversoul.

chapter sixty-five

In the year that elapsed between the murders and the upcoming Ferrell trial, Heather visited her parents' grave only once, on Easter Sunday. When she had been deposed in October of 1997, it was the first thing Rod's defense attorneys asked her about.

Her visit to the grave, without so much as a simple flower, was proof of Heather's nonchalance, of her heartless mentality. People were even more suspicious because Heather had a team present for her deposition. Really, it was just her attorney, James Hope, along with her psychologist, Larry Shyers, who was there for emotional support.

All the defense attorneys had been court-appointed, each had their own successful practice in Lake County, and from the looks of things, they were preparing to go to trial. There was no talk of plea bargains—Brad King wasn't offering anything—and everyone's job there, at the five-hour deposition, was seemingly, to implicate Heather.

The defense attorneys were jaded, they had a hard time sitting in a room with the girl they held almost entirely responsible for their clients' problems. If not for Heather, the other four would never have gone to the Wendorfs', the other kids would still be free. This was the consensus among attorneys. Each "vampire" defendant had an entire team working for them, but just six lawyers were in the spotlight: Candace Hawthorne and Bill Lackay, representing Rod; Thomas Carle, representing Charity; Mary Ann Plecas, representing Dana; and Michael Graves and Harry Hackney, representing Scott.

As the deposition progressed, they asked Heather about being caught at the Howard Johnson's parking lot in Baton Rouge, and about her treatment in the juvenile detention center. They asked about things that had little to do with the murders, such as the weeks she spent at her grandmother's house in Orange City and the whole incident with Granny's gun. They pussyfooted around all kind of subjects for a while, including the religious beliefs of Heather's aunt Lily and Heather's stay in the "loony bin" in the Volusia Medical Center.

They wanted to know if Heather, after she had been released from the detention center, the day of her grand jury testimony, had been in contact with Rod. They were surprised to learn that there had been no letters, no telephone conversations, no contact whatsoever.

"Are you aware of any proceeds from life insurance from either your mom or your dad that would be available to you?" Bill Lackay asked.

"I'm not sure. There's so many different things that my father had. I can't hardly keep count of it all."

"As a result of your parents' death," Lackay prodded, "what is your understanding? How much money will you receive? And when I say money, any stocks, bonds, CDs, interest in property, vehicles, life insurance proceeds, the whole ball of wax."

"About a half a million, and my sister will get a half a million. Because my dad basically had a million dollars' worth of everything."

"Does that include the home out on Greentree?"

"Yes."

"And that home on Greentree, is that now in you and your sister's name?"

"Yes."

"Are you all going to put it up for sale?"

"We decided that we don't want to sell it. We are going to fix it up and rent it out."

Her response created side glances. Some of the attorneys rolled their eyes. Heather said she wanted people to live in the place on Greentree. She said that she and her sister sometimes went to visit the house, admitting that they both liked to spend time there. When she said it, it caused the attorneys to bristle; their backs were up.

Apparently it never occurred to any of the adults questioning her that Jeni and Heather were revisiting the only place they knew as "home." To the girls, even though a horrible murder had happened there, it was still the only house they had grown up in, the last remnants of their family.

But the defense attorneys did not seem to understand that. They would later spread the word: Heather's comments proved she was disturbed, and evil to the bone. That she could enjoy one moment in a house of murder . . . that was just too much.

"Tell me how you would go about cutting yourself to drink your blood," Hawthorne said, her voice accusatory.

"Just take a razor blade, cut, drink," Heather said. "It's not like a process or anything."

"Did you drip your blood or drain your blood into a goblet or some type of glass?"

"No."

"You just sucked it right off your skin?"

"I just licked it off my arm or licked it off the cut."

"And did you drink Jeanine's blood?"

"Yes."

"And what was the purpose of this?"

"No real purpose, just the taste."

"Do you like eating rare steak?"

"No, actually, I eat it well-done."

"Is blood something you would develop a craving for?"

"Yeah. It has a distinct taste, but I don't know how to describe it."

"Did you consider yourself to be a *vampire?*" Hawthorne wanted to know.

"No, I mean, not really. I didn't really know that they were real. I just thought about them."

"Do you think they're real now?"

"No."

"Did you? At some point in time?"

"At some point in time I did. But I don't think so anymore."

"Tell me when you thought they were *real.*"

"After I met Rod, I thought they were."

For the panel of attorneys, Heather talked about how she didn't want to have a mundane life, about how she didn't want to "jump on the bandwagon" with all the typical kids at school. She said she wore things that would make her stand out: things like black tights with cutoff shorts and combat boots. She said she dyed her hair red and purple and blue and turquoise, all the colors of the rainbow, that she liked to wear hats. Heather claimed her mother and father didn't mind the way she dressed. They thought it was just a phase. In discussing her sister, the cheerleader, Heather didn't know why Jeni would make the statement about "plotting" their parents' death. Heather had thought about it, she had remembered a chat she and Jeni had had about plotting the death of one of Jeni's ex-boyfriends, because he was threatening her, but that was about it.

Heather told the attorneys that she had suggested Rod Ferrell could either kill Jeni's ex-boyfriend or, at least, beat him up. Heather admitted that she thought Rod was a violent person, because Rod had bragged about beating up his friend. For the same team of attorneys, Matt Goodman would later confirm that, for no apparent reason, Rod knocked his front teeth out.

The attorneys wanted Heather to explain the witch's handbook, and she said it was used for casting spells, invoking spirits. They asked her why she kept gargoyles in her room. She said that in Gothic times, they were used to scare away evil spirits, to protect the home. "That's why they put them on cathedrals," she explained, mentioning that she had received the ceramic gargoyles from her dad as a Christmas gift.

Local newspapers continued to print stories about what investigators thought had happened the night of November 25, 1996. Though none of the four codefendants corroborated it, local news reports stated that Heather Wendorf was believed to be "waiting in Anderson's Buick Skyhawk with Cooper and Kessee, while Ferrell and Anderson went into her home."

It wasn't great journalism; the press didn't even get the make of Anderson's car straight, but there was nothing stopping it. Part of the problem was that local news had to wait weeks for deposition transcripts. In the interim, they relied on trumped-up police theories.

chapter sixty-six

As things were coming down to the wire, the defense attorneys decided to bring Heather in for a second round of questioning. They had her begin with the night of the murders, take them through her ride to Jeremy's. They made her relive the whole course of events that evening.

They discovered that Heather began "putting things together" when she saw Rod and Scott driving the Explorer without shirts on. She testified that the only reason the guys wouldn't be wearing shirts was "there was something on them."

By the time she suspected anything, however, Heather was already in the backseat of the Buick, being told they were on their way to New Orleans. With about fifty dollars in her pocket, Heather testified, she never expected to make it as far as Louisiana. She figured they were bound to run out of gas, because, for one thing, it turned out that none of the others had any cash left.

"Why, did you understand why the boys were being left there at your house?" Dana's attorney, Mary Ann Plecas, wanted to know.

"I didn't think they were being left at my house," Heather explained. "We discussed that they would go and get Jeanine, while me and Charity and Dana went to Jeremy's house."

"And how were they going to get to Jeanine?" Miss Plecas wondered.

"Walk. They were going to walk."

"Is that something, realistically, that can happen between your house and her house?"

"Yes, because I've walked there myself."

"Okay. Did you have any reason, Heather, whatsoever, to believe that anything other than that was going to happen?"

"No."

"Is there anything about Dana Lynn Cooper's behavior that would cause you to think that she believed anything other than that was going to happen?"

"No."

Dana and Charity's lawyers were trying to establish that the other two girls knew nothing about murder until the group was already on their road trip. Unfortunately, Heather wasn't really sure. She thought the two girls found out about it when the guys had switched license plates, but that was only her impression. Heather didn't believe that Dana and Charity were a part of stealing the Explorer, but she couldn't really say.

Charity's attorney, Tommy Carle, wondered how long Heather had been planning to run off with Rod. Heather tried to tell him that they had no concrete plan, that running away was just something Rod always talked about, but the lawyer wanted her to get specific. The fact was that, once Rod appeared in Eustis, Heather did agree to take a trip with him to New Orleans.

"When Rod called that evening," Carle asked, "what did he have to say?"

"That we had to leave that night. That he couldn't wait a week."

"And did you tell him you'd meet him?"

"Well, I wasn't going to go until I knew all the facts. If I had to leave that night, I was going to know why, because I was promised a week. So I told him to come meet me. I gave him sort of directions, not to come directly to my house, I met him down the road."

Heather described meeting Rod and Scott at the end of Greentree. She called the boys "paranoid" and said they were worried about driving in Anderson's stolen car. At the time, Heather had not spoken to Charity or Dana. Heather said she left believing that Rod and Scott were heading over to Jeanine's, and a half hour later, when she jumped the fence with her two backpacks and teddy bear, she saw Charity and Dana driving slowly past the house. The girls stopped at the edge of Heather's driveway, and she jumped in the Buick.

"Okay, did you or *anyone else* in the group, after that time, ever talk about your parents being murdered?"

"Yeah, here and there."

"Okay, so before the arrest, if it was here and there, just explain to me what that means."

"I didn't really like to talk about it, so it wasn't really brought up that much."

"Okay. After Rod told you in Louisiana, did you believe him?"

"Yeah, because he started giving details that sounded right. He started saying how my dad slept on the couch, and my dad always fell asleep in the couch, and . . ."

"Had Rod ever been in your house before that?" Carle interrupted.

"No."

"Your parents, did they even know who Rod was?"

"They knew I had a friend named Rod, but it was really vague for them. They knew I talked to him on the phone, but they never saw him."

Both the defense and law enforcement, the defense attorneys
...

chapter sixty-seven

Even more than law enforcement, the defense attorneys fostered the theory that Heather was a conspirator. Both Candace Hawthorne and Scott's attorney Michael Graves had clients facing execution. They felt Heather should be indicted on two counts of first-degree murder as well.

Hawthorne and Graves filed written arguments outlining the reasons that Heather's grand jury testimony should be turned over to them, but Brad King opposed the idea, and in the end Judge Lockett refused to release the transcripts. The judge didn't agree that her testimony should become a matter of public record.

Arguably, of all the defense attorneys, Mike Graves and his cocounsel, Harry Hackney, had the saddest case to deal with. Scott Anderson was a lost soul who had somehow fallen under Rod Ferrell's spell, even though Scott never believed Rod was a vampire.

The sixteen-year-old participated in Vampire: The Masquerade, enjoyed role-playing and sparring with Rod in the western-Kentucky hills, and had helped with the "strange book" that Rod was working on, the *Book of the Undead*. However, before Rod came back to live in Murray, in the days when Rod lived in Eustis, Scott was a "normal boy."

His foster mom, Karen Puckett, had told police that Scott was not particularly violent, at least, not in the year he was living with her family. Mrs. Puckett recalled that Scott would sometimes get into fights with his younger brothers, but said it was just "typical kid stuff." While in the Puckett home, Scott attended the Church of Christ, studied tae kwon do, and was basically doing very well. In the care of the Pucketts, Scott was a good kid, earning average grades in school. He was never in any kind of trouble.

"Scott said he wasn't ever going back to his parents," Mrs. Puckett confided, "but he changed his mind when his father started buying him things."

"I'm not really sure why the authorities in Kentucky returned him to the Andersons," Hackney later reflected. "If Scott was in foster care and he was doing well, why they would put him back in the violent environment of the Andersons' household is beyond me. His dad went out and got him an old Buick and fixed it up, and I think he used it, trying to entice Scott back."

Getting a car was a big deal, especially for Scott, since he lived out in the sticks, in the little town of Mayfield, more than thirty minutes away from civilization. At least in Murray, there were college kids around, there were pool halls and other decent places to have fun. There was Jaden's crypt, the basement where Rod and Jaden and everyone hung out, and there was Sondra's place at Southside Apartments. Then of course, there was Dana's place, where Scott and Rod could pursue anything that was taboo, where they had the greatest freedom of all.

"Scott basically followed Rod around like a little puppy dog," Hackney concluded. "It might be difficult for adults with stronger personalities to understand, but he had some kind of strange attachment to Rod, where he just followed him around. When you think of the murders in that context . . . the fact that Rod was armed and obviously in a violent rage, it was probably hard for a kid like Scott to do anything."

Although Scott was facing death, to his attorneys, that sentence hardly seemed appropriate. After all, Scott didn't even strike a blow. But Anderson had participated by entering the house and stealing the Explorer, and therefore, under the law for felony murder, he was subject to the same penalty as Ferrell.

Of course, Brad King was relentless in his prosecution of Ferrell and Anderson. King habitually made the victims a part of the penalty process, and clearly, the Wendorf family didn't think the lock-'em-up-and-throw-away-the-key punishment was sufficient for these boys. The Wendorfs expected both Rod Ferrell and Scott Anderson to pay big, and they were putting the pressure on, full throttle.

At a pretrial hearing, the boys' defense attorneys argued that the confessions the teens had given police in Baton Rouge should be nullified. In front of Judge Lockett, Ms. Hawthorne and Mr. Graves sought to block the state attorney from using the police interviews, contending that, under Louisiana law, statements made by juveniles were automatically excluded. When that tack didn't work, Michael Graves suggested the detectives had coerced the confessions. Graves asserted that Detective Gussler led Scott to believe that he'd be spared the death penalty in exchange for his cooperation.

Judge Lockett ruled that Florida law would pertain to all four "vampire teens" involved. Since the crimes had been committed in Florida, they would each be tried as an adult and each be tried separately. All of their confessions were deemed valid and were being edited. These confessions would be shown on a movie-size screen in the Lake County courtroom.

The Public Defenders' Office sent out two thousand questionnaires to test prospective jurors, hoping to find a handful of people who had not already formed an opinion about Ferrell's guilt. With all the extraordinary publicity about the case, it would be almost impossible to find local people who had not read the newspapers or watched any TV coverage. If Roderick Ferrell was to be convicted, the attorneys hoped that, at least, they would be able to spare his life.

But Rod's legal team was having problems. Their change-of-venue request had been denied, their motion to sequester the jury had been denied, and through it all, the pretrial publicity raged on.

Meanwhile, Michael Graves had done the math on Anderson: on a good day, he would get life without the possibility of parole. Of course, there had been a time when a life sentence in the state of Florida had meant twenty-five years, but those days were over. For Scott, a life sentence without parole would mean just that. On a bad day, Scott would be sentenced to death. Those were the choices.

For both Roderick Justin Ferrell and Howard Scott Anderson, the news that Brad King wasn't willing to budge, that the prosecutor expected an eye for an eye, came as a total and complete shock. Both boys had been holding on to the hope that their youth would save them. Neither of them seemed to really listen, even when their lawyers tried to make things plain.

As Rod's trial date closed in, Sondra and Harrell paid more visits to Rod. Up until then, Sondra Gibson hadn't seen her boy all that much. She couldn't, because she had spent part of the year sitting in jail in Calloway County awaiting her own fate. Ms. Gibson was facing felony charges regarding her letters to Jaden's fourteen-year-old brother, Jamie, and eventually plead guilty to soliciting rape and soliciting sodomy, for which she served six months. Each count carried a twelve month sentence, but her plea deal allowed her to spend the rest of her time out on parole.

Sondra tried to comfort Rod. At one point, she told him he was immortal, that it didn't matter what happened in the courtroom. She would be eternally waiting for him, with Jaden, his sire.

chapter sixty-eight

Harrell and his wife offered their prayers. They wanted Roderick to turn to God. Sondra felt sorry for her son. She had plead guilty, using mental illness as a defense, just so she could travel to Florida to stand by Rod, just so she could visit him every day. A court-appointed expert had filed a report in Calloway County saying that Ms. Gibson was "delusional." Now, it would be Rod's turn.

The morning of his trial, February 5, 1998, Rod kept his head down. He really wasn't looking at the Wendorfs, who occupied the two front rows on the left. On the right, directly behind him, sat his grandparents, his mother, and his aunt. It was all hitting him, the reality of the chair, and he was squirming for his life.

For weeks, he had talked about pleading guilty, he had

brought it up with his defense team. He thought a guilty plea would save him. Now, as Brad King began his opening statement, Rod eyeballed the boxes of files, all the evidence, all the mass preparation.

King had come heavily armed. From his viewpoint, the road to justice would be swift. A genetics scientist linked blood and skin found beneath Ruth's fingernails to Ferrell. The odds that anyone else could have that same DNA were 15 million to one. A shoe print linked Ferrell's boots to prints found near Ruth's body. And of course, there was Ferrell's videotaped statement, most of which would be shown to jurors.

The crowd that had filtered into the small courtroom had no idea what was happening, however, when out of nowhere, Rod's defense team asked the judge to halt King's opening statement. All of a sudden, they wanted to stop the trial, a thing never done, and for a moment, there was mass confusion.

Assistant Public Defender Bill Lackay approached the bench, and a few minutes later, with Rod and Candace at his side, he made the pronouncement: Roderick Justin Ferrell wished to change his plea to guilty to the murders of Richard Wendorf and Naoma Ruth Queen.

Before God and everyone else, Rod's voice cracked as he whispered, "Yes," he knew he was waiving his rights to a trial. The jury was promptly escorted out of the room, the crowd dispersed, and Sondra broke down in tears. She wanted to touch her son, but court deputies wouldn't allow it. Sondra, along with the rest of the Gibsons and the Wendorfs, was cleared out of the courtroom.

"We live forever," Sondra defiantly hissed at reporters, stepping into the gallery, taking her fifteen minutes of fame. "He's a good boy," Harrell added, moving toward the cameras into the spotlight. "He said he did it," Harrell said flatly, "now, we're going on from there."

Bill Lackay later admitted that his client was "scared to death" but decided to gamble, hoping his honesty would bring forgiveness. After all his talk about immortality, after all his boasting about death being a "formality," Rod didn't want to die. He was fighting for life in prison.

Brad King told the press that Ferrell's plea wouldn't be admissible against the other three teens who awaited trial. Those trial dates would not be set, he told reporters, until Rod Ferrell's sentencing hearing was done with. Roderick Ferrell's fate would be determined first.

Even though Ferrell plead guilty, Brad King was still obligated to go through the presentation of all the evidence. He still needed to show the jury the degree of Rod's guilt, the monstrosity of the crime. For seven days, as the sentencing phase progressed, every state's witness would testify, just as if it were an actual trial. Pictures, tapes, blood, DNA experts, all of this would be presented for the jurors before they would make their ultimate recommendation.

At times, the evidence was so gruesome, it made the worst horror movie seem tame. When the courtroom was darkened so jurors could watch Ferrell's confession, people were actually gasping. It was difficult to watch Ferrell, a thin-lipped, long-haired freak, gloat about the brutal murders. Among other things, jurors watched Rod tell Lake County law enforcers that killing the Wendorfs gave him a rush:

"You have any other aliases or go by any other name?" Wayne Longo asked calmly.

"No, just Rod."

"Okay. And did you change? Didn't you say you had

blood all over you when you were up in the house? Did you stay that way?"

"No, right before we stopped the Buick, like unpacked everything, it was on the way that we were going to Jeanine's house, we stopped at a gas station, I think it was Circle K. I had Scott go in and get wet rags."

"Okay."

"And I just took my shirt off and threw it."

"So, now, you are bare back?"

"I was bare back and totally wet from washing myself."

"Is that where you threw the shirt, in the outside garbage can or in the woods?"

"No, I set it on fire and threw it out in a field, so it's all ash now. Look, I'm being very congenial and cooperative, so that's why I'm wondering about these shackles, I'm like . . ."

"Well, you've got to understand you're in Louisiana now," the Lake County lawman told him, "you're not in Florida and we have no control right now. You know, we've got to play by their rules."

"Rod, if you could just tell me one thing. If you would?"

"Anything."

"You said when you started swinging the crowbar on the male subject, that you really felt, I was trying to think of the word. You felt good? You felt . . ."

"There was a rush."

"A rush, okay."

"To actually feel that I was taking a life because that's just like the old philosophy: if you can take a life, you can become a god for a split second. And it actually kind of felt that way for a minute," Rod said, "but if I were a god, I wouldn't exactly be here, would I?"

"How many times did you hit him?"

"Around fifty."

"Together, total, or each?"

"Total for him. For her, it was about thirty. They were really fucking hard hits because his face was just, it looked like a rubber mask, it didn't even look real. And her head, her brains were just, like, oozing out of her skull."

"Did Scott do anything? Stopped you from doing it? Watched you?"

"He just watched and smiled."

"He got a rush then, obviously? Is that what kind of smile you are referring to?"

"He was, like, just really happy. Almost like a kid at an amusement park for the first time."

As Rod continued to boast, to make outrageous statements, people in the courtroom were floored. Rod claimed that all the law enforcement officials in Murray were a part of a cult.

For the Lake County audience, it was not only horrifying to watch the boy pat himself on the back, it was maddening.

chapter sixty-nine

After Brad King proved that Rod acted with premeditation, establishing that Rod acted with unusual malice and cruelty, it was time for the public defenders to put on the Rod Ferrell show.

On Rod's behalf, everyone from Jaden Murphy to Matt Goodman testified as the defense paraded up a line of people, including Sondra and even Charity, who, against her attorney's advice, took the stand wearing shackles. Pleading for Rod's life, Charity called her boyfriend "sensitive."

The only person absent from the proceedings, it seemed, was Heather.

As Ferrell's history was unveiled, the psychological experts testified that Rod practiced "dark magic" because he intended to "release evil into the world." Dr. Harry Krop talked about Rod's upbringing, touching on the claims of sexual abuse, blaming Sondra Gibson for spending more time with her boyfriends than she did with her son. Krop testified that Sondra had her own schizotypal personality disorder and called the Gibsons "one of the most dysfunctional family situations I've ever experienced."

Shannon Yohe, who had already testified for the prosecution, took the stand to talk about her happier days with Rod. For the court, Shannon pointed to photographs of herself, when she and Rod attended Sondra's wedding in Daytona. It was a second marriage for Sondra, one that would only last a couple of weeks.

As Jaden Steven Murphy was about to take the stand, he blew a kiss at Rod from across the courtroom. He told the court that he still loved Rod and asserted that he was "the closest thing to a father" that Rod had ever known. "We don't kill," Murphy testified, "we're supposed to have the highest admiration for life." Murphy told jurors that Ferrell violated their vampire codes, admitting that he himself still participated in "vampirism."

"I'm nineteen, not thousands of years old," Jaden testified, flashing his pierced tongue at news cameras, making bizarre faces. "I know I can die," Jaden insisted, telling the court that unlike Sondra Gibson, he was not afraid of garlic or sunlight. Jaden admitted that he was known as the Prince of the City in Murray and said that Rod's mother was in love with him, pulling a brand-new valentine card from his pocket, which contained a "nice little love letter" from Sondra.

Jaden looked over at Sondra with a smirk, calling her "messed up in the head," testifying that Sondra had made insane promises about the three of them "living together" when Rod got out of jail. Sondra even proposed marriage, telling Jaden she would love him "for eternity." Jaden handed the valentine letter over to the court to be logged as evidence:

[Brad King] wants everyone to believe Rod's to blame for all the crimes, not Scott or Heather, and that I raised him real main stream, which, with my help, Rod's lawyers are going to get me up on the stand for 4 hours and blow the idea of me raising Rod in a normal home—clear out of the water!!

When Sondra finally took the stand, complete with dark eye shadow, a black suit, and black fingernails, her testimony was tearful. She obviously felt violated by Jaden's cavalier attitude. The boy had embarrassed her. It was also apparent that she cared about her son, but had no logical or reasonable way of showing it.

Responding to Hawthorne's carefully prepared questions, Sondra Gibson told the court about Rod's sweet childhood, about how "Roddie" was so concerned for life, he actually dug up a fish one day. Apparently, the boy had caught it, but the fish was too small to eat, so first he buried the creature, but then he wanted to see if it was okay. With big tears in her eyes, Rod's grandmother Rosetta would tell the court the same story. "Roddie didn't want the fish to be so cold down there," Rosetta testified. "He would go in the backyard and dig it up to see if it was all right. He never hurt nobody."

For the jurors, Sondra (calling herself "Star") pointed to posters filled with various pictures of her son. She described the photos of Rod and all the stages of his childhood: the freckle-faced, strawberry-blond five-year-old who was pudgy; the infant Rod with Sondra and Rick in the hospital delivery room; the adolescent Rod having a birthday party; the clean-cut Rod, in a family portrait with Harrell, Rosetta, and Sondra.

There was even a photo of Rod, age fourteen, wielding a sword, shrouded in dark clothes, his face completely hidden by a black mask. But the eeriest picture, a photo that was put into evidence but never discussed openly in court, was one of "Roddie" at age two, taken in Winter Garden, Florida. Dressed up like a street prostitute, the toddler wore full makeup—painted lips, rouge, eye shadow—and was dressed in a tiny, sheer, black negligee, accessorized with a beaded choker and silver high-heeled shoes.

In her testimony, Sondra claimed that Rod was born with the umbilical cord wrapped around his neck, cutting off oxygen at birth and possibly causing brain damage. She also mentioned Rod's alleged case of encephalitis, another potential cause for Rod's disturbed mind. Under cross-examination, however, these claims could not be substantiated. Brad King held up a copy of Rod's "baby book," which recorded the child's growth, milestones, and medical particulars. The prosecutor also had a copy of Rod's birth record, of Rod's "Newborn Assessment Sheet."

Sondra reviewed the documents and admitted that there was no mention of Roddie's afflictions. She told the court the medical records were invalid, that someone must have filled them out incorrectly.

"When you lived in Winter Garden," Hawthorne asked, "Rod was admitted into the hospital with a severe illness?"

"Yes. He started going into convulsions at the house, so we rushed him to the hospital and they said they didn't expect him to live overnight. They thought he had some type of disease. I don't know exactly what it was."

"And how old was he?"

"He was two."

"Now, were you using drugs at that time?"

"Well, I was addicted to phenobarbital and I was drinking a lot."

"After the Winter Garden hospitalization, were you dating men at that time?"

"Yes."

"About how many boyfriends did you have during that time?"

"I couldn't count."

As Hawthorne moved Sondra through Rod's troubled times, his mother admitted that, because the Gibsons moved around so often, it was difficult for little Rod to develop a sense of roots. She herself was never around on weekends, she testified. She admitted that at one time she had been a "prostitute," that she had worked in a nightclub called Faces as a "dancer."

Sondra talked about an incident that occurred when Rod was fifteen and suddenly became emotional, breaking down in sobs. Apparently, after Sondra married husband number two, Darren Braven, she decided to move up to Michigan with him, leaving her son back in Murray with her folks, which was a turning point for Rod.

"Why did you leave Rod behind?" Hawthorne wondered.

"Because he was going to school and I didn't want to keep moving him," Sondra said, her tears flowing. "But Darren had a whole other story. I didn't know at the time, but Darren took Rod aside. I found out after I had already got to Michigan, and Darren told him that I was never coming back."

Sondra cried uncontrollably, promising the defense attorney that when she found out what Darren had said, she got on a Greyhound bus and immediately returned to Murray. As she testified, Sondra looked over at her son—who was sitting erect and staring at her from behind the defense table. She just started wailing. The court had to give her a moment to calm down.

"Now, Rod began having trouble at school when he

was fifteen, didn't he?" Hawthorne continued, trying to bring Sondra back down to earth.

"He started having trouble in middle school."

"But when you moved back to Murray, he *especially* started having trouble?"

"I wouldn't say especially, no."

"He was cutting classes?"

"Yes."

"He was sleeping all day long?"

"Yes."

"When he was going to school, he would dress in all black?"

"Yes."

"He was being disrespectful to the teachers?"

"To one that I know of."

"And you approved of him smoking?"

"I let him smoke in the house, but he wasn't supposed to smoke at school."

"Were you aware that your son was having drug problems at this time?"

"Yes."

"Were you aware that he was using acid and LSD?"

"Not at that particular time."

"Were you aware that he was drinking alcohol?"

"Not when he was going to school, no."

"And were you dating throughout this period?"

"Yes."

"And, in fact," Hawthorne asked, her voice filled with distaste, "wouldn't you go to social functions with your son and his girlfriend?"

"Yes."

"Did you ever tell anybody about your son and others *drugging* you and having sex with you?"

"I never told anyone that my son had sex with me," Sondra quipped, "that's ridiculous."

"Did you ever tell anybody that the reason you wrote the letter to the fourteen-year-old was because you were trying to get into the cult?"

"I may have said that to someone, but I don't recall saying that, no."

But of course, Sondra "Star" Gibson *had* said it. She had said it to the press, to her defense attorneys, and to anyone who would listen. According to Sondra, the only reason she had approached Jamie, the *only reason* she had written the letters and sent Jamie her key, was because she was trying to gain access to Rod's coven. She needed to get involved with his vampirism, she claimed, so she could figure out how to get Rod to stop participating in blood rituals.

"You knew your son was using drugs at this time?" Hawthorne asked again.

"At the time, I knew he was using heroin and LSD, yes."

Sondra admitted that she hadn't placed Rod in any kind of treatment center, implying that her fifteen-year-old was unreachable. She told the court that she had taken Rod to the Department of Children and Family Services in Kentucky, that she had filed documents to declare her son an "uncontrollable minor." She said she tried to place Rod in counseling, that she herself had begun attending a parenting class, but it was all "a big joke" and "a total waste of time."

"During this time, did your son have an upside-down cross hanging in his room?" Hawthorne wondered.

"Yes, uh-huh."

"And he had his room draped in black?"

"Yes."

"And he had an altar with the Necronomicon on it? Do you know what the Necronomicon is?"

"Yes, I know what the Necronomicon is," Sondra huffed. "He had a table with candles and symbols on it, yes."

"Okay. And he was cutting himself?"

"Yes."

"And he was engaging in the ritual of drinking blood with others?"

"Yes."

"And you didn't have him hospitalized?"

"No."

Sondra claimed she hadn't actually seen any of Rod's drugs, except for a joint in the living room. She admitted that she allowed Rod to dye his hair black, to dress in black bodysuits, to paint his face with makeup, in the image of the main character from the movie The Crow. Sondra told the court that she allowed her boyfriend Kyle to tattoo symbols on Rod, that she saw nothing wrong with being involved in the occult.

"You indicated earlier that you filed a complaint with the juvenile courts in Kentucky?" Brad King asked on cross-examination.

"Yes," Sondra told him, sounding sheepish.

"That was in order to have your son, basically, controlled by the court, since you couldn't do it? Correct?"

"That was the General Work Court, yes."

"And, as a part of that, you told them about the things he was doing? The drugs and the self-mutilation and all that, correct?"

"I went a little bit beyond that, but, yes."

"And that was done so that, in your opinion, so that somebody could help him, right?"

"So that someone actually could help me and him both," Sondra told King, feeling sorry for herself, "but especially Rod."

Under this line of questioning, Brad King established that, because of Sondra's complaint filed with the juvenile courts, Roderick Ferrell had been required to appear before a judge in Calloway County on November 25, 1996.

King produced a state's exhibit, flashing the document at Sondra, asking her to read, for the court, the date that Rod was supposed to appear. She looked it over, glanced it up and down, and spoke to the prosecutor in a childlike voice.

"I know he was supposed to write this paper, and he didn't write the paper," she testified, referring to the document. "It says he was supposed to come back November fourth. I know he didn't write the paper and he went to court. I know this for a fact."

"Doesn't it say at the bottom," King asked, pointing to the document, "that he is ordered to appear back in court on November twenty-fifth?"

"Yes, it says that."

"That's the same Monday that these murders were committed, correct?"

"I have no idea, actually. I'd have to see the documents."

"Your Honor," the prosecutor muttered, "I have nothing else."

chapter seventy

Usually, defense attorneys like to have a trial, they know it's important, regardless of how much evidence is stacked up, to allow the jury to come to the conclusion that a person is guilty. That way, the jury can get out all their anger and frustration, they can feel, in part, that they have performed their sense of "civic duty" in the guilt phase.

If Rod had allowed the trial to proceed, the jury would have viewed the posters of the bloody bodies, they would have watched the videotape of his arrogant bragging, they would have listened to the testimony by DNA experts, and then, a week or so would have elapsed before they would have to consider Rod's sentence. The time gap between the end of the trial and the start of the sentencing hearing would allow the twelve jurors to digest things. That week could have proven to be critical in Rod's case.

But when Rod pulled the plug on the trial, he had set

himself up, because now, the jury would see blood and gore and cocky attitudes during the time when they would be asked to recommend a penalty. There would be no cooling-off period. Rod had yanked the rug out from under them in the most poignant of circumstances.

After they viewed a portion of Ferrell's videotaped interview for the second time, after they reconsidered the psychological aspects of Rod's borderline personality, the jurors rejected the notion that he was psychotic and unable to determine right from wrong. After reviewing the grainy black-and-white police tape, where Rod Ferrell blew cigarette smoke and referred to himself as "God," the jury of twelve voted unanimously to sentence the seventeen-year-old to die in Florida's electric chair.

"Ferrell knew that his victims were real people," Brad King later told the press, "he wore his victims' real blood on his clothes after his crimes."

The Wendorf family wept and held hands as the advisory sentence was announced. Roderick Ferrell, wearing a starched white shirt and a tie, his formal attire including a black velvet jacket, had no real reaction at all. Even Brad King was reduced to tears, but not Rod. When he saw his mom sobbing, Rod's eyes welled up, but then Rod's veneer, his public mask, recaptured his strange face.

Ferrell's attorneys told media that a sentence of death would be "too harsh" a punishment for the boy. They requested a delay in the sentencing hearing, telling reporters that execution in the electric chair was "cruel and unusual punishment" for such a young offender, but they were denied any special considerations by the judge.

Jury foreman Joseph Crumpton told reporters that the strength of the prosecutor's evidence was "insurmountable." Despite the highly charged emotions of the jurors, egged on by the subject of *Heather*, two jury members initially thought Rod should be sentenced to life. However, when it came time to actually cast the ballots, all twelve agreed on the death penalty.

"The defense absolutely pushed Heather on us," the foreman said, "trying to make us believe Heather manipulated Rod, but I think it was vice versa."

It was true, Candace Hawthorne had done everything possible to shift some of the blame to Heather. She reminded jurors that Miss Wendorf didn't flee or try to talk to police when she ran away with Ferrell. She brought witnesses forward, Jennifer Wendorf among them, to testify that Heather had talked about it, that she wanted her parents *dead*.

Evidently, the defense didn't concern themselves with the implications of their stampede on Heather. If Heather really *had* talked to Rod about the killings months before, if she had seriously *plotted* their murders with him, as they tried to make it appear, that would only make Rod Ferrell all the more culpable. That would certainly create less room for leniency.

Even though Rod had been convicted of the two counts of first-degree murder, Judge Jerry T. Lockett still had to make the final decision about the sentence. Though everyone expected Lockett to be strict, the Lake County judge had the authority to overrule the jury, to sentence Roderick to life without parole. At Ferrell's Spencer Hearing, a proceeding enacted by the Supreme Court of Florida to allow the defendant the opportunity to be heard *one last time*, the defense team did their best to present additional evidence before the judge. The public defenders were taking their best shot.

* * *

A teary-eyed Charity Kessee testified that Rod suffered from "mood swings," that he made "bizarre statements." Charity said she could sometimes reason with Rod, but had to plead the Fifth on most questions. Charity was still awaiting her own trial, and her lawyer was furious about her testimony. Charity hadn't been handed a subpoena. She hadn't been given immunity. She was there to testify of her own free will. In her petite little voice, she wanted to tell the court that Rod was "usually normal." Charity thought Rod should never have been thrown out of Calloway High School. She thought that was where all of Rod's problems really started.

The next morning, when Roderick Justin Ferrell took the stand, in a striped, preppy, button-down shirt, wearing his hair short and slicked back, he was as polite as he could be. He spoke softly into the microphone, taking an oath to tell the truth, the whole truth, and nothing but . . .

Rod said he finally realized the Wendorfs were "three-dimensional people" when he saw the Wendorf family grieving in the courtroom. Of everyone, Rick's twin brother, Billy, seemed the most outraged and upset about the crime. Billy looked identical to Rick, but even that didn't fluster Rod.

A sensitive man, Billy could hardly bear the pain of his loss. He cringed and wept bitterly throughout the proceedings, and when it was his turn to make a victim's statement, he told the judge that Roderick should be executed. He did not want Rod to have the privilege of seeing sunshine, of hearing birds chirping, of weight lifting in prison.

The state relied upon six aggravating circumstances to secure a death sentence, but by taking the stand, Rod thought he could negate them. The only thing he wouldn't elaborate on was the "rape" he had supposedly suffered. He said he "blocked most of it out" of his memory.

But his aunt Lyzetta had already testified during the sentencing phases. She had told the court that Harrell Gibson had tried to kiss her, that her father was "sexually inappropriate." Having received a subpoena, having been forced to air her childhood trauma, Lyzetta testified that Harrell had laid her down on the bed and "rubbed himself against" her, that he "rubbed his hands up and down" his own child. Meanwhile, outside the courtroom Harrell vehemently denied Lyzetta's abuse claims.

Of course, Rod didn't really want to talk about his grandpa, nor did he have much to say about his own dad, Rick. Rod had a clear memory of playing Dungeons & Dragons with him, but that was about it. Hawthorne asked Rod to talk a bit about the game, about creating a character on paper and then pretending to *be* that person, so Rod described D&D the best he could. It was obvious that Rod didn't really care to describe role-playing, that he had moved far beyond childhood pastimes.

chapter seventy-one

"Now, did you have a conversation with Heather Wendorf in the late spring, early summer of 1996?" Hawthorne asked, being very dramatic with Rod, who sat on center stage for Court TV, the rest of the media, and all the courtroom to watch.

"Yes."

"Would you tell the court about those conversations?" she asked, using a motherly voice.

"At this time, I was actually having more correspondence with Heather than with Jeanine, and she would express about the vampirism, her questioning about that. Basically her lust for that lifestyle," Rod said, hesitating, "and also, she had told me that her problems with her family were increasing."

"Did she tell you what kind of problems she was having?"

"No."

"All right. Tell us about some of the things that she said about her family. What would she tell you?"

"She really didn't state much about her family. The most I recall, she said that her father was okay, but that her mother, she didn't like her."

"Did she ever tell you that her family was hurting her?"

"Yes."

"Did she ever tell you that she wanted to run away?"

"There were times when she would actually cry," Rod testified, sneering at the Wendorfs. "Heather would get hysterical over the phone, and me, coming from an abusive life, and being around people that have had abuse like Scott Anderson. I took the symptoms from her crying as being real. It seemed like she was really being abused."

Candace Hawthorne had a litany of questions, all designed to make Heather look guilty. The defense attorney tried to get Rod to explain the type of abuse Heather complained about, but Rod had no details. Hawthorne was doing her best to put Heather on trial, to make sure the judge realized how unfair a death sentence would be, particularly since Heather was the alleged instigator in this case. Heather was the one who had two sides, Hawthorne wanted to imply. Heather was the one who used her magical side to coax Rod.

"Did Heather ever say anything about the fact that her parents would never let her go, and she would like to actually get rid of them in order to leave?"

"Yes," Rod said.

"Did she ever talk about her family's money?"

"No."

"Now, when you came to Florida in November, did you and Heather have a conversation in the cemetery?"

"Yes, we did."

"Did Heather know you were coming to Florida?"

"Yes, her and Jeanine LeClaire both, but no one was really sure when."

"Tell us about the conversation you had with Heather Wendorf in the cemetery."

"That day, I believe it was Monday. We walked over to the cemetery to initiate her crossover."

"Did she say anything about her parents?"

"No, just the fact that her mother was going to pick her up that day."

Under oath, Rod claimed that he had been using all kinds of drugs on his trip down to Florida—LSD, marijuana, and various pills—but none of the other kids in the car seemed to notice. Charity, in particular, felt sure that Rod was straight, even though Rod maintained he swallowed eight hits of acid that disastrous Monday.

Rod also told the court that Heather condoned the theft of her parents' Explorer, stating that she "didn't have a problem with it." He asserted that Heather directed him to the car keys in her home—on the dresser in the master bedroom—but in reality, the Wendorfs kept their keys inside their automobiles. The whole family was aware of that.

Later, a fuss was made about Heather supposedly sending Rod into her house for the keys. Defense attorneys for the remaining "teen vampires" would provide each other with theories that Heather Wendorf was basically sending Rod into the house to kill her parents. They were sure Heather was deliberately setting the scene for an altercation by giving Rod the command to take the Explorer keys.

The only problem with these theories: they couldn't be proven.

Heather said she never knew about the plan to steal the Explorer, and Howard Scott Anderson would later reconfirm that. Indeed, if Rod was now telling this story, it appeared to be a device he'd thought of as a way to save his own skin. He certainly had reason to believe that pinning things on Heather might help.

"She also asked me to grab her father's knife and her mother's pearls," Rod told Hawthorne, gazing directly at the jury, "and I asked her, after she had asked about the pearls and the knife, I said, 'since you have spoken so much about killing your parents over the past year, do you still want me to?'"

"And what did she say?" Hawthorne asked, her eyes bulging.

"She said yes."

"Did Scott overhear this portion of your conversation?"

"Not that part."

"Okay. Shannon Yohe testified that you made statements in her kitchen regarding the Wendorfs. Would you tell the court what you all talked about, specifically, in that regard?"

"I do remember making comments about killing people in general, but, to my recollection, I don't remember specifics about the Wendorfs."

The following day, newspapers in Lake County ran full-color pictures of Rod on the witness stand. One headline was worse than another. From the Orlando paper:

FERRELL BLAMES HEATHER.
DO YOU WANT ME TO KILL YOUR PARENTS?
SHE SAID "YES."

chapter seventy-two

On the day before final judgment, newspapers ran stories that Rod was "a little bit disappointed" with the jury's recommendation. The night before, Rod had decided to hold a little news conference from jail, telling the press, "I really and truly thought they didn't weigh the factors out."

Not once did Rod say he was sorry for what he had done. He had a cavalier attitude, even about his own impending doom. The jail guards and chaplain had tried to prepare him: Judge Lockett was not expected to reverse the jurors' recommendation. The judge had already sent eight others to death row.

"I don't hate Heather," Rod told reporters. "I'm sorry she can be free and make money off her parents and not feel any guilt for the death of her parents."

Rod said he still considered himself a vampire, but told

the press he was "never in a cult." He hoped to improve his public image and wanted the news to get to the judge.

"When I came here, I was in a state of dementia," Ferrell was quoted. "I had many delusions about life. But over the course of a year, I have had the time to see the reality about things. There's been a very drastic change."

Sondra wore a frilly, white blouse, her bra straps hanging out, her black, kinky hair all the more flagrant. Her tiny five-foot frame sat hunched over in the front row of the courtroom, her dark purple fingernails clasped together, her hands positioned in prayer, like an angel. She was waiting for her son to be led in by the bailiffs. She hardly looked at her sister, Lyzetta, a tall strawberry blonde, the opposite of Sondra in every way. Their dad, Harrell, sat next to them, sporting a pin-striped suit and flashy tie. The old man sat erect with his head up high, but his eyes were troubled. He seemed like a figure frozen in a tableau, unaware of what his part really was.

The evidence on the tables in the courtroom sat wrapped in brown paper. Because Rod had confessed, because every little detail didn't need to be proven, much of the evidence hadn't been opened. The official red tape remained intact, so in a weird way, the items looked almost like Christmas or birthday packages, all ready to be shipped in the mail.

When Candace Hawthorne waltzed into the courtroom, her long blond hair flowing against a cherry-red wool suit, she looked strained. The woman was clearly worn-out. She had an expression of knowing.

Brad King had already made his statement during the sentencing phase. He told the judge and jury to "do what's right."

Speaking just above a whisper, King reminded the

court of the five state's witnesses who had testified, who had brought hard evidence into the courtroom—the tiles from the Wendorf house, the combat boots—they had lined it all up. He had asked that the sentence be determined based on scientific principle, not emotion. King called Ferrell a liar and a manipulator. He reminded the court that Ferrell had come up with every excuse to blame others, that he had refused to accept responsibility.

Holding up a poster-board diagram of the Wendorf house, the prosecutor showed where Ferrell found the murder weapon, where Anderson pulled the phones, where Ferrell stopped in the kitchen to get himself a drink. King described the confrontation with Ruth, showing how Ferrell had almost decapitated her, which was Rod's "favorite method of killing," according to what he told Shannon.

The crime was cold, calculated, and premeditated, King repeated once again, insisting that there had been a plan beforehand, that each fact proved the following aggravating circumstances: the homicides were committed during a burglary, making them felony murders; the crime was committed for the purpose of avoiding lawful arrest; the crime was committed for financial gain; and as to Naoma Ruth Queen, the crime was especially heinous, atrocious, and cruel.

By then, Roderick Justin Ferrell had been blown up larger-than-life. Everyone had seen the newspaper and magazine clips featuring pictures of Rod as a vampire. Jaden had turned them over to the press and to the public defender, boasting about the night he and Rod had posed for each other in the Old Salem Cemetery. Back then, Rod seemed to be having great fun with it. Rod was hanging upside down, Rod held a wooden stake above a coffin,

Rod was even flying off tombstones. The photos would become legend. They were living proof of Rod's vampiric ways.

Then, just as the court was called to order, just as everyone stood watching the judge enter in his flowing black robe, when the stillness hung over the room like a shroud, the cameras all turned to Rod. For what seemed an eternity, there was dead silence.

As Roderick stood before Judge Jerry T. Lockett's packed courtroom, February 27, 1998, Lockett warned the audience that there would be "no loud outbursts." Ferrell had been convicted on four counts: two counts of murder in the first degree, two counts of armed burglary.

Under the watchful eye of strong bailiffs, Rod looked small and thin. Garbed in jailhouse orange and wearing spectacles, Rod looked flimsy. All of a sudden, he was just a kid, just another person who had fallen through life's cracks. He didn't look like a killer.

But Rod had admitted to murder. He had bragged that he beat the Wendorfs until "they finally stopped breathing," that he "smacked the fuck out of them." And now, Judge Jerry T. Lockett sentenced him to death.

Heather later admitted that she once thought "Rod was deep, Rod was emotional." Heather had really believed that "Rod had more character than most people," that he was "poetic."

After the sentence was pronounced, Heather received the news by phone. She was relieved, yet sad. Nothing had really changed for her. She had wanted to be present for the pronouncement, but there was no way for her to be physically in the courtroom. The media would have eaten her alive.

Afterward, Rod was totally without remorse, without

any visible sign of emotion. When he reflected on the murders, he told reporters, "At the time, I was very evil. I had been evil for many years. I enjoyed my evil."

Of course, Sondra had managed to hang on to her own fantasy, remembering Rod just the way she wanted to. "Rod slept with a little teddy bear ever since he was a child," she told the cameras, pretending she'd always have her little boy. However, the dark circles under her eyes told a different tale. The whites of her pupils were streaked with blood vessels, yet Sondra insisted that she could sleep with herself. The woman's left eye had a frightening blood speck near the left pupil. As Sondra pontificated about her son's innocence, about how unfair the justice system was, her pale white skin grew even paler.

Rod Ferrell had been held accountable, and Sondra's fantasy world no longer mattered. Rod would no longer be subject to her erratic behavior. For Rod, the fantasy bond had finally ended. For years, he had blamed the world, he had thought he could correct his life by focusing on social evils, by being an assassin.

The grandiosity of being immortal, the ecstasy of sexual conquests with teenage girls, the fulfilled sense of taking someone's blood, all of that magical possession that Rod thrived on was over. He was destined for separation and aloneness, destined to solitary confinement, as the youngest of 350 inmates on Florida's death row.

Rod would later describe it as "hell" but would insist that he had "no regrets." He would assert that if he hadn't killed the Wendorfs, he would have been "propelled" to kill someone else, "at some other place." He admitted that for him, committing murder was "inevitable."

"Ricky's brothers, I have no sympathy for," Ferrell told

filmmaker Ed Robbins, for a documentary to be aired on Court TV.

"William felt no sympathy for me," Rod pouted, "and the other one, Bobby, he's a *really good* actor.

"I believe you reach true life through *death*, so there's really no consequence," Rod insisted. "Pain and regret equals a cancerous disease," he said, smiling, "so, why bother?"

For her part, Heather would tell people that she "didn't have a role" in the murders, but most folks didn't believe her. They didn't believe that she loved her parents. They didn't believe that she never wanted to see them hurt. They didn't care that her whole world was gone. Of the Wendorfs, only her grandfather, Jim, had pity for the girl. So, Heather had to start from scratch.

"I miss my parents so much," Heather said later, a single teardrop streaming down her face, "I think of them all the time."

Though Heather was offered all kinds of money, thousands of dollars, from tabloid TV shows, she turned everything down. Though she had received requests from *around the world* to tell her story, Heather wasn't interested in getting any kind of press. She had hired an attorney to keep the media away; she wanted to get on with her life. Really, Heather had more important concerns, because Jerry Lockett had requested that Brad King consider reopening the case against her.

Sheriff George Knupp was still after Heather; he had managed to rile up the judge, the public, and the local media. The lawman and his investigators felt sure they could get Heather convicted, and they were doing everything possible to bring a second grand jury into session. They were questioning people all over Lake County and even considered asking people to sign a petition to go after

Heather. They were badgering out-of-state witnesses to return to Lake County to elaborate on their testimony against Heather. They were collecting hundreds of pages to resubmit to the state attorney. To Brad King, they handed over deposition transcripts, personal letters, just anything that they thought hadn't been presented to the grand jury the first time. The sheriff and his men were out for the kill.

It took months before Brad King reconvened a second grand jury, before he honored the sheriff's request and presented the whole case again. On the day the story hit the news, December 8, 1998, the local paper featured a picture of Knupp holding a "strategy session" with his team of investigators. They were looking for a way to get Heather Ann Wendorf indicted as an accessory to murder.

"I think we'll be able to show," Knupp said, "in our testimony, that Heather put Ferrell in a confrontation scenario when she asked him to go into her home and take her mother's necklace, a knife of her father's, and also the keys to the car."

James Hope wondered publicly why Sheriff Knupp wasn't out trapping bank robbers, why Knupp wasn't busy executing the backlog of eight thousand warrants in his office. Mr. Hope told reporters that Knupp's report was a "manifesto."

Indeed, the new grand jury would be presented with three and a half inches of support documents, which they would have to consider.

chapter seventy-three

While awaiting their trials, Scott Anderson, Charity Kessee, and Dana Cooper were all treated like celebrities by fellow inmates. Housed in the Lake County Jail, they received special requests from the media, were the topic of conversation for corrections officers, and the envy of prisoners' eyes.

None of them said they were vampires, but people wanted to believe that. People wanted to think they were housed with supernatural beings. For the three teens, it wasn't amusing. They were in deep trouble and were scared, especially after hearing about Rod's sentence.

Dana, in particular, was having trouble dealing with long-term imprisonment. Her attorney, Mary Ann Plecas, had explained things, and Dana said she understood her involvement, but really, she didn't. Dana couldn't comprehend that because she had asked to "go with" Rod and

Scott to the Wendorfs', because she had participated in the conversation at Shannon's, because she was a part of the plan, she was guilty.

There was no doubt that Cooper would serve time, but Plecas would assure the twenty-one-year-old that she would be shown mercy. The attorney was preparing for a big trial. Other defense attorneys made fun of Plecas for talking about getting a face-lift. She had the wrong priorities, they thought, as she readied herself for a media exploit. Having worked with F. Lee Bailey on a prior case, Plecas was pulling out all the stops. She wanted Bailey to act as an outside adviser.

Howard Scott Anderson, meanwhile, was telling fellow inmates that he was a master of black magic and voodoo. He was claiming to suffer from "multiple personalities," hoping to pull off an insanity defense, and because of Scott's strange mental state, his attorney, Mike Graves, had a difficult time getting through to him.

Apparently, Scott had taken a "vow" of secrecy regarding his vampirism, it wasn't something that was to be discussed with outsiders. It took a while for Graves to work through that, mostly because Scott still believed Rod could walk on water. The way Scott talked about his "sire," it seemed Scott would have jumped off a bridge if Rod told him to.

"I think Scott was surprised, to some degree, that this all happened," Graves confided. "I think, from everything he's told me, what happened in that house was, to him, a surreal experience."

Mr. Graves saw his client as someone who enjoyed hearing Rod "talk." Scott liked Rod's "hyperdramatic" dialogue, but thought it was all playacting. According to Graves, Scott never thought any of their words would come to blows. The attorney surmised that when it *actually happened*, when Rod started to bludgeon Rick Wendorf, Scott froze because he couldn't believe his eyes.

"It all just kind of moved around him," Graves concluded.

Of course Graves had to listen to Anderson's story with a grain of salt, there was so much fantasy going on, so much confusion. But in the end, he determined that Scott was basically a good kid who was just "socially bereft."

Being a vampire allowed Scott, like Dana, to be a part of something for the very first time. Both had been outcasts. Both had no idea what it was like to have the attention of others. When Rod came along with his magical promises, acting like a father figure, they thought they had a new *family*. And Scott, in particular, became utterly devoted.

As the spring of 1998 moved forward, as the impending "vampire" trials drew near, a strange thing happened. Following a yearlong halt in executions in Florida, in a nine-day period in late March, four death-row inmates were sent to Florida's electric chair. One of the prisoners was Judy Buenoano, a black widow who, despite last-minute pleas, would become the first woman executed in the state in 150 years.

On April Fools' Day, at the same time that serial killer Daniel Remeta was being put to death, eighteen-year-old Howard Scott Anderson withdrew his not-guilty plea in exchange for life without parole. He pleaded guilty to two counts of first-degree murder and accepted two consecutive life terms. The plea bargain would mean no chance for appeal. Scott Anderson would spend the rest of his days behind bars. His attorney was broken up about it, but the Wendorf family was elated. Afterward, Graves would comment about how unfair he thought the sentence was. It irked him that Brad King insisted on sentencing Scott so harshly, without any compunction. The defense attorney felt that if Scott Anderson were to be let out on parole, he could become a productive member of society.

Of course, at the time of Anderson's plea, Mary Ann Plecas, whose client was merely an "accessory suspect," told the press she had no interest in plea deals. In fact, in April, Ms. Plecas held a mock-trial outside of Lake County, because, with Cooper's trial scheduled to begin in July, Plecas wanted to try out her defense strategies.

The attorney convened enough people to play the principal court roles: she portrayed herself, two Lake County attorneys played Judge Lockett and Brad King, and a couple of teenagers stepped in as Scott and Heather. According to press reports, the mock-trial was "funded with county-paid meals," but Plecas felt the expense was justified.

As it turned out, Dana Cooper's lawyer was granted a change of venue. Dana's trial was scheduled to be held in St. Augustine, with Judge Lockett presiding, but in the weeks prior, while media folks were making their plans to arrive, the whole interstate surrounding historic St. Augustine caught on fire. Lightning had struck, the woods were burning, and people wondered how they would gain access. The flames were jumping across the state highway, just completely out of control.

Of course all the cameras and microphones never made it down there. The media people didn't have to brave the raging brushfires because Dana Lynn Cooper, the most unlikely "vampire" of them all, changed her plea to guilty just days before the jury selection was to begin. Dana's belongings, which included five bags of clothes, costume jewelry, Anne Rice books and videos, and her Kentucky records and files, remained locked away with the Lake County sheriff. No one in her family would even bother to retrieve them.

Dana Cooper would be sent off to serve a seventeen-and-a-half year sentence in a female facility in Lowell, Florida. From prison, Dana would pray that "God bless" all the people hurt by her actions. Then, a few weeks after her arrival, she received a letter, supposedly written by Brad King, stating that the charges against her would be dropped. It was a dirty trick, but Dana desperately wanted to believe it. Miss Cooper wrote to the judge, just hoping, and Judge Lockett's clerk was forced to respond to the prisoner, explaining that no such letter had been generated by the state attorney.

Almost expectedly, the trial for Charity Lynn Kessee never came to pass. Like Dana Cooper, Charity backed down at the last minute. On August 13, Brad King agreed to reduce the charges to third-degree murder in exchange for a guilty plea. Kessee was guilty of driving Heather Wendorf from her home the night of November 25, for which she would be sentenced to serve ten and a half years in prison. Even with eighteen months already under her belt, Charity would not be out on parole until she was twenty-five.

"She is a little girl," Brad King told reporters, "but she allowed herself to become involved in things that were not little-girl things."

Wearing a flower-print dress, dressed in stockings and high heels, the seventeen-year-old cried bitterly as she received her sentence. She too would spend her time in the women's facility in Lowell. Months later, people would bristle at the news that Charity and another female inmate were caught *exchanging blood* in the dormitory bathroom area. Prison officials initially accepted calls from newspapers, but refused to comment further on the matter.

In mid-December, when the grand jury was reconvened regarding Heather Wendorf, the twenty-one people spent days reviewing evidence and listening to testimony. Even though the holiday celebration for 1998 was upon them, the new grand jury spent their time, they did their homework. The panel wanted to be able to assure Lake County residents that they had considered *all* the evidence, including the testimony of one witness who hadn't gone before the first grand jury.

Handwriting experts had been hired, all kinds of accusations were being made, but ultimately, it could not be established that Heather Wendorf drew the map of her house, that she had ever corresponded with Rod Ferrell in writing, that she had ever ordered her friends to enter the Wendorf house.

After three hours of deliberation, the panel filed a two-page report stating that they agreed with their predecessors. There was no hard evidence against Heather. They could not find probable cause.

"Each witness was allowed to testify fully, and we have asked such questions as we felt appropriate," the grand jury wrote. "We find the evidence identified as new is not credible and we will not act upon it."

Heather was no ringleader. Heather was a victim.

The people had spoken.

epilogue

The arrests of the five teenagers in the Wendorf murders created a certain anxiety among the Gothic subculture in America. Goth people were afraid that the event would get hung on them. Anne Rice commented that she wanted nothing to do with the story, that it was unfortunate that her books were found among the belongings confiscated from the blue Ford Explorer. In particular, people who practiced witchcraft felt violated by the associations to Heather Wendorf. Because she had dabbled in earth magic, because a witch's handbook was found in her room, they too were getting flak.

Gothic teenagers seemed scary enough, other people would say, with or without capes. The tie-in between vampires and a group of disturbed teens became too overwhelming for mainstream America to assimilate. The infamous case brought to light the members of an underground teen world, with its own jargon, hierarchy, and dress. Mainstreamers didn't want to deal with it. Vampires were only romantic and enticing in movies, not in real life.

"The vampire thing was something that was thrust upon Rod by his mother," one observer noted. "God help us if any of our parents ever forced us to play this game. For him, it became a way of life because his mother made it a way of life."

"In my view, Rod is like most children," one of Rod's defenders said, "they always need a sense of worth that can only come from parents. But Rod's mother had done everything within her power to keep anyone from having a positive influence on him."

"Rod got hold of people who were pretty much pathetic," a Lake County source commented. "These were kids interested in country music and McDonald's and all the things that normal teenagers are. They were average teenagers, not crazed, wild vampires."

"Rod was a child being sent to prison, he felt he got a raw deal and was looking for someone to blame," Heather's guardian surmised. "In his strange mind, Rod may have absolutely believed that he was the knight on the white horse saving this poor intelligent girl from these Neanderthal parents. He couldn't understand why Heather didn't see him as her savior."

"It was really strange because back then, Rod was really my whole life," Heather would admit. "The whole vampire thing was my life at that point, because I didn't have other factors to go into. I didn't have an adolescent life. I wasn't social. I didn't have many friends."

In spite of the whole ordeal, Heather was undergoing

her own metamorphosis. She had given up witchcraft, given up bloodletting, and had transferred to an arts school in North Carolina to finish up her high school education.

"My specialty was being a vampire," she reflected. "I was Zoey. I wasn't Heather. Zoey could handle it. Zoey was the cucumber. Zoey could be wild, but Heather isn't any of these."

Also from

APHRODITE JONES

All She Wanted

The *only* book on
the "Brandon Teena" case.

POCKET BOOKS

2806